"In the same clear and careful way that Richard McBrien helped Catholics of the 1980s understand the richness of their doctrinal tradition, Tom Rausch offers in this volume a way for Catholics to navigate that same tradition in this second decade of the twenty-first century. Rausch pays close attention, however, not only to the tradition's content but also to its context of postmodernity, cultural diversity, gender awareness, and sensitivity to sexual orientation. Although sometimes controversial, Rausch is always thorough and fair. This will be a helpful book for students and teachers alike."

— Stephen Bevans, SVD
   Louis J. Luzbetak, SVD, Professor of Mission and Culture, Emeritus
   Catholic Theological Union, Chicago

"Rausch has produced a first-rate introduction to Catholic systematic theology. This book provides a cogent and up-to-date summary of the conversation in every major branch of systematic theology while also explaining the methods, biblical bases, historical development, and ecumenical perspectives that inform the debates. Rausch's writing is clear and engaging, making this text an excellent book for undergraduates. At the same time, it provides substantive contributions useful to advanced scholars. This book should be the top choice for anyone who wants to get the 'lay of the land' in contemporary Catholic theology."

— Mary Doak
   Associate Professor, Theology and Religious Studies
   University of San Diego

"Thomas Rausch is a masterful teacher. With this book he offers a clear, well-informed introduction to contemporary Catholic systematic theology. Rausch insightfully maps its key areas, major figures, and frontier issues."

— Robert P. Imbelli
   Associate Professor of Theology Emeritus, Boston College
   Author of *Rekindling the Christic Imagination*

"Thomas P. Rausch, one of American Catholicism's finest writers, provides a solid introduction to the study of systematic theology, one that is attentive to its complex historical evolutions and contemporary face, while taking seriously its faith-filled, ecclesial, and contextual character. Educators and students alike will welcome his balanced presentation of the plurality of contemporary systematic theologies that carry forward the pastoral effort of mediating the meaning of a life in communion—with the Christian God, with other human persons in the church and society, and with the whole of creation—to the women and men of our time."

   — Catherine E. Clifford
    Saint Paul University, Ottawa

"Covering every major topic in Catholic theology with his signature accessibility and insight, this treatment of systematic theology is Thomas Rausch's *chef d'oeuvre*. Students and teachers looking for a reliable overview of historical and contemporary approaches to theology will find no single volume better than this."

   — Michael Downey, editor of *The New Dictionary of Catholic Spirituality*

Systematic Theology

A
Roman Catholic
Approach

Thomas P. Rausch, SJ

A Michael Glazier Book

LITURGICAL PRESS
Collegeville, Minnesota

www.litpress.org

A Michael Glazier Book published by Liturgical Press

Cover design by Jodi Hendrickson. Image courtesy of Wikimedia Commons. Peter Lombard, *Sententiae* (*The Sentences*), Bibliotheque Municipale at Troyes MS900, fol. 1r.

On the cover is Peter Lombard (1096–1169), a scholastic theologian at Notre Dame in Paris. His *Four Books of the Sentences* could be considered one of the first comprehensive texts on systematic theology. University students prepared commentaries on its overview of Christian doctrine down to the sixteenth century.

Library of Congress Cataloging-in-Publication Data

Names: Rausch, Thomas P.
Title: Systematic theology : a Roman Catholic approach / Thomas P. Rausch, S.J.
Description: Collegeville, Minnesota : Liturgical Press, 2016. | "A Michael Glazier book."
Identifiers: LCCN 2015035247| ISBN 9780814683200 | ISBN 9780814683453 (ebook)
Subjects: LCSH: Catholic Church—Doctrines. | Theology, Doctrinal.
Classification: LCC BX1751.3 .R388 2016 | DDC 230/.2—dc23
LC record available at http://lccn.loc.gov/2015035247

For my graduate students

Contents

Acknowledgments

I am grateful first of all to my graduate students who encouraged me to write this book. Some of the material in the chapters that follow has appeared in earlier forms. I want to thank the editors of these works for graciously allowing me to include this material. Among them are Matt Malone for "Theology's New Turn," *America* (February 2, 2015); John J. Piderit and Melanie M. Morey, "Catholic Anthropology," which appeared in their *Teaching the Tradition: Catholic Themes in Academic Disciplines* (Oxford University Press, 2012); and Jeremiah J. McCarthy for "Vatican II on the Priesthood: Fifty Years Later," published in *Seminary Journal* (Winter 2012).

Thanks also to my friends at Liturgical Press, Hans Christoffersen for his encouragement and Patrick McGowan for his careful copy editing. Two of our graduate assistants, Raymond Camacho and Alan Flower, helped with the proofreading. I very much appreciate their assistance.

I am also grateful for the advice of colleagues and friends here and across the country who reviewed parts or chapters of the manuscript. They include Susan Abraham, Catherine Clifford, John Connolly, Michael Cook, SJ, Nicholas Denysenko, Michael Downey, Mark Fisher, Dorian Llywelyn, SJ, Marie Anne Mayeski, Peter Phan, and Terrence Tilley. Their suggestions have been invaluable, while responsibility for what appears must rest with the author.

Thomas P. Rausch, SJ
Loyola Marymount University

Abbreviations

Documents of Vatican II

AG   *Ad Gentes*: Decree on the Mission Activity of the Church

DH   *Dignitatis Humanae*: Declaration on Religious Freedom

DV   *Dei Verbum*: Dogmatic Constitution on Divine Revelation

GS   *Gaudium et Spes*: Pastoral Constitution on the Church in the Modern World

LG   *Lumen Gentium*: Dogmatic Constitution on the Church

NA   *Nostra Aetate*: Declaration on the Relationship of the Church to Non-Christian Religions

SC   *Sacrosanctum Concilium*: Constitution on the Sacred Liturgy

UR   *Unitatis Redintegratio*: Decree on Ecumenism

Other

CDF   Congregation for the Doctrine of the Faith

ITC   International Theological Commission

CIC   *Codex Juris Canonici*

DI   *Dominus Iesus*

DS   Denzinger-Schönmetzer, *Enchiridion Symbolorum* 33rd ed. (Freiburg: Herder, 1965).

WCC   World Council of Churches

Introduction

How does one characterize Roman Catholic theology? In his study, *Catholicism*, itself a work of systematic theology, the late Richard McBrien describes Catholicism as having a philosophical focus rooted in a Christian realism and three theological foci: sacramentality, mediation, and communion.[1]

Its philosophical focus rejects both idealism and naïve realism. Idealism limits knowledge to the phenomena perceived by the senses; ultimate reality remains unknowable. Naïve realism is a common sense approach that reduces knowledge to what appears at first glance, ignoring the capacity of intelligence to discover the intelligibility in the data and to form explanatory concepts. This includes a biblical or doctrinal fundamentalism which takes a text literally, without examining conditioning factors such as language, literary form, or historical context. Thus Catholicism's philosophical focus is concerned with a critical realism.

Theological foci include sacramentality, mediation, and communion. Sacramentality sees material realities, whether nature, art, symbol, story, or persons as able to mediate or bring about an encounter with the transcendent mystery of God. Mediation, a corollary of sacramentality, serves as a bridge to join or bring about some effect. Just as Jesus mediates God's grace to humankind, sacramentality not only symbolizes that grace but also makes it effective in our lives. In a secondary sense, God's grace is mediated by the church as well

---

[1] Richard P. McBrien, *Catholicism*, rev. ed. (San Francisco: Harper San Francisco, 1994), 1192–99.

as by human kindness, compassion, and care for the other. Communion expresses the idea that Catholicism is essentially a communal experience of Christian faith; it always takes the social seriously. Rejecting a radical individualism, it recognizes that we are essentially social beings who need community to survive and flourish. To be "in Christ" is to be in his body, the church.

A Catholic systematic theology should always be informed by these markers of Catholic identity: a critical realism, an appreciation of sacramentality which lights up the world with traces of the divine, mediation which ennobles both creation and human agency, and communion, underlining Catholicism's deep sense for the importance of community and the union with God and all people to which we are called.

This communal dimension of Catholic theology coincides well with the recent efforts of Pope Francis to shift from an understanding of Catholic life focused on doctrine to one that sees pastoral care as the center of the church's life. As he puts it, realities are more important than ideas.[2] Catholic theology, with its stress on a gracious God who respects human freedom and is constantly reaching out to creation, its sense that human nature even if flawed is also graced, its conviction that grace builds on the human, and its conviction that faith and reason must work in harmony undergirds rather than displaces a greater emphasis on the church's pastoral mission.

A word on structuring a systematic theology. Thomas Aquinas divided his classic *Summa Theologica* into three parts. The First Part (*Prima Pars*) treats the one God and God's trinitarian nature, then creation, the angels, and the human person. The Second Part, divided into two parts (*Prima Secundae, Secunda Secundae*) considers human acts, general principles of morality, morality in particular, and the virtues. The Third Part (*Tertia Pars*) which remained unfinished takes up the person and work of Christ, the sacraments, and the last things: death, judgment, heaven, and hell. Thus there is a cyclic movement from God to humankind and then through Christ back to God.

---

[2] Francis, *Evangelii Gaudium*, Apostolic Exhortation on the Joy of the Gospel, no. 231, http://w2.vatican.va/content/francesco/en/apost_exhortations/documents/papa -francesco_esortazione-ap_20131124_evangelii-gaudium.html.

The present work follows that basic structure but with some differences. The first two chapters deal with the nature and changing contexts of theology. The next two focus on the divine mystery, the Trinity, and Jesus the Christ, including his mission of proclaiming the kingdom of God. The next three chapters focus on humankind in relation to God. One treats revelation and faith; the next deals with sin, grace, and the human person; the third looks at how grace as a share in the divine life becomes fruitful in the lives of human beings, and more specifically, Mary and the saints. The next three chapters treat the church and the sacraments, while the final chapter treats creation and eschatology, bringing God's creative work to its ultimate fulfillment or what might be described as the fullness of salvation. If there is an overarching theme, it is mission, the mission of the church as a share in the mission of the Word and Spirit in the world. Thus systematic theology describes how God's grace moves from eternity into space and time, gathering creation into the fullness of the divine mystery.

This volume is not intended to be encyclopedic; it is a modest effort to construct a systematic theology alert to the pluralism of contemporary theology. It cannot explore in depth all the issues raised by cultural and methodological shifts today, for example postcolonial, feminist, queer, eco-theology, and comparative theology, though it will consider them briefly. The intention is to present a text that is relatively concise and mainstream, an introduction to explore basic themes in Catholic systematic theology from a biblical, historical and contemporary perspective, though always aware of today's theological pluralism. A manageable text also makes possible the inclusion of other articles and texts that might expand on any particular topic. Each chapter includes recommended readings for further study.

Chapter 1

Systematic Theology

The English word "theology" is derived from the Greek *theologia*, which in turn comes from two Greek words, *theos* (God), and *logia* (words, utterances, or speech). Thus theology can be translated as talking about God. Plato used it in this sense in the fourth century BCE in his classic work, *The Republic*.[1] The classic Christian definition of theology comes from Anselm of Canterbury (d. 1109), who said that theology was *fides quaerens intellectum*, faith seeking understanding.

The Nature of Theology

What is important about Anselm's definition is that it underlines that theology in the Christian tradition is always a critical reflection on the faith of the community, an effort to bring the faith-experience of God and God's grace to expression, clarity, and deeper understanding. It means asking questions, probing more deeply into our beliefs, trying to bring our sense for God and God's graciousness toward us to more adequate levels of expression.

The emphasis on faith, received and handed on is what distinguishes theology from religious studies; it is a confessional approach. To do theology is to stand within a faith tradition and reflect on it critically. Religious studies means studying the same from outside—so to speak—as one might study sixteenth-century English literature

---

[1] Plato, *Republic* 2.18.

1

or German history. There is no personal investment. As Pope John Paul I reportedly said: "Theologians talk a lot about God. I wonder how often they talk to God." Several points about Christian theology are important.

First, theology, even when done by individuals, is always rooted in the community of faith. The Christian theologian reflects on the faith received and to which he or she remains committed. In the Judeo-Christian tradition, revelation is always to a people, to Israel, to the disciples of Jesus, to the church. Thus theology implies a knowledge that is more personal than objective, for God is not an object, a phenomenon, or a behavioral pattern like the objects studied by the empirical or social sciences; God is a subject, whose self-disclosure is always free and intersubjective. While individuals often play important roles—for example, one thinks of the dominating presence of Moses in the Pentateuch, the importance of the prophets, and of course Jesus—their teaching always arises out of the experience of the people of which they are a part and to which they remain bound. It cannot be reduced to something entirely subjective and individual.

In the Judeo-Christian tradition, God's self-disclosure is always mediated communally by the people of Israel and later by the community of the church, with its Scriptures, its sacraments, and its apostolic ministry. Thus Karl Rahner defined theology as "the conscious and methodological explanation and explication of the divine revelation received and grasped in faith,"[2] while Karl Barth, the premier Protestant theologian of the twentieth century, called his multivolume work *Church Dogmatics*. Theology is a work of the church.

Second, theology is always a second-order language, removed by several levels of abstraction, metaphor, or analogy from the faith experience to which it gives rise. What the first disciples of Jesus experienced in their encounter with Jesus was healing, forgiveness, freedom, reconciliation, and new life—in a word, salvation. When Paul, perhaps the first Christian theologian, attempted to describe the meaning of the Christ event to others, he used terms rooted in his Jewish imagination and hallowed by use in his Jewish tradition, terms such as justification, reconciliation, expiation, salvation, re-

---

[2] Karl Rahner, "Theology," in *Encyclopedia of Theology: The Concise Sacramentum Mundi*, ed. Karl Rahner (New York: Seabury Press, 1975), 1687.

demption, freedom, sanctification, transformation, new creation, and glorification.[3] Similarly, the medieval church adopted the language of transubstantiation in an effort to safeguard its eucharistic faith in Christ's presence in the Eucharist. But this philosophical language, using the categories of Aristotle and the notion of a change of substance, was considerably removed from the experience of the first Christians who recognized the presence of the risen Jesus in the meal (1 Cor 10:16-17; Luke 24:31, 35).

Third, theology is always contextual; it represents an effort to reflect on the Gospel message in a particular historical situation or context. A criterion of the adequacy of a theological statement is its ability to speak to the concerns of contemporary people. As Karl Rahner once said, all theology is pastoral. For example, liberation theology speaks to this concern for context with its emphasis on praxis.

Finally, theology is a critical discipline, a science with its own methods and "specialties," even if different from the empirical sciences. It seeks always to reflect on the church's language, to refine it so that it might more adequately proclaim and express the good news of the Gospel in the various cultures and different historical contexts in which the church is living. Often it must distinguish between popular belief or theological opinion and the church's official teaching, and sometimes it helps to amend that teaching.

Theological Disciplines

In his important work *Method in Theology*, Bernard Lonergan lists eight functional specialties, referring to different moments in the doing of theology.[4] A traditional division of the theological disciplines has included fundamental theology, biblical theology, historical theology, pastoral theology, and systematic theology, but the divisions are not always precise, and there is often overlap.

Fundamental theology includes natural or philosophical theology, fundamental theology itself, and apologetics. Natural theology asks

---

[3] Joseph A. Fitzmyer, "Pauline Theology," in the *New Jerome Biblical Commentary*, ed. Raymond E. Brown, Joseph A. Fitzmyer, and Roland Murphy (Englewood Cliffs, NJ: Prentice Hall, 1990), 82.67.

[4] See Bernard Lonergan, *Method in Theology* (New York: Herder and Herder, 1972).

what we can know about the mystery of the divine in light of philosophical reflection; it relies on natural reason, not revelation. Fundamental theology seeks to establish the historical and philosophical grounds for the fundamental doctrines of the faith: God, Christ, the Spirit, the church, and so on. It presupposes revelation. Apologetics, today often considered a part of fundamental theology, at its best seeks to enter into a dialogue with culture by showing the reasonableness of Christian faith and its teaching. Some classic examples of fundamental theology would include Karl Rahner's *Foundations of Christian Faith*, Joseph Ratzinger's *Introduction to Christianity*, Hans Küng's *On Being a Christian*, and Gerald O'Collins's *Fundamental Theology*.

Biblical theology investigates Christianity's sacred writings or "scriptures," thus the story of Israel and the early Christian community, its memory of Jesus and his ministry, and the initial development of its theological language. Scripture obviously is ingredient in all theological disciplines, but there are many different theologies in the Old and New Testaments, and Scripture always needs to be interpreted. Biblical theology's primary concern is the historical meaning of the text, the meaning intended by the biblical author, using the various historical and literary disciplines of the historical-critical method. Catholic theology is also sensitive to the "fuller" sense that emerges as a particular text is reread in the light of the tradition.

Historical theology studies how the church's faith has developed and its theological language has changed in different periods in the church's long history. It includes various subsets—for example, patristic, medieval, reformation, modern, and nineteenth-century theology. Moral theology, often called Christian ethics today, seeks to understand what it means to live life "in Christ," guided by the Holy Spirit. Thus it includes both the personal and social dimensions of Gospel living.

Pastoral theology includes a number of disciplines. Pastoral theology itself seeks to nurture and deepen the practical life of Christians and their communities. Liturgical theology is concerned with the theology and expression of the church's worship. Spirituality examines different ways of expressing a life of prayer, discipleship, Christian service, and growing in the Spirit. Finally, there is systematic theology.

Systematic Theology

Systematic theology, sometimes called constructive theology, dogmatic theology, or systematics (Lonergan), seeks to understand and render more intelligible the central doctrines of the faith and show how they are related to each other. Focusing primarily on theology in the contemporary life of the church, it tries to show how the church's doctrinal tradition grows out of its roots in Scripture and develops in the history of the church; most importantly, it strives to more adequately express and sometimes reinterpret that tradition, always in the interest of better communicating the mystery of salvation and bringing it into a dialogue with culture. Systematic theology is truly evangelical; for this reason it is also concerned with how to relate faith to culture.

First, systematic theology is concerned with understanding the basic doctrines of Christian faith and, thus, the meaning or truth of those doctrines. According to Lonergan, both doctrines and systematics aim at understanding the truth but do so in different ways. "Doctrines aim at a clear and distinct affirmation of religious realities: its principal concern is the truth of such an affirmation. On the other hand, systematics aims at an understanding of the religious realities affirmed by doctrines," though he notes that systematic theology is aware that its understanding remains imperfect, analogous, and no more than probable.[5] "Doctrines are correlated with judgment, systematics with understanding. Doctrines are affirmations. Systematics attempts to understand what has been affirmed."[6]

Second, systematic theology is concerned with how the basic doctrines of the faith relate to each other. What is the relation between Christology and pneumatology or between the theology of creation and eschatology? Again, Lonergan: "The aim of systematics is to present an 'assimilable whole,' and so a unified understanding of Christian doctrine; but the core meanings that were explicitly affirmed

---

[5] Lonergan, *Method*, 349; Lonergan finds this distinction in Aquinas's *Summa Contra Gentiles*, bk. 6; see Lonergan, *Method*, 336–37.

[6] Robert M. Doran, *What Is Systematic Theology?* (Buffalo, NY: University of Toronto Press, 2005), 8.

by the Christian church in the kairos moments of its self-constitution are to form the core of that synthetic statement."[7]

Finally, systematic theology is comprehensive. In its efforts to understand Christian doctrine, it necessarily incorporates the data of biblical, historical, and doctrinal theology. Perhaps Origen (c. 184–253), who sought in his theology to develop a complete Christian worldview using biblical exegesis, hermeneutics, philosophical theology, and spirituality could be considered the first systematic theologian.

A precursor to the development of systematic theology might be found in the third-century catechetical schools of Alexandria and Antioch, with their different concerns and approaches to affirming both the divinity and humanity of Jesus in an integrated theology. The school at Alexandria was founded in 195 by Clement of Alexandria (d. 215); Origen was its great light. The basic concern of the Alexandrians was the divinity of the Logos, which had in some way entered into or become joined to flesh in the person of Jesus. Believing that human souls preexisted in a world of spiritual beings, Origen taught that the Logos became fused with the soul of Jesus.[8] Thus Alexandria was clear on the divinity of the Logos, but its way of describing the mystery of the incarnation risked denying the full humanity of Jesus, as later happened with Apollinaris. The school at Antioch, probably founded in the second half of the third century by Lucian of Antioch (d. 312), was concerned with affirming the full humanity of Jesus. To safeguard confession of both his divinity and his humanity, Antioch used the language of "two natures," divine and human, joined in a substantial (hypostatic) union.

These different approaches have been characterized as word-flesh (Alexandria) and word-man (Antioch). In spite of the rivalry between the two schools, some of it political, their dispute was fundamentally a struggle over theological language that was eventually resolved by the Council of Chalcedon (451).

From these earliest days of the church, Catholic theology has made room for various theologies and schools: Augustinian, Thomistic,

---

[7] Ibid., 9; see also Lonergan, *Method*, 162.

[8] J. N. D. Kelly, *Early Christian Doctrines* (London: Adam and Charles Black, 1958), 154–55.

Franciscan, and Scotist. At the Council of Trent, the bishops were careful not to canonize one particular theology of justification. As theologian Avery Dulles says, "The Council wished to present a coherent Catholic doctrine that would exclude the errors of the Reformers without condemning the positions of any of the recognized Catholic schools."[9] In the seventeenth century, Jesuits and Dominicans argued over grace and free will; the twentieth century saw a host of schools that looked to Rahner, Lonergan, or Ratzinger, or to the new theologies of liberation. This pluralism within unity exemplifies what it means to be catholic.

Francis Schüssler Fiorenza points to three classic paradigms within the Western theological tradition, the Augustinian, the Thomistic, and the neoscholastic.[10] Since these schools offer different approaches to the mystery of the divine, and their influence continues to be felt in different ways even today, we should consider each one briefly. We will also consider scholasticism and Baroque scholasticism, which could be seen as transitional stages.

Augustine: *Theology as Wisdom*

Few have had more influence on theology than Augustine of Hippo (354–430). His epistemology was basically Platonic, envisioning two worlds, one the intelligible world in which truth dwells, the other the sensible world which we perceive by sight and touch.[11] Understanding meant moving from the visible to the invisible and intelligible. Most important was his distinction between knowledge (*scientia*) and wisdom (*sapientia*). While knowledge offers rational insight into the visible, changeable, and temporal things of this world, this was not yet wisdom. The object of wisdom is the eternal and unchangeable realities. Knowledge comes from experience, authority, and signs. Experience leads from the visible to the intelligible. Knowledge based on experience is better than that based on human

[9] Avery Dulles, *The Assurance of Things Hoped For: A Theology of Christian Faith* (New York: Oxford University Press, 1994), 48.

[10] Francis Schüssler Fiorenza, "Systematic Theology: Tasks and Methods," in *Systematic Theology: Roman Catholic Perspectives*, ed. Francis Schüssler Fiorenza and John P. Galvin (Minneapolis, MN: Fortress Press, 2011), 6–22.

[11] Augustine, *Contra Academicos* 3.27.37.

authority, but Christ's authority is divine. Signs also contribute to a knowledge that goes beyond direct experience. Some signs are natural, like smoke as a sign of fire. Others are "given" either by humans or by God, as in the words of Scripture which refer to the transcendent, to God.

Scripture, for Augustine, holds the highest authority (*Confessions* 16.1). Scripture witnesses to God's revelation in Christ—the invisible Divine Wisdom become visible—and to Christ's authority. Scripture is interpreted not only in its literal or historical sense but also in reference to the transcendent. The task of biblical scholars is to interpret the signs that point to divine truth. But the authority of Scripture is an "interpreted authority," effective "only as it is extended into the interpreting community of the Church through the rule of faith." [12] In Catholic terms, Scripture does not stand alone.

There is a voluntarist dimension to Augustine's epistemology, especially to his view on how we know the transcendent. In the search for truth, the will has a certain primacy over the understanding. "What is known cannot be divorced from what is loved." [13] To know the truth one must love the truth and believe in what God has revealed. This is very different from the intellectualism of Aristotle's epistemology as well as the "objective" approach of contemporary scientific method. In the Prologue to Book 15 of his treatise on the Trinity, Augustine quotes from the Septuagint translation of Isaiah 7:9: "Unless you believe you shall not understand." [14] In Schüssler Fiorenza's words, "Knowing the eternal reality requires a spiritual ascent and purification. Such a spiritual purification is, therefore, a presupposition for interpreting Scripture." [15]

Augustine's influence was to play an enormous role in the development of theology in the Western church. The doctrine of the Trinity, original sin and grace, thus theological anthropology, the church, and

---

[12] See Howard J. Loewen, "The Use of Scripture in Augustine's Theology," *Scottish Journal of Theology* 34 (1981): 207.

[13] Robert E. Cushman, "Faith and Reason," in *A Companion to the Study of St. Augustine*, ed. Roy W. Battenhouse (Grand Rapids, MI: Baker Book House, 1979), 289.

[14] Augustine, *The Trinity* 15.2, trans. Edmund Hill (Brooklyn, NY: New City Press, 1991), 395.

[15] Schüssler Fiorenza, "Systematic Theology," 10; see also Loewen, "Scripture in Augustine's Theology," 218–19.

the efficacy of the sacraments all were important themes in his work. The Reformers, especially Luther and Calvin, were deeply influenced by Augustine's understanding of original sin. His distinction between the reality (*res*) and signs (*signa*) of Christian doctrine and the order of his treatment influenced the medieval *summas*. Joseph Ratzinger could stand as an example of a contemporary Augustinian.

Scholastic Theology: Theology in the Universities

For much of the twelfth century, theology was still basically Augustinian. Taught in the monasteries and the ecclesiastical schools, with Scripture being the primary text, the discipline was called *sacra doctrina*, sacred doctrine, or sometimes *sacra pagina*. In the schools of the twelfth century, the forms of instruction were the *lectio, disputatio,* and *praedicatio*, a reading, debate, and sermon focused on the text of Scripture.[16] But with the development of the universities in the late eleventh and twelfth centuries, *sacra doctrina* began to undergo a transformation into what became known as scholastic theology, a discipline done by the *magistri* (masters) or "scholastics" as they were called, men of the "schools" who were the university professors. The *magistri*, with a *licentia docendi* (license to teach), were authoritative interpreters of revelation.[17]

Two theologians played an important role in the development of theology from a spiritual to a more critical discipline, Peter Abelard (1079–1142) and his student Peter Lombard (1096–1164). Abelard's book *Sic et Non* (yes and no) was a compilation of passages from the church fathers on Christian doctrine and life, not all in agreement with each other. Under his influence, the *disputatio*, an examination of a topic approached in the form of a particular *quaestio* or question, became increasingly a vigorous academic debate. Various positions or objections from different authorities would be brought forth under the *sed contra*, the "on the contrary," in the effort to arrive at an agreed

---

[16] Ulrich G. Leinsle, *Introduction to Scholastic Theology* (Washington, DC: The Catholic University of America Press, 2010), 122.

[17] Marie-Dominique Chenu, *Nature, Man, and Society in the Twelfth Century* (Chicago: University of Chicago Press, 1957), 274–76.

upon understanding. By bringing these differences in opinion and approach into view, Abelard was working toward common understanding and agreement, thus, toward a more critical theology. As Chenu says, "The criteria of truth were no longer based solely on the rule of faith as operative in the revealed texts but also upon the rational coherence of propositions taken from a philosophy of man and here used as the minor premises of syllogisms."[18]

In the thirteenth century, the mendicant orders, the Dominicans and Franciscans, began to establish themselves at the universities, arriving in Paris as early as 1217, originally to form houses of study for their own younger members. They tended to emphasize biblical exegesis. But others were increasingly emphasizing the *Four Books of Sentences* of Peter Lombard as a systematic work, another compilation of biblical texts with passages from the fathers and medieval thinkers. Like Augustine, it moved from the Trinity to creation, to Christ and the virtues, and then to the signs or sacraments. Before long, the *magistri* were lecturing less on the Bible, taking instead the *Sentences*. It became the standard textbook for theology in the medieval universities. Even Luther and Calvin commented on it.

The status of theology as a university discipline, however, was not yet clear. Was it a science distinct from *sacra doctrina*, the interpretation of Scripture? How was it related to the other sciences? The introduction of Aristotle, already available in translation since the mid-twelfth century, was to play a role in this controversy. By the thirteenth century, Aristotle's *Posterior Analytics*, with its concept of science based on experience, logical demonstration (the syllogism), and self-evident principles was widely accepted. This not only played an important role in the developing Western understanding of science but also provided a new model for theology. In the university, theology was becoming a science in the Aristotelian sense.[19]

Thomas Aquinas: Theology as a Science

The Dominican Albert the Great (1200–1280) was one of the first to incorporate this Aristotelian perspective into the doing of theology.

[18] Ibid., 288.
[19] Leinsle, *Introduction to Scholastic Theology*, 122.

But it was his student, Thomas Aquinas (1225–1274) who from early in his career worked to place *sacra doctrina* or theology as a distinct science alongside philosophy and the natural sciences. The introduction of Aristotle was opposed by both the church and the university, with the Franciscan Bonaventure—who held fast to an Augustinian epistemology—leading the resistance. Bonaventure rejected the idea of a self-sufficient philosophy. Since Christ was the center of all things, philosophy had to be radically Christian and christological. But by 1255, the curriculum included the entire Aristotelian corpus.

While there remains considerable controversy about how Thomas understood *sacra doctrina*, according to Schüssler Fiorenza, he located it as a distinct science (*scientia*) alongside philosophy, using Aristotle's distinction of two kinds of science, one based on principles of natural reason such as mathematics or geometry, the other proceeding from a superior knowledge, what Aristotle called a subaltern (or subordinate) science. *Sacra doctrina* was such a subaltern science based on what God has revealed, on revelation. Thus faith was involved, for faith gives the Christian both certainty and participation in divine knowledge. Since *sacra doctrina* had its origin in revelation, its primary authority was Scripture. But scholastic theology also recognized the work of commentators who were themselves recognized as authorities, as did Thomas. He also distinguished between the magisterium of the doctors or theologians and the pastoral magisterium of the bishops, thus between a magisterium based on scholarship and another based on office.

Sacra doctrina also had a hermeneutical task—to interpret a prescientific faith. Philosophy could help in the understanding of the truths of faith, but it could not demonstrate them, since they were based on revelation. Its authority was limited. As the *magistri*, the professors of the day, increasingly focused on the disputed questions instead of the texts of the Scriptures, exegesis of the *lectio* gave way to the *quaestiones* and the *disputatio*. The *magistri* often collected their questions into a *summa*, which developed from simple collections to a rational ordering of the truths of revelation. The discipline was increasingly identified by the term theology, a term used since Anselm in the sense of an ordered body of knowledge about God. As it focused less on authority and more on dialectics and disputation, theology was becoming a critical discipline.

Baroque Scholasticism

While medieval scholastic theology had known a diversity of schools, in the modern period the *Summa Theologica* of Aquinas replaced the *Sentences* of Peter Lombard as the basic theological text. But controversies between the councils and the papacy as well as between the papacy and the universities as well as those caused by the Reformation and the Renaissance led to a multiplication of theological authorities in the sixteenth and seventeenth centuries in the period known as Baroque Scholasticism. Typical was Melchior Cano's (1509–1560) *De locis theologicis*, listing ten sources of theological authority, including oral tradition, councils, and the Roman church, and with an emphasis on the importance of historical sources. Characteristic of this period were commentaries on the *Summa* of Thomas. The works of Robert Bellarmine and Francis Suarez were also significant.

The work of Parisian theologian Denis Petau (1583–1652), a French Jesuit also known as Petavius, sought to establish the scientific character of theology by employing a process of reasoning that deduced theological conclusions from the certain principles of faith using the syllogism. His deductive method was to shape neoscholastic theology. But he was also the first to attempt a study of Christian doctrine from a historical perspective.

Neoscholasticism

The neoscholasticism that emerged in the nineteenth century presented a Catholic theology that had become a far less creative discipline. Much of it was polemical and apologetic; it sought to clarify church teaching and defend it against the teachings of the Protestants. It took its point of departure not from Scripture like the Protestants but from church teaching, which it held to be the proximate rule of faith. The *quaestio* of medieval theology was replaced by the thesis, to be defended and proved by appeals to church authority. Passages from Scripture or the fathers were reduced to proof texts; investigation had become demonstration. Rather than prizing historical research into the sources, its approach was abstract and ahistorical, influenced by the Cartesian ideal of clear and distinct ideas and Petau's deductive method. Pope Leo XIII's encyclical *Aeterni Patris* (1879) sought to ensure that all those preparing for the priesthood would study Thomistic philosophy, though it was really a neo-thomism.

Leinsle summarizes neoscholasticism's approach as idealizing the thirteenth century, subjecting not just theology but also philosophy to the magisterium, rejecting Protestant theology for not conforming to magisterial teaching, and emphasizing a strict distinction between the natural and the supernatural orders. At the same time, it did inspire some research into medieval philosophy and theology.[20] Neoscholasticism's characteristic work was the manual, a textbook used mostly in seminaries. The result was what became known as the "textbook theology" of seminaries and the Roman schools.

A classic example, referred to simply as "Denzinger," is the *Enchiridion Symbolorum et Definitionum*, a collection of the decrees, definitions, and canons of the councils, condemned propositions, and papal declarations compiled by Heinrich Joseph Dominicus Denzinger (1819–1883). The most recent edition, prepared by Adolf Schönmetzer in 1963, is referred to by the abbreviation DS, for Denzinger-Schönmetzer. Theology done in the neoscholastic mode too often resolved questions by citing the appropriate DS numbers, that is, by appealing to church authority, though the work remains an important compendium of church teachings.

Joseph Ratzinger once characterized the theology of the first half of the twentieth century as living inside the box of neoscholasticism; it had a greater certainty and logical lucidity than today's theology but was "far removed from the real world."[21] It was still present in many of the initial texts drafted by the Theological Commission for the Second Vatican Council. For example, Yves Congar criticized the first draft's chapter on the laity for being very much in the scholastic mode, like "chapters from a good manual." Largely a summary of papal documents, the source of its teaching "is never the Word of God; it is the Church herself, and even the Church reduced to the pope." And there was nothing ecumenical about the text.[22]

---

[20] Ibid., 359.

[21] *30 Dias* (April 1994): 62, http://www.traditioninaction.org/ProgressivistDoc/A_018_RatzingerScholasticism.htm.

[22] Yves Congar, *My Journal of the Council* (Collegeville, MN: Liturgical Press, 2012), 47.

Counter Currents

There were some significant counter currents to the neoscholastic dominance. One came out of the Catholic faculty of theology at Tübingen in Germany. The work of John Henry Newman represented another. The Transcendental Thomists, influenced by Blondel, sought to enter into a dialogue with modern philosophy. There was also the *ressourcement* movement. Based largely in France, it was commonly called the *"nouvelle théologie"* before Vatican II.

Tübingen School

The Catholic Tübingen School, founded by Johann Sebastian von Drey (1777–1853), began as a reaction to the rationalism of the Enlightenment.[23] Most important to Drey was his understanding of history and the historical method. Ecclesiology was a particular focus—not the juridical ecclesiology of the nineteenth century, but the church as a spiritual community formed by the biblical idea of the kingdom of God. For Drey, God's progressive, historical revelation of the kingdom of God reaches its definitive communication in the Catholic Church. His student Johann Adam Möhler (1796–1838) completed his studies at Tübingen and became one of its most distinguished graduates. Both Möhler and Drey saw how the new emphasis on history, including the historical nature of theological statements, could aid in the understanding of revelation.

Möhler's great works (in English) were *The Unity of the Church* (1825), *Athanasius the Great* (1827), and *Symbolism, or the Exposition of Doctrinal Difference* (1844). He took seriously the notion of doctrinal development and saw tradition itself as developing. In *Symbolism*, perhaps his most influential work, he studied doctrinal differences between Catholics and Protestants. Understanding symbols as the confessional statements of the different communities, he made the important distinction between the substance of a doctrine and its historical form. His ecclesiology also took seriously the work of the Holy Spirit. He understood the church not as a juridical society, as in neoscholasticism, but as the body of Christ.

---

[23] See *The Legacy of the Tübingen School*, ed. Donald J. Dietrich and Michael J. Himes (New York: Crossroad, 1997).

In his earlier works, Möhler focused on the pre-Nicene church, which seemed to be more open to the Spirit's influence, though in his later works he shifted to a word-centered, incarnational ecclesiology. His incarnational approach and emphasis on ecclesial communion anticipated the *ressourcement* movement which developed in the next century just as his organic ecclesiology was to help decenter Bellarmine's juridical model. Today, in spite of his strong commitment to the Roman Catholic doctrinal tradition, his work is recognized as an attempt to mediate between the Catholic and Protestant traditions.

John Henry Newman

Another theologian who took history seriously and provided an alternative vision to the narrow dogmatic orthodoxy of Roman neo-scholasticism was John Henry Newman (1801–1890).[24] Born into an Anglican family and educated at Oxford in the Greek and Latin classics, Newman was ordained an Anglican priest in 1825. Newman's view of faith was personalist rather than propositional, rooted in a relationship with the God revealed in Jesus. While dogma was important, it was secondary to the divine mystery to which dogmatic truths were to serve as a guide. His book *An Essay on the Development of Christian Doctrine* (1845) was a classic, the fruit of his long involvement with the Oxford Movement and the personal struggle that led him into the Catholic Church. Newman was perhaps the first to systematically treat the development of doctrine. Especially significant was his maintaining the right of the laity to be consulted in matters of faith, using the example of the fourth-century Arian crisis in which many of the bishops were Arian and the faith was kept by the laity. Newman also struggled for years with various Roman congregations that remained suspicious of his orthodoxy. Thus he remains a figure with much to teach the church of today.

Transcendental Thomism

At the beginning of the twentieth century, some Catholic scholars sought a path beyond neoscholasticism by placing an emphasis on

---

[24] John R. Connolly, *John Henry Newman: A View of Catholic Faith for the New Millennium* (Lanham, MD: Rowman & Littlefield, 2005).

human experience, using the intellectualism of Thomas. Like Kant, Jesuits Pierre Rousselot (1878–1915) and Joseph Maréchal (1878–1944) turned to the human subject and the transcendental reach of consciousness. Both saw the dynamism of human understanding as disclosing far more than the object known. They sought to overcome the neoscholastic split between nature and the supernatural by showing that the supernatural was grounded in the natural.[25]

Rousselot worked to reinterpret Aquinas by studying his intellectualism. Like Thomas, Rousselot distinguished between intellect (*intellectus*) and reason (*ratio*). While discursive reason was important, giving us knowledge of the world, concepts, science, and symbols, he identified the intellect as an intuitive faculty inclined toward the "First Truth," God, an inclination or appetite he found in all things. Maréchal's great work was his five-volume *Le Point de depart de la metaphysique*. In the fifth volume, he argued that Kant had erred by not following the reach of reason beyond the natural realm to the intimations of the Absolute that it disclosed. The dynamism of human understanding showed a desire to move beyond the objects known, beyond finite existence, to unlimited Being as such, the existence of which was the *a priori* condition of possibility for every speculative judgment.[26] Maréchal's influence on Karl Rahner and Bernard Lonergan was considerable.

Nouvelle Théologie

The *nouvelle théologie* was a name given to the work of a number of theologians associated with the Saulchoir, the Dominican study center in Paris, and Fourvière, the Jesuit theologate in Lyons in the period from 1935 to 1960. In part, their work was a reaction to the dominance of neoscholasticism, enforced by the anti-Modernist measures put in place after Pope Pius X's encyclical *Pascendi Dominici Gregis* and the decree of the Holy Office, *Lamentabili Sane* (1907). In

---

[25] See Stephen M. Fields, "*Ressourcement* and the Retrieval of Thomism for the Contemporary World," in *Ressourcement: A Movement for Renewal in Twentieth-Century Catholic Theology*, ed. Gabriel Flynn and Paul D. Murray (Oxford: Oxford University Press, 2012), 355–58.

[26] Gerald A. McCool, *Catholic Theology in the Nineteenth Century* (New York: Crossroad, 1977), 256.

part, it represented an effort to overcome the rupture between theology and life and enter into dialogue with contemporary thought. Foremost representatives included Jean Daniélou and Henri de Lubac (both Jesuits), and the Dominicans Yves Congar and Marie-Dominique Chenu. De Lubac, Chenu, and Congar were all influenced by Möhler. Also associated with the movement were Hans Urs von Balthasar, Karl Rahner, Louis Boyer, and Joseph Ratzinger.[27]

An appreciation for history was central to the work of these theologians. Their method was a *ressourcement,* a French term for a "return to the sources" of Catholic faith and life in the Scriptures, the liturgy, and the fathers of the church. Ecclesiology was a key issue; other topics included the development of doctrine, creation and evolution, original sin and grace, and the Eucharist. De Lubac's *Le surnaturel* was an attempt to overcome the separation between the natural and the supernatural that had ruled Catholic theology since the controversy with Baius and Jansenius in the sixteenth and seventeenth centuries. Congar wrote on the nature of tradition, church reform, the theology of the laity, and ecumenism. Chenu compared changes in thirteenth-century society and church to those in the twentieth century.

The term *nouvelle théologie* was apparently used for the first time, pejoratively, by the Holy Office's Msgr. Pietro Parente in February 1942 in an article in the *L'Osservatore Romano,* the official Vatican newspaper, though the theologians themselves did not consider their theology as really new. But because it was biblical and historical rather than neoscholastic, it was seen as a threat to Roman orthodoxy. After *Humani Generis* (1950), the encyclical of Pope Pius XII condemning methods that departed from neoscholasticism, a number of these theologians "were removed from their professorial chairs, prevented from upholding their views in lectures or writings, condemned to silence and inactivity."[28]

But theology was already changing. The church's traditional emphasis on neoscholasticism had already given way to the work of

[27] Hans Boersma, *Nouvelle Théologie and Sacramental Ontology: A Return to Mystery* (Oxford: Oxford University Press, 2009), 11.

[28] Carlo Falconi, *The Popes in the Twentieth Century* (London: Weidenfeld & Nicolson, 1967), 283.

theologians whose work would so enrich the Second Vatican Council. Among them were Karl Rahner, Edward Schillebeeckx, Joseph Ratzinger, Hans Küng, and especially the *ressourcement* theologians we have been considering. Their work, along with the work of scholars in the modern biblical movement and the liturgical movement, both cautiously embraced by Pope Pius XII, was to be vindicated at the council.

Contemporary Theology

In the days after Vatican II, Catholic theology, reenergized by the council, underwent a further transformation. First, the locus for theological reflection changed, as theology began moving out of seminaries and into universities and graduate schools. Second, it would no longer be done chiefly by priests. The council's document *Gaudium et Spes* had encouraged the laity to receive "a sufficient formation in the sacred sciences" and expressed the hope "that some will dedicate themselves professionally to these studies," along with affirming that "all the faithful, whether clerics or laity, possess a lawful freedom of inquiry, freedom of thought and of expressing their mind with humility and fortitude in those matters on which they enjoy competence" (GS 62). In response, Marquette University established the first doctoral program open to laymen and women in 1963, and other universities quickly followed suit. Before long, laymen and especially laywomen were graduating with doctoral degrees and began moving into universities and graduate schools. As Catholic theology underwent a simultaneous declericalization and laicization, it began to develop new methodologies and approaches.

Transcendental Theology

As noted earlier, Joseph Maréchal's Transcendental Thomism was an effort to bring theology into dialogue with modern philosophy, particularly Kant, by analyzing the conditions for the transcendental reach of human understanding. The premiere example of Transcendental Thomism in contemporary theology is the work of Karl Rahner, who adopted Schleiermacher's transcendental point of departure.

His theological anthropology, drawing on both Aquinas and Heidegger, describes the human person as a radical openness to transcendence, grasped non-thematically in every act of knowing, and thus, as an openness toward God and the possibility of God's self-communication. Rahner's classic text is his *Grundkurs* or *Foundations of Christian Faith*, a modern day *Summa*.[29]

Liberation Theology

Arising out of the postconciliar ferment in Latin America, liberation theology developed as a radically contextual theology, rooted in the social *realidad* of the often oppressive Latin American societies. Its key figures were the Uruguayan Jesuit Juan Luis Segundo, who even before Vatican II was calling for the church to address the poverty and injustice of so much of the continent, the Peruvian Gustavo Gutiérrez, whose book *A Theology of Liberation* is its most famous text, and the German Johann Baptist Metz, who began asking after the Second World War how it was possible for German Christians to continue their untroubled believing and praying during the war, singing Gregorian chant with their backs to Auschwitz.[30] Metz broke with the Transcendental Thomism of his mentor Karl Rahner to develop what became known as political theology. Gutiérrez defined theology as "a critical reflection on Christian praxis in the light of the Word."[31]

With this emphasis on praxis, liberation theology takes as its starting point an analysis of the concrete sociopolitical situation in which the Gospel is actually being lived and that which frustrates the embodiment of Gospel values. Theology should be done from the side of the oppressed with liberation as a goal. What do the Scriptures have to say about salvation in the real lives of a people? Jon Sobrino describes the task of liberation theology as a reflection on praxis, its *locus theologicus* as the poor of this world, and its goal "taking the

---

[29] Karl Rahner, *Foundations of Christian Faith: An Introduction to the Idea of Christianity* (New York: Seabury Press, 1978).

[30] Johann Baptist Metz, *The Emergent Church* (New York: Crossroad, 1986), 27.

[31] Gustavo Gutiérrez, *A Theology of Liberation: History, Politics, and Salvation* (Maryknoll, NY: Orbis Books, 1973), 13.

crucified peoples down from the cross," a phrase he borrowed from Ignacio Ellacuría. Sobrino emphasizes the historical Jesus, the church of the poor, martyrdom, and salvation as liberation from all oppression, always in the context of the reign of God.[32]

The fact that liberation theologians often used a Marxist hermeneutic made the movement suspect in Rome, especially with Polish Pope John Paul II, whose experience of communism was anything but positive. Latin American liberation theology was the first of many contextual theologies of liberation—black, Hispanic, Asian, gay or "queer," or feminist, the last further divided into *"mujerista"* (Hispanic) or "womanist" (African American) theologies.[33]

Analytical Approaches

Francis Schüssler Fiorenza outlines two types of analytical approaches, one using an epistemological metatheory as a basic method and another using models and paradigms for theological reflection. As an example of metatheory, he takes Lonergan's study of human understanding, *Insight*, as well as his understanding of critical realism as a transition from a classical Aristotelian understanding of scientific method to a modern empirical method.[34] His metatheory includes an analysis of the intentionality of conversion as multidimensional—intellectual, moral, religious, and some add affective or psychic (Robert Doran)—and the biases that can introduce a blindness (scotoma) on any of these levels. His emphasis on modern empirical method has been adopted by theologians such as Roger Haight and Paul Lakeland, who seek to do ecclesiology "from below," an inductive or empirical ecclesiology.[35]

---

[32] Jon Sobrino, preface to *Systematic Theology: Perspectives from Liberation Theology*, ed. Jon Sobrino and Ignacio Ellacuría (Maryknoll, NY: Orbis Books, 1996), ix–x, at ix.

[33] Alfred T. Hennelly, *Liberation Theologies: The Global Pursuit of Justice* (Mystic, CT: Twenty-Third Publications, 1995).

[34] Schüssler Fiorenza, "Systematic Theology," 36–40; I am dependent on Schüssler Fiorenza's analysis for what follows. See also Bernard Lonergan, *Insight: A Study of Human Understanding* (New York: Philosophical Library, 1957).

[35] Roger Haight, *Christian Community in History*, vol. 1, *Historical Ecclesiology* (New York: Continuum, 2004), 4–14; Paul Lakeland, *Church: Living Communion, Engaging Theology: Catholic Perspectives* (Collegeville, MN: Liturgical Press, 2009), 120–23.

The use of models in theology was pioneered by Avery Dulles, who adapted the concept of models or paradigms from the physical and social sciences in his classic *Models of the Church*, returning to it again in *Models of Revelation*.[36] For example, he described the church as institution, mystical communion, sacrament, herald, and servant, later adding community of disciples, while using the models of doctrine, history, inner experience, dialectical presence, or new awareness as different ways of characterizing revelation. Priesthood can be understood on the basis of a sacerdotal, community leadership, or representative model. Each model concretized an approach in imaginative and theological terms, leading to comparative appreciations and deeper understandings. Similarly, theological analysis can proceed using diverse categories. Christology can be described in ontological or functional terms; original sin may be described as an ontological, existential, or social reality.

Method of Correlation

Much of modern theology traces its roots to Friedrich Schleiermacher's starting point in human experience. To mediate between this and a more traditional starting point in Scripture, German Protestant theology in the mid-nineteenth century developed a "mediation theology" (*Vermittlungstheologie*) to mediate between science and faith as well as Scripture and reason. Paul Tillich's further development of this method led to its wide acceptance by many Roman Catholic theologians. Hans Küng used it to show the critical relation between the historical Jesus and the present. Edward Schillebeeckx looks at the correlation between the experiences of the tradition and present-day experiences, sometimes bringing about a critical confrontation. Rosemary Radford Ruether brings about a correlation between feminist perspectives and the prophetic principle, using the latter to critique whatever in the Bible might privilege one social group over another. David Tracy seeks a critical correlation between an interpretation of the Christian tradition and an interpretation of

---

[36] Avery Dulles, *Models of the Church* (New York: Doubleday, 1974); Dulles, *Models of Revelation* (New York: Doubleday, 1983).

the contemporary situation, appealing to mutually critical correlations between two sets of interpretations.[37] What is common to these theologies of correlation is the emphasis on experience, the fruit of modernity's "turn toward the subject."

Roger Haight has pointed to three important dimensions or "gifts" of American intellectual culture to the world church; they include a feminist perspective, openness to pluralism, and the rise of the laity.[38] In the area of ecclesiology especially, an emphasis on experience means an attention to ethnography, that is, direct observations of developments or situations. Joseph Ratzinger also does a theology of correlation, without the emphasis on experience, which for him is a product of German Enlightenment thinking. Correlation, for Ratzinger, is between philosophical and theological inquiry, showing how faith illumines reason.

Conclusion

Theology begins with a critical reflection of the church on its faith. Thus it is a communal enterprise, even when it remains bound to the work of individual scholars. Systematic theology seeks a comprehensive understanding of the realities affirmed by faith—God, Jesus, sin, grace, church—and how they relate to each other.

One of the first great theologians in Christian history, Augustine, saw theology as wisdom, the hidden Wisdom of God become visible in Christ and witnessed to by Scripture. Scripture points to transcendent truth and is interpreted in light of the church's rule of faith. Knowing the truth is contingent on loving the truth, which for Augustine gives a certain epistemic priority to will over intellect.

Thomas Aquinas, using the recently introduced work of Aristotle, placed greater emphasis on the intellect in his approach. He saw *sacra doctrina* as a distinct science alongside philosophy; in the university

---

[37] Schüssler Fiorenza, "Systematic Theology," 41–46.

[38] Roger Haight, "The American Jesuit Theologian," in *Jesuit Postmodern: Scholarship, Vocation, and Identity in the 21st Century*, ed. Francis X. Clooney (Lanham, MD: Lexington Books, 2006), 98.

it was increasingly called theology. Part of its task was to interpret a prescientific faith, and as the *magistri* increasingly turned from commentaries on Scripture to the opinions of the authorities listed in Lombard's *Sentences*, using the *disputatio* to examine disputed questions, theology was becoming an increasingly critical science.

In the centuries following the High Middle Ages, Catholic theology seemed to freeze into Baroque or neoscholastic forms. Aside from some significant commentaries, it became an increasingly ahistorical and deductive discipline, looking not to Scripture but primarily to church authority. But there were some exceptions. A new appreciation for history was evident in von Drey and Möhler at Tübingen in Germany, Cardinal John Henry Newman in England, and especially the *ressourcement* theologians in France. At the same time, the Transcendental Thomists sought to begin a dialogue with modern philosophy and Thomas by investigating the transcendental reach of human understanding.

One result of this history is that the relation between theology and Scripture has taken different forms. With Augustine, Scripture was testimony to the Divine Wisdom become visible in Christ. The task of theology was to interpret the text and the transcendent wisdom to which it referred. The primary method was the commentary (*lectio*). With Aquinas and his distinction between faith knowledge, based on Scripture, and scientific knowledge, theology became more critical, using the *disputatio* and arguing not only from the text but also from authorities. Still, Scripture remained the primary rule of faith. But under the influence of scholasticism, especially after the Reformation and its appeal to *sola Scriptura*, Catholic theology increasingly appealed to church teaching as the primary authority for Catholic theology, with Scripture used as a proof text.

The modern biblical movement gradually restored Scripture to its rightful place. Pope Pius XII's encyclical *Divino Afflante Spiritu* (1943) gave Catholic scholars freedom to use modern historical-critical methods, leading to a renewal of biblical scholarship within the church. *Dei Verbum*, the Second Vatican Council's Constitution on Divine Revelation, reaffirmed the central place of Scripture in the church's life and its place as the foundation for theology, along with tradition (no. 24). But contemporary theology, both Protestant and Catholic, too often risks ignoring the revelatory character of Scripture, reducing it to one more historical source,[39] rather than interpreting it within the life of the church and its living tradition.[40]

If Catholic theology has rediscovered the importance of Scripture, its task has become even more complex as the intellectual climate of the West changed, with modernity giving way to postmodernism and theology becoming increasingly contextual, pluralistic, and post-colonial. We will consider these changes in the following chapter.

For Further Reading

Boersma, Hans. *Nouvelle Théologie and Sacramental Ontology: A Return to Mystery*. Oxford: Oxford University Press, 2009.

Chenu, Marie-Dominique. *Toward Understanding Saint Thomas*. Chicago: Henry Regnery, 1964.

Denziger, Henrichs, and Adolf Schönmetzer, eds. *Enchiridion Symbolorum*. Barcione: Herder, 1965.

Doran, Robert M. *What Is Systematic Theology?* Buffalo, NY: University of Toronto Press, 2005.

Dulles, Avery. *The Craft of Theology: From Symbol to System*. New York: Crossroad, 1984.

Fiorenza, Francis Schüssler, and John P. Galvin, eds. *Systematic Theology: Roman Catholic Perspectives*. Minneapolis, MN: Fortress Press, 2011.

Jenson, Robert W. *Systematic Theology*. New York: Oxford University Press, 1997–1999.

Kasper, Walter. *The Methods of Dogmatic Theology*. Shannon, Ireland: Ecclesia, 1969.

Kerr, Fergus. *Twentieth-Century Catholic Theologians: From Neoscholasticism to Nuptial Mysticism*. Malden, MN: Blackwell Publishing, 2007.

---

[39] See Sandra M. Schneiders, *The Revelatory Text: Interpreting the New Testament as Sacred Scripture* (Collegeville, MN: Liturgical Press, 1999); see also Brevard S. Childs, *Biblical Theology in Crisis* (Philadelphia, PA: Westminster Press, 1970).

[40] Pontifical Biblical Commission, "The Interpretation of the Bible in the Church" (Vatican City: Libreria Editrice Vaticana, 1993).

Leinsle, Ulrich G. *Introduction to Scholastic Theology*, Washington, DC: The Catholic University of America Press, 2010.

Lonergan, Bernard. *Method in Theology*. New York: Crossroad, 1972.

Mettepenningen, Jürgen. *Nouvelle Théologie: Inheritors of Modernism, Precursor of Vatican II*. London/New York: T & T Clark, 2010.

Ratzinger, Joseph. *Principles of Catholic Theology: Building Stones for a Fundamental Theology*. San Francisco: Ignatius Press, 1987.

Sobrino, Jon, and Ignacio Ellacuría, eds. *Systematic Theology: Perspectives from Liberation Theology*. Maryknoll, NY: Orbis Books, 1996.

Tanner, Norman P., ed. *Decrees of the Ecumenical Councils*. Vol. 1, *Nicaea to Lateran V*; Vol. 2, *Trent to Vatican II*. Washington, DC: Sheed and Ward and Georgetown University Press, 1990.

Chapter 2

Changing Cultures, New Hermeneutics

If Catholic theologies during and after the Second Vatican Council were different from the abstract, nonhistorical arguments of the neo-scholastics, they were still largely European works, universal in conception, focused on the church and its tradition as understood in the West. But theology cannot be simply universal. It is of necessity affected by social location, with different concerns if it is done in the context of the social iniquities of Latin America or the changing culture of Africa or the many disadvantaged in India by its caste system and its culturally sanctioned treatment of women.

In this chapter we will consider the transition from modernity to postmodernity, including a new emphasis on historical consciousness. Then we will look at how these changes have contributed to the emergence of new hermeneutical perspectives and new disciplines. Finally we will note the new pluralism in theology as theologians, working out of a contemporary self-understanding, strive to hold on to their faith in what God has done in Christ Jesus.

From Modernity to Postmodernism

The terms modernity and postmodernism suggest a chronological development in which that characteristic way of thinking or intellectual culture known as modernity is succeeded by a later ethos called postmodernism. And as a generalization, such a scheme works. But in fact, both mindsets, often unacknowledged, can be found in representatives of contemporary culture.

Modernity

Modernity describes the mentality that developed in Europe following the scientific revolution in the seventeenth century and the Enlightenment (*Aufklärung*) in the eighteenth.[1] Modernity is characterized by an unbounded confidence in what human reason, once freed from the confines of faith, ecclesiastical authority, and religious doctrine, could accomplish on its own. A type of optimistic rationalism, blissfully unaware of how much it was itself culturally conditioned, this mentality saw the self as autonomous and humankind as capable of mastering nature and enhancing human life, creating in the process a just and equitable society. Or as Joseph Ratzinger has described it, "Modernity, which has discovered progress as the law of history, is by nature optimistic."[2] Increasingly God was seen as an unnecessary hypothesis.

The roots of modernity can be traced to the Renaissance, the Protestant Reformation, and the scientific revolution. The Renaissance sought to move beyond medievalism, exalting the human by appealing to classical Greco-Roman culture. In their effort to reform the church, the Reformers exalted individual conscience over against church authority, which in the Enlightenment would lead to an emphasis on human autonomy. In their emphasis on "faith alone" and "Scripture alone," they contributed to the separation of faith from reason that would be carried through more radically in modernity.

The scientific revolution, with its emphasis on observation and empirical demonstration, was to result in the triumph of the scientific method as the exclusive avenue to truth. Advances in science seemed to undermine the authority of both Bible and church. Copernicus (1473–1543) challenged the biblical view that the earth was the center of the universe. Galileo's condemnation in 1633 was to embarrass the Roman Catholic Church down to Pope John Paul II's 1992 statement, acknowledging that errors had been committed by church officials.[3]

---

[1] See Timothy G. McCarthy, "The Church and Modernity," in *The Catholic Tradition: The Church in the Twentieth Century*, 2nd ed. (Chicago: Loyola Press, 1998), 23–55.

[2] Joseph Ratzinger, *Salt of the Earth: The Church at the End of the Millennium; An Interview with Peter Seewald* (San Francisco: Ignatius Press, 1997), 25.

[3] Alan Cowell, "After 350 Years, Vatican Says Galileo Was Right: It Moves," *New York Times*, October 31, 1992; John Paul II, "Message to the Pontifical Academy of Sciences: On Evolution."

Darwin (1809–1882), with his theory of evolution, seemed to many Christians to have challenged the biblical doctrine of creation, while his theory of natural selection often led to a "survival of the fittest" view of human society.

The Turn to the Subject

The Enlightenment, basically hostile to Christianity, suggested the dawning of a new era of freedom and light following the darkness of medieval Catholicism, though its real product was a profound skepticism about ultimate reality. The intellectual revolution begun by Descartes (1596–1650) and continued by Locke, Hume, Kant, Hegel, and Feuerbach has been described as a "turn to the subject." No longer was human understanding seen as fundamentally receptive, determined by the world it apprehended, what Bernard Lonergan called the "already-out-there-now-real."[4] Instead, after Kant, consciousness was seen as constructive, even constitutive; humanity increasingly became the measure of all things.

Descartes's "systematic doubt" made certainty and truth dependent on what the mind could grasp on its own ("I think, therefore I am"), thus relativizing the authority of Scripture and church. The British empiricists made knowledge completely dependent on experience derived through the senses. Kant (1724–1804) argued that the mind projects intelligibility on the phenomenal world rather than grasping it in its understanding process; ultimate reality (the *noumenal*) remains unknown. He reduced religion to ethics (the perennial temptation of liberal theology). Hegel (1770–1831) identified the absolute Spirit with human consciousness itself, expressing itself historically in art, culture, science, political institutions, and philosophy. Religion he identified as consciousness of the Absolute—but consciousness still in alienation from itself; thus religion is a form of alienation. The concept of alienation was to become increasingly important. Feuerbach (1804–1872) secularized Hegel's metaphysical Absolute; the Absolute was not different from humanity but only a projection of humanity's own need. Thus modernity's turn to the

---

[4] Bernard Lonergan, *Insight: A Study of Human Understanding* (New York: Longmans, 1958).

subject meant that the human person became the creator of meaning rather than its discoverer. As Aidan Nichols has said, "The more the Enlightenment advanced in history, the more it tended to whittle down the concept of reason which was its foundation."[5]

Those Catholic thinkers who sought to reconcile modernity with Christian faith were called Modernists. While they legitimately sought to use modern methods of biblical and historical investigation, they accepted without question too many of the rationalist presuppositions of the Enlightenment, which too often led them to rationalize doctrines and reduce revelation to subjective human experience. Their work represented a sincere but not sufficiently critical effort to enter into a dialogue with modernity. The church condemned what it understood to be the heresy of Modernism in 1907.[6]

Classicist versus Historical Consciousness

One important result of modernity was what Bernard Lonergan has described as a shift from a classicist worldview to historical mindedness or historical consciousness.[7] The classicist worldview is basically static and essentialist; it ignores the importance of history. Like classical Greek and scholastic philosophy (Plato, Aristotle, Aquinas), it stressed the abstract or universal. Its perspective assumes that the human person, morality, theology, church, and sacrament are static, unchanging realities, like Platonic forms or Aristotelian universals. Methodologically, it proceeds deductively, from the abstract or universal to the particular case. Thus it emphasizes absolute laws, a perennial philosophy (Thomism), perfect definitions (man is a rational animal), and a Cartesian clarity. As we saw earlier, this was largely the method of neoscholasticism.

By contrast, historical consciousness stresses the concrete and particular; it presumes development and change, is open to new insights,

---

[5] Aidan Nichols, *The Thought of Benedict XVI: An Introduction to the Theology of Joseph Ratzinger* (New York: Burns and Oates, 2005), 256.

[6] See Gabriel Daly, *Transcendence and Immanence: A Catholic Study of Modernism and Integralism* (Oxford: Clarendon, 1980).

[7] See Bernard Lonergan, "The Transition from a Classicist World View to Historical Mindedness," in *A Second Collection*, ed. William F. J. Ryan and Bernard J. Tyrrell (London: Darton, Longman and Todd, 1974), 1–9.

higher viewpoints, and reinterpretations of traditional positions. It proceeds not deductively from universal natures (man, society, church) but inductively from empirical observation, critical investigation, historical evidence, and personal experience. Meaning is constituted by a historical process that is changing and developing, sometimes becoming frozen and even going astray, but always capable of reinterpretation, more accurate formulation, and the discovery of deeper meaning. We have seen a sense for historical consciousness at work in the works of Drey and Möhler, Newman, and those committed to the *ressourcement*.

Historical consciousness presumes that the church's self-understanding develops and its structures emerge historically; not all is given at the beginning. Thus ecclesiology is a historical discipline involving specific communities. Similarly, Christology develops through stages, the preaching of the Jesus of history, the proclamation of the early Christian communities, the constructive work of the church fathers and the early councils. Michael Novak's concept of "non-historical orthodoxy" represents a key insight.[8] It refers to an opinion or belief that over time has assumed the certainty of a doctrine; it is held to be orthodox and its opposite heresy, even though as a belief it lacks biblical or historical foundation. An example would be the "doctrine" that there are two sources of revelation, long presumed in post-Reformation Catholicism to be the teaching of the Council of Trent. Trent never used this language; nevertheless, the first draft of what became *Dei Verbum*, Vatican II's Dogmatic Constitution on Divine Revelation, titled its first chapter "The Two Sources of Revelation," though this draft was rejected by the council fathers.

The Catholic Church acknowledged the historical, and therefore limited, character of its teaching in the Congregation for the Doctrine of the Faith's 1973 declaration *Mysterium Ecclesiae*. After affirming the infallibility of the universal church and its magisterium, the declaration stated that the transmission of revelation encounters difficulties not only because the mysteries of God far exceed the human intellect but also because of "the historical condition that affects the expression of Revelation." Expressions of revelation might include Sacred Scripture, the creeds, as well as the dogmas, doctrines, and teachings of the magisterium. The declaration then suggested four

---

[8] Michael Novak, *The Open Church* (New York: Macmillan, 1964), especially chap. 5.

factors that might limit an expression historically.[9] We can illustrate them here, drawing on ecclesiology for examples.

First, the CDF referred to "the expressive power of the language used at a certain point of time." For example, terms such as kingdom of God, grace, or righteousness may have to be retranslated for different ages and cultures. Second, it noted that "it sometimes happens that some dogmatic truth is first expressed incompletely (but not falsely), and at a later date, when considered in a broader context of faith or human knowledge, it receives a fuller and more perfect expression." Vatican I's definition of papal infallibility was true but needed to be complemented by Vatican II's emphasis on the bishops' share in the exercise of the church's magisterium and charism of infallibility.

Third, it noted that when the church makes a pronouncement concerning Scripture or the tradition, it "usually has the intention of solving certain questions or removing certain errors. All these things have to be taken into account in order that these pronouncements may be properly interpreted." In other words, one has to be aware of the specific concerns or contexts that motivated the statement. Vatican I's emphasis on papal infallibility was in good part a response to French Gallicanism's exaggerated emphasis on the rights of national hierarchies and the state vis-à-vis the pope. Finally, the truths which the church intends to teach sometimes bear traces of the "changeable conceptions" of a given epoch. Certainly the monarchical concept of the church in the nineteenth century is inappropriate for understanding the church after the Second Vatican Council. And if an expression of revelation is limited historically, it might also be limited by the patriarchal culture from which it originated.

The Shift to Postmodernism

What is known as postmodernism is more of a sensibility, mentality, or ethos than a coherent philosophy. It is often seen as a reaction to modernity's unbounded confidence in humankind's ability to

---

[9] Congregation for the Doctrine of the Faith (hereafter CDF), "Declaration in Defense of Catholic Doctrine on the Church against Certain Errors of the Present Day," no. 5, http://www.vatican.va/roman_curia/congregations/cfaith/documents/rc_con_cfaith_doc_19730705_mysterium-ecclesiae_en.html.

perfect itself through the use of reason. That optimistic outlook had already begun to break down in the nineteenth century as a result of the work of thinkers like Kierkegaard, Nietzsche, Marx, and Freud. These "masters of suspicion" sowed the seeds of doubt in the enlightened character of human reason, revealing other, more sinister drives at work.

Søren Kierkegaard (1813–1855) dramatically illustrated the absolute solitude of the person before God who, like Abraham, must set forth at God's command into the unknown. Friedrich Nietzsche (1844–1900) argued that it was not reason but the will to power that drove the Enlightenment thinker. He saw modern culture as making God irrelevant. In the new world that resulted, values could not be imposed but only chosen, created by the "superman" who lived beyond good and evil. Karl Marx (1818–1883) secularized Hegel's dialectic; it was not the Absolute that governed the world but social interests and economic relationships. The point of philosophy was not to interpret the world but to change it. And finally, Sigmund Freud (1856–1939) analyzed the human person not as a rational animal but as driven by subconscious psychological dynamisms—the id, the superego, and the pleasure principle, beneath which lurked the death wish. Common to these thinkers was the conviction that rather than a self-possessed rational being, the human person was in a state of alienation, driven by unconscious dynamisms, subject to various illusions, far less free than most thought but called to become a true self.

But more than anything, it was the tragedies of the twentieth century that put an end to modernity's unquestioned confidence in the perfectibility of humanity and the world by the use of an autonomous reason.[10] Two devastating world wars, crushing poverty, state-supported torture, and numerous genocides—from the Armenian genocide during the First World War to Rwanda and Burundi at the end of the century, but dominated always by the Holocaust or Shoah which took place in a supposedly Christian Europe—brought home again how much irrationality and evil is present in the human heart.

---

[10] Benedict XVI critiqued this secularized notion of Christian hope in his encyclical *Spe Salvi*, nos. 16–23, http://w2.vatican.va/content/benedict-xvi/en/encyclicals /documents/hf_ben-xvi_enc_20071130_spe-salvi.html; see also Thomas P. Rausch, *Faith, Hope, and Charity: Benedict XVI on the Theological Virtues* (New York: Paulist Press, 2015), 61–64.

The use of nuclear bombs on Hiroshima and Nagasaki, the threat of nuclear annihilation during the Cold War, and the AIDS pandemic— to mention only a few examples—suggested that confidence in science and technology was misplaced, destroying the illusion that human- kind was constantly improving.

What emerged was what has been called the postmodern sensibil- ity, a less objective epistemology that sees all knowledge as "socially constructed" on the basis of one's social location, meaning that the biases of gender, race, ethnicity, and sexual identity that come from our own particular circumstances filter how we perceive the world. Postmodernism received its philosophical formulation from French poststructuralists like Derrida and Foucault. The structuralists agreed that all cultural phenomena are primarily linguistic in character. Jacques Derrida taught that all phenomena are "texts," outside of which reality itself remains unknowable. Michel Foucault maintained that knowledge is always an expression of power relationships; there- fore texts are always politically constructed on the basis of one's social location.

Postmodernism's characteristic method is deconstruction: tearing down privileged systems, rules, established meanings built on the hegemony of power relationships and privileged value systems. In a world where all reality is textual, literature becomes the central discipline, not as a study of story, drama, and art to be enjoyed for its own sake or for its insight into the human, but rather as an inves- tigation into relations of power and oppression. Hence the dominance of "culture studies" in the modern university. "Binary oppositions" (body/soul, male/female, culture/nature, objective/subjective, center/margin) are particularly suspect, as they reflect social location, making the first element in each pair formative, while still dependent for its definition on the less valued term. So are metanarratives sus- pect—explanatory stories considered universally valid and true.

The postmodernist sensibility should not be seen simply as nega- tive. It takes evil seriously and recognizes the episodic, irruptive, discontinuous character of history, and it is suspicious of any claim to objectivity. Its inherent skepticism has restored a measure of humility to Western thought, stressing the socially constructed character of our knowing, its tentative quality, the limited nature of our perspec- tives, and the importance of experience. Recognizing that our systems of meaning are influenced by social location has given new hope to marginalized groups and helped uncover the dynamics that oppress them.

At the same time, a healthy skepticism has too often given way to a pervasive relativism, suspicious of all truth claims and metanarratives. The deconstructionist impulse sees power relationship everywhere and is constantly finding new victims. Today there are only "truths," multiple and diverse. What is at risk is the very concept of truth.

New Hermeneutics

The postmodern sensibility also finds expression in a number of new hermeneutical disciplines sensitive to issues of how theology is shaped by historical consciousness and social location. They include postcolonial theory, feminist studies, queer studies, eco-theology, and comparative theology.

Postcolonial Theory

Recognizing what they see as the negative impact of Western colonialism on literature, history, politics, and cultures and their peoples, postcolonial theorists seek to decolonize or "deconstruct" Western ways of knowing as well as restrictive identities constructed on mutually exclusive "binaries" such as male/female, white/black, First World/Third World, heterosexual/homosexual, and so on. But postcolonial theory is not easy to grasp. It employs an abstract, postmodern language and a lexicon of bewildering terms. Its practitioners speak of difference, agency, whiteness, hybridity, homogenization, recoding, social location, heteronormativity, and hegemony, and they employ strategies such as deconstruction, dispossessing of the self, and border crossings. They have moved beyond the identity politics of the 1980s and early 1990s to a focus on culture, which for them involves more than geography, politics, religion, and ethnicity. They see it as a complex web of relationships shaped by race, class, gender, and sexuality which influence our thinking and result in privilege and marginalization.

Thus postcolonial theorists challenge Western, universalist ways of thinking that ignore social location, the effects of colonialism, and its new form of globalizing capitalism that displaces women, people of color, and others who are different. Methodologically they use deconstruction, not to destroy, but to reveal the exclusionary character of imperialism and privilege and the constructed character of much that is considered normative, making room for the disadvantaged other.

Many of these theorists are determinedly secular, ignoring "the potency of religion and theology among Third World peoples,"[11] though as Susan Abraham observes, their work reflects a "neo-colonial" secular culture in its efforts to eliminate the religious.[12] But as postcolonial theory became increasingly popular in the academy, it was not long before its methods were adopted by theologians and began moving into the church. Two areas of theological concern particularly influenced by postcolonial theory are feminist studies, already energized by Vatican II, and queer studies.

Feminist Studies

Vatican II turned the focus of the church away from itself and toward a needy world, especially in *Gaudium et Spes*, the Pastoral Constitution on the Church in the Modern World. Among the socially conscious movements it inspired was feminist theology. While some feminist theologians, for example, the late Mary Daly, would eventually move beyond Christianity and the church, most Christian feminists have sought to empower women and renew the church from within. They reject defining women in terms of their reproductive function, insisting that their value cannot be determined simply by biology. They want to help women discover their own spiritual power and critique arguments about women's roles in the church that seem

---

[11] R. S. Sugirtharajah, "Complacencies and Cul-de-sacs: Christian Theologies and Colonialism," in *Postcolonial Theologies: Divinity and Empire*, ed. Catherine Keller, Michael Nausner, and Mayra Rivera (St. Louis, MO: Chalice Press, 2004), 36.

[12] Susan Abraham, "Purifying Memory and Dispossessing the Self: Strategies in the Postcolonial Classroom," *Spiritus* 13 (2013): 59.

to be based on traditional attitudes rather than cultural studies and critical theology.

While biblical scholarship was long dominated by the supposedly objective approach of the historical-critical method, in the 1980s a new feminist hermeneutic emerged, developed by women to uncover the suppressed presence of women in the New Testament texts.[13] Elizabeth Johnson has outlined some presuppositions and strategies for overcoming patriarchal interpretations of Scripture and promoting the dignity of women.[14]

Presuppositions:

1. For the most part, the books of the Bible were written by men, for men, from a male perspective, in a sociopolitical culture dominated by men.

2. The flip side of this patriarchal stamp on biblical texts is that they pay little or no attention to women.

3. In addition to this fact, we also have to contend with the fact that the later history of the text continues in the hands of men, interpreting, preaching, and translating these texts within a patriarchal society and church.

4. Given the above presuppositions, the Word of God itself needs to be liberated from its overarching patriarchal bias.

Strategies:

1. If women are in a biblical text at all, they must have been even more powerfully present in the original event.

2. If women are not in a text, this does not necessarily mean that they were not present and active during the event (cf. Mark 6:34-44).

3. When male gender-specific words are used in an obviously inclusive sense, women should be read into the text as being included (Rom 8:14).

---

[13] For example, Elisabeth Schüssler Fiorenza, *In Memory of Her: A Feminist Reconstruction of Christian Origins* (New York: Crossroad, 1985).

[14] Elizabeth A. Johnson, "Feminist Hermeneutics," *Chicago Studies* 27 (1988): 129–34; I have paraphrased somewhat Johnson's principles.

4. Texts which lay down norms for women's roles should be analyzed in order to distinguish between prescriptive and descriptive functions. Most of these texts are prescriptive, written by men to order or persuade women to act in certain ways that men would like (1 Cor 14:34).

5. Texts which speak in a subordinationist way of women should be reinterpreted, if possible, to reveal a positive content (1 Tim 13-14).

While some feminist biblical scholars focused on biblical hermeneutics, others began to elaborate a feminist spirituality, raising consciousness by sharing personal stories, particularly their experience of disempowerment, taking women's embodied existence seriously, including those aspects of female sexuality often ignored or viewed negatively by religion, for example childbirth and menstruation, and emphasizing the goodness of the material and the bodily, including nonhuman nature, thus with ecology, what is often called eco-feminism. Finally, feminist spirituality seeks to develop communities that are participative and inclusive rather than patriarchal and dominative.[15]

By the late 1980s and early 1990s, the voices of postcolonial theorists, many of them women of color, began to challenge these early feminists. They noted the liberal and secular framework of their work and that it was largely a Western phenomenon. It assumed a universalist posture, embracing all women, not recognizing the privileged position these critics enjoyed on the basis of their whiteness. Among early efforts to include women of color were womanist and *mujerista* theologies, for black and Hispanic women, respectively. A second generation of postcolonial critics, among them Kwok Pui-lan, Tina Beattie, Gale Yee, and Musa Dube highlighted new concerns such as hybridity, deterritorialization, hyphenated or multiple identities, and the relations between race, colonialism, and patriarchy, for example, seeing the biblical story of Rahab the prostitute in the book of Joshua

---

[15] See Sandra M. Schneiders, "Feminist Spirituality," *The New Dictionary of Catholic Spirituality*, ed. Michael Downey (Collegeville, MN: Liturgical Press, 1993), 400.

(2:1) as a story of the sexual and territorial dispossession of native women.[16]

More radical secular feminists argue that not just gender but our understanding of nature itself is socially constructed. Concerned to reject the claim that anatomy is destiny, they end up failing to acknowledge the significance of the body, denying any real meaning to nature. These feminists, including some Christian ones, show a resistance to theology more characteristic of the Enlightenment, even to the extent of silencing the voices of women of faith.[17]

Not all feminists are allergic to feminist theology, with its stress on relationality, interdependence, and vulnerability. Tina Beattie argues that the feminist theological body is neither the disembodied body of the gender theorists nor the essentialized body of some Catholic feminists. Rather, it is a sacramental body which, while questioning the patriarchal and clerical dynamics of exclusion and control, discovers its true meaning by its incorporation into the Christian story in prayer, worship, and daily life. She cites, though in a critical way, Pope John Paul II's theology of the self as gift precisely in our creation as male and female.[18]

Queer Studies

Developing in the early 1990s out of feminist studies with its argument that gender and sexual identities are socially constructed, queer studies seeks to deconstruct conventional notions of "heteronormativity." Reclaiming the term "queer" as a term for studies on homosexuality is deliberately provocative, and some of its practitioners are clearly hostile to Christianity. But many are practicing Catholics who are also homosexual. They represent a community that, in spite of a number of positive statements from the American bishops such as the 1997 *Always Our Children*, is often marginalized in the church.[19]

---

[16] Musa W. Dube, *Postcolonial Feminist Interpretation of the Bible* (St. Louis, MO: Chalice Press, 2000), 122.

[17] See, for example, Tina Beattie's critique in her *New Catholic Feminism: Theology and Theory* (London and New York: Routledge, 2006), 26–29.

[18] Ibid., 45–48.

[19] USCCB, *Always Our Children: A Pastoral Message to Parents of Homosexual Children and Suggestions for Pastoral Ministers* (1997), http://www.usccb.org/issues-and-action/human-life-and-dignity/homosexuality/always-our-children.cfm.

Their language is frequently off-putting, for example, speaking of "queering" theology or even "queering Christ." They see homosexuality as a socially constructed category of exclusion.[20] Their intention is neither to attack the church nor to reject all sexual norms but to make room for those whose gendered and sexual identities make them "other" by finding resources within the tradition that may have been overlooked.

Queer theory theologians like Carter Heyward, Robert Gros, Gary David Comstock, and Graham Ward seek to reconfigure the valuing of Christian relationality beyond reproductive difference, stressing the inability to set limits to the church's inclusivity by setting boundaries that may be based on privileged notions of normativity. And they stress that human relationality reflects the relationality of our Triune God. For example, Graham Ward seeks to move to a broader understanding of relationality by reflecting on the "displacement" of the risen body of Jesus into the church, which in the process becomes multigendered—not just male and female—but embracing many expressions of being sexual,[21] like the now ubiquitous initials LGBT for Lesbian, Gay, Bisexual, and Transgendered (many add Q, for queer). Some surveys today ask, "With which gender do you identify?" listing, male, female, and other.

Ward argues that being male or female exceeds its anatomical reference; the malleability of the body opens up to a broader, eschatological sociality that signifies partnership, covenant, fellowship, and helpmates. For him, same-sex relationships reveal a love that goes beyond biological reproduction on the way to the redemption represented by the coming of the kingdom. Thus he envisions the church as an erotic community; "Our desire for God is constituted by God's desire for us such that redemption which is our being transformed into the image of God, is an economy of desire."[22]

James Alison is a gay theologian (he uses "gay" rather than "queer") who writes frequently about the pain and anguish especially felt by gay and lesbian people, especially gay priests who are not able to be honest about who they are. Yet he is optimistic that God is in the process of revealing that gay people are just like others, invited

---

[20] Beattie, *New Catholic Feminism*, 36.
[21] Graham Ward, *Cities of God* (London and New York: Routledge, 2000), 183.
[22] Ibid., 172; see also 196–202.

to the wonderful party God hosts, a God who is promiscuous in his invitations.[23] At the same time, some postcolonial scholars note critically that queer theology as a Western movement too often ignores the voices of gay men of color and pays insufficient attention to the complex relation between homoeroticism, race, religion, and colonialism.

Eco-theology

Other theologians are focusing their concerns on the life of our fragile planet. Elizabeth Johnson asks what has happened to our belief that the natural world is God's creation, which means that God is its beginning, its continuing existence, and its goal. Without God's sustaining presence, creation would cease to exist, for God not only sustains it at every moment but also, in some mysterious way, brings it to completion in the divine life.

Johnson argues that Greek dualistic thinking led to the medieval distinction between the natural and the supernatural, with the result that nature was excluded from the realm of grace. The modern era transformed the biblical mandate of "dominion" over nature (Gen 1:26) to domination. Nature was to be used, not cared for, and as Europeans began to colonize other lands, they assumed the right to dominate their darker, indigenous peoples.[24] She goes on to uncover the Spirit's life-giving presence in the natural world, in a creation groaning like a woman in childbirth, longing to be set free (Rom 8:18-25). And she reminds us of Pope John Paul II's words, "respect for life and for the dignity of the human person extends also to the rest of creation which is called to join humanity in praising God."[25] So dominion is not quite right; we are a community in partnership with creation, a complex mutually dependent network of living beings, an ecosystem reflecting the glory of God.

---

[23] James Alison, *Undergoing God: Dispatches from the Scene of a Break-In* (New York: Continuum, 2006), 166–72.

[24] Elizabeth A. Johnson, *Creation: Is God's Charity Broad Enough for Bears?*, ed. Theresia De Vroom (Los Angeles: Marymount Institute Press, 2014), 6–15; see also Johnson, *Ask the Beasts: Darwin and the God of Love* (London: Bloomsbury, 2014).

[25] Johnson, *Creation*, 32–33.

Besides their concern for the protection of the planet, some eco-theologians have taken on the cause of animal welfare, appealing to the example of Mahatma Gandhi and Albert Schweitzer. Gandhi's principle of *ahimsa*, nonviolence, embraced the animal kingdom as well as the human. His vegetarianism was a consequence of *ahimsa*, as was his objection to using animals in medical experiments, though he made an exception to killing them when they posed a serious threat to humans.

Gandhi's principle influenced Albert Schweitzer, the Protestant theologian who spent most of his life tending the sick at Lambaréné in Africa. From his youth, Schweitzer had shown a concern for animals. Later he wrote, "There slowly grew up in me an unshakeable conviction that we have no right to inflict suffering and death on another living creature unless there is some unavoidable need for it."[26] This conviction grew into a reverence for all living things, from the amoeba to the human, and led him also to embrace vegetarianism. According to Catherine Keller, some postcolonial theorists like Gayatri Spivak even dream of an animist liberation theology for an ecologically just world, though Spivak would reject "theology" as alien to her secular thinking.[27]

Comparative Theology

Nostra Aetate, the Second Vatican Council's Declaration on the Relation of the Church to Non-Christian Religions, both anticipated and contributed to the new attitude toward religious pluralism that is seen as increasingly important in the twenty-first century. It called Catholics to a new respect for religious pluralism, noting that other religions often reflect a ray of that truth that enlightens all people. And it encouraged Catholics to dialogue and cooperate with the followers of other religious traditions (NA 2). Thus to enter into inter-

---

[26] Thomas Kiernan, ed., *Reverence for Life: An Anthology of Selected Writings* (New York: Philosophical Library, 1965), 5, cited in Ryan P. McLaughlin, "Non-violence and Nonhumans: Foundations for Animal Welfare in the Thought of Mohandas Gandhi and Albert Schweitzer," *Journal of Religious Ethics* 40, no. 4 (2012): 678–704.

[27] Catherine Keller, "The Love of Postcolonialism," in Keller, et al., *Postcolonial Theologies*, 237.

religious dialogue is itself a religious act, seeking out the truth that may be embodied in another religious tradition.

Comparative theology, associated in its first generation with the work of Francis Clooney and James Fredericks, is one significant response to religious pluralism. It is postmodern in that it recognizes that truth can have multiple expressions and postcolonial in its attentiveness to new insights coming from theologies of others continents and religious traditions. Comparative theology differs from comparative religion by its committed stance within one tradition in order to explore how another tradition might shed greater light on one's own through dialogue with its teachings and traditions. But it requires honesty about one's own beliefs. Fredericks insists that Christian theologians should not feel obliged to reformulate their own beliefs to make them more acceptable to a dialogue partner, for example, making Jesus into an *avatar* of Vishnu. The same is true of course for those who follow another tradition. As Fredericks says:

> If a theology of religion can become a way to avoid dealing with the moral, intellectual, and spiritual demands religions make, so also it can act as a mask for a subtle form of religious intolerance. If we should believe that all religions are ultimately saying the same thing or responding to the same ultimate reality, then there is nothing a Buddhist or a Confucian or a Muslim could say that would require me, as a Christian, to change my mind, at least regarding matters of great theological importance.[28]

Thus comparative theology is different from some all-embracing theology of religion. Rather, it seeks to show how one religion in its uniqueness might lead to a deeper understanding of one's own tradition. For example, its method is to ask how Muslims understand the mystery of God, or how Buddhists understand death, or how the divine love is understood in Hinduism.

---

[28] James L. Fredericks, *Faith among Faiths: Christian Theology and Non-Christian Religions* (New York: Paulist Press, 1999), 164; see also Francis X. Clooney, ed., *The New Comparative Theology: Interreligious Insights from the Next Generation* (London: T & T Clark, 2010).

Theological Pluralism

If we consider the variety of theological disciplines today and how theology, like all the humanities, has been influenced by postmodernism, postcolonial theory, a new concern for the excluded other, and the life of the planet itself, it becomes apparent how pluralistic theology has become. This is the argument of David Tracy in his book *Blessed Rage for Order*. He begins by situating the contemporary theologian between his or her faith in what he calls the "modern experiment," a postmodernist world shaped by the Enlightenment and a personal faith in the God of Jesus Christ. The Enlightenment, with its demand for rationality, has contributed to a "disenchantment of the world," leaving no room for the supernatural or the mystical. The result is not so much a crisis of faith as it is a crisis of cognitive claims made in the Christian Scriptures which cannot be sustained by the findings of history and the natural sciences.[29] The morality of scientific knowledge means that the theologian can no longer maintain intellectual integrity simply because this is what the tradition has believed. Intellectual integrity demands a new commitment, not to what authority teaches, whether Protestant or Catholic, but rather to what autonomous, critical inquiry demands. Thus theologians and their secular contemporaries share a commitment to scientific knowledge that forces them to assume a critical attitude toward their own tradition's beliefs.

Still, these "revisionist theologians" are not reduced to the same level as their secularist critics, for what the secularists cannot acknowledge is that without a proper understanding of revelation, God, or Jesus Christ, they cannot provide an adequate understanding of the very faith of secularity itself. Indeed, revisionist theologians point out that the secularists' rejection of God and Christianity leaves them unable to give an account of our common experience that can affirm the final worthwhileness of existence.

At the end of the article, Tracy introduces what he calls the disenchantment with disenchantment as the crisis of the modern secular mind. He points to the critical social theory of the Frankfurt School

---

[29] David Tracy, "The Pluralist Context in Contemporary Theology," in *Blessed Rage for Order* (New York: Seabury Press, 1975), 4–5.

as the most telling critique of the Enlightenment, not from the right, but from the radical left. These thinkers—all Marxists—argue that "the reification of reality enforced by modern scientific processes of demystification and rationalization is in fact responsible" not only for some of the horrors of the twentieth century but also that this process, instead of developing symbols that might lead to personal and social liberation, has given us impoverished symbols that "continued the domination of the developed powers in modern technological society."[30] In other words, the rich and the powerful continue to rule.

In his encyclical *Spe Salvi*, Pope Benedict XVI observes that technical progress without progress in ethical formation and moral growth remains a threat for both human beings and the world, citing Theodor Adorno of the Frankfurt School, who calls it progress "from the sling to the atom bomb" (no. 22). Or as Pope Francis says in *Laudato Sì*, "Following a period of irrational confidence in progress and human abilities, some sectors of society are now adopting a more critical approach. We see increasing sensitivity to the environment and the need to protect nature, along with a growing concern, both genuine and distressing, for what is happening to our planet" (no. 19).

Conclusion

Modernity's Enlightenment-driven confidence in what reason could accomplish on its own began to break down as scholars such as Kierkegaard, Nietzsche, Marx, and Freud presented a picture of the human person driven by dynamisms deeper than unfettered reason, while the atrocities and violence of the twentieth century challenged the idea that scientific progress was leading to a better life for all. The result was postmodernism, with its suspicion of metanarratives, skepticism about truth claims, and concern with power relationships of privilege that disadvantaged others.

The gradual move from a classicist approach to one characterized by historical consciousness in Catholic theology was to prove enormously important in moving beyond an abstract neoscholasticism.

[30] Ibid., 13.

This move bore fruit at the Second Vatican Council, especially in the work of the *ressourcement* theologians. Yet Catholic theological scholarship was still largely Western in its provenance and universalist in expression. In the postconciliar period, the churches of Africa, Asia, and Latin America began to find their own voices; some were quick to embrace the postcolonial turn we have been considering.

If these postcolonial theologies remain controversial, they occupy an increasingly prominent place in both the East and the West. Their emphasis on social construction seems to deny the existence of any truth to which all might be accountable; still, they are correct in recognizing how our ideas and values are shaped by issues of gender, ethnicity, social status, and sexual orientation as well as by the plurality of social and religious contexts that inform our theologies today. And they point out that if today we are beyond European colonialism, empire has not vanished but only been replaced by global capitalism and American military power.

It is also true that postcolonial theory, with its concern for the marginal and the disadvantaged, can challenge the church to a greater inclusivity. In including all those who follow Jesus, the church embraces all God's children, women and men, gay and straight, the gifted, the wounded and hurting, and those on the periphery. Even more, the challenge to greater relationality is grounded in the relationality of the Triune God. The fact of religious pluralism today calls theologians to a new sensitivity to the truth that may be present in the religious other.

Nor can the earth be excluded from our concern. From eco-theology we can learn to see ourselves as caretakers rather than masters of the fragile ecosystems of the beautiful blue planet we are accustomed to seeing today against the blackness of space. It is our home, and it is under threat.

For Further Reading

Abraham, Susan. "What Does Mumbai Have to Do with Rome? Postcolonial Perspectives on Globalization and Theology." *Theological Studies* 69 (2008): 376–93.

Beattie, Tina. *New Catholic Feminism: Theology and Theory*. London and New York: Routledge, 2006.

Clooney, Francis X., ed. *The New Comparative Theology: Interreligious Insights from the Next Generation*. London: T & T Clark, 2010.

Fiorenza, Elisabeth Schüssler. *In Memory of Her: A Feminist Reconstruction of Christian Origins*. New York: Crossroad, 1985.

Francis, Pope. *Laudato Sì*. Encyclical Letter on Care for Our Common Home. 2015.

Fredericks, James L. *Faith among Faiths: Christian Theology and Non-Christian Religions*. New York: Paulist Press, 1999.

Johnson, Elizabeth A. *Ask the Beasts: Darwin and the God of Love*. London: Bloomsbury, 2014.

———. "Feminist Hermeneutics." *Chicago Studies* 27 (1988): 123–35.

Keller, Catherine, Michael Nausner, and Mayra Rivera, eds. *Postcolonial Theologies: Divinity and Empire*. St. Louis, MO: Chalice Press, 2004.

Lonergan, Bernard. "The Transition from a Classicist World View to Historical Mindedness." In *A Second Collection*. Edited by William F. J. Ryan and Bernard J. Tyrrell. London: Darton, Longman and Todd, 1974. 1–9.

Tracy, David. "The Pluralist Context in Contemporary Theology." In *Blessed Rage for Order*. New York: Seabury Press, 1975. 3–21.

Chapter 3

The Divine Mystery

Rudolf Otto, in his book *The Idea of the Holy*, pointed to an experience, both fascinating and terrifying, arguing that it was to be found in all religions. He called it the numinous, using the related word "numen" to refer to the mystery of the divine or God.[1] St. Catherine of Siena, Doctor of the Church, captures beautifully this experience of the mystery of God from a Christian perspective. It is the experience of God who cannot be known directly but in drawing near awakens in us a hunger that can never be stilled, a desire that can never be satisfied.

> You are a mystery as deep as the sea; the more I search, the more I find, and the more I find the more I search for you. But I can never be satisfied; what I receive will ever leave me desiring more. When you fill my soul, I have an even greater hunger and I grow more famished for your light.[2]

Contemporary culture has too often substituted another deity for the true God, not a God of awe and transcendence, but a comfortable God who is "always there for me" and demands little. The old God of punishment and retribution, supported by a moralistic theology of rules and prohibitions, is long gone. But gone also is the divine mystery. Or the culture remains comfortably agnostic. The challenge

[1] Rudolf Otto, *The Idea of the Holy* (London: Oxford University Press, 1950).
[2] Catherine of Siena, *Gratiarum action ad Trinitatem*, cap. 167.

for a Christian understanding of God is to do justice to the divine otherness without reducing the God of the biblical tradition to the domesticated "personal" God of popular culture. In this chapter, we will consider a God who is transcendent and incomprehensible and yet disclosed in history as Father, Son, and Spirit, a God whose very nature is relational.

A Transcendent God

The Christian experience of God has its roots in the Hebrew Scriptures and the experience of a God who is "holy" or other. When Moses stands before the burning bush, symbolic of God's presence, he is told to take off his sandals because the place where he stands is holy ground (Exod 3:5). Two aspects of the divine mystery stand out throughout the Bible. One is God's otherness and unknowability, in short, God's transcendence. The other is that God is personal, seeking always a relation with the people who are the work of God's hands.

Transcendence

The idea of God's holiness, from the Hebrew root *qds*, meaning separate, emphasizes God's otherness, apartness, and difference from all that is created, limited, and imperfect. God is the "wholly other" (*totaliter aliter*), the transcendent. The Israelites were forbidden any attempt to represent their God with images "of anything in the sky above or on the earth below or in the waters beneath the earth" (Exod 20:4; cf. Deut 5:8), a prohibition also incorporated into the Qur'an. To look upon God's face was life threatening; it could bring about death (Exod 33:20; Judg 13:22). Even God's holy name, YHWH, was not to be pronounced; the texts read in the synagogues provided alternatives. And unlike the gods of the nations (for example the gods of the Greeks and Romans), Israel's God did not have a sexual partner or enter into sexual relations with humans.

Related to God's transcendence is God's unknowability. In the book of Job, when Job in a *crie du Coeur* demands an explanation for his suffering, God answers him in a wonderful poetic passage which suggests our inability to understanding the divine mystery:

Where were you when I founded the earth?
   Tell me, if you have understanding.
Who determined its size; do you know?
   Who stretched out the measuring line for it?
Into what were its pedestals sunk,
   and who laid the cornerstone,
While the morning stars sang in chorus
   and all the sons of God shouted for joy?

And who shut within doors the sea,
   when it burst forth from the womb;
When I made the clouds its garment
   and thick darkness its swaddling bands?
When I set limits for it
   and fastened the bar of its door,
And said: Thus far shall you come but no farther,
   and here shall your proud waves be stilled. (Job 38:4-11)

The answer is simple and yet profound. How can a mere human being understand the God who created the heavens and the earth? The transcendent God is unknowable. The Old Testament describes God as hidden in an impenetrable cloud (Exod 20:21; 24:15). Other images for God's unknowability include light and darkness, both of which impede vision. Thus, the author of 1 Timothy speaks of God as dwelling "in unapproachable light" (1 Tim 6:16). Gregory of Nyssa (c. 335–395) speaks of God hidden in "luminous darkness." Echoing 1 Timothy, Anselm (1033–1109) pictures God as dwelling in "inaccessible light" that blinds the human intellect:

Surely, Lord, inaccessible light is your dwelling place, for no one apart from yourself can enter into it and fully comprehend you. If I fail to see this light, it is simply because it is too bright for me. Still, it is by this light that I do see all that I can, even as weak eyes, unable to look straight at the sun, see all that can be seen the sun's light.[3]

A fourteenth-century mystical text describes God as approached through a "cloud of unknowing."

[3] Anselm, *Proslogion* 16.

Late in his life, Karl Rahner spoke increasingly about the incomprehensibility of God, God as absolute mystery, basing himself on the teaching of Thomas Aquinas. For Thomas, God is incomprehensible not only because the finite mind cannot know God who is pure being but also because even in the immediate vision of God (the beatific vision), God's self-communication reveals God's total simplicity, and thus, God's even greater incomprehensibility. For Thomas, this is primarily an anthropological teaching about the finite character of the human person rather than a "negative" quality of God. But this finiteness is positive rather than negative; it reflects the way human intelligence works, with "the ultimate and fundamental movement of the spirit and its activity (*intellectus agens*) toward the infinite being of God in his incomprehensibility, and this is the ground of all knowing."[4] It also reveals the transcendence of the intellect, constantly moving beyond what it knows. As Rahner says in his *Foundations of Christian Faith*, we are oriented toward mystery, toward God.[5]

Knowing the Transcendent God

If the transcendent God is unknowable, how, then, can we come to any knowledge of God? Catholics and Protestants have answered this question differently. While both acknowledge the importance of revelation, Catholic theology with its emphasis on the incarnation has tended to stress the divine immanence, while Protestant theology from its origins in Luther and Calvin has placed great emphasis on God's transcendence and tended to rely on "Scripture alone." In part, this was a reaction to what the Reformers saw as the abuses in Catholic popular devotion and its sacramental system. And in part, they were shaped by the late medieval philosophy they inherited, with its univocal concept of being and nominalism, the legacies of Duns Scotus and William of Ockham, respectively.[6] Catholic theology,

[4] Karl Rahner, "Thomas Aquinas on the Incomprehensibility of God," *Journal of Religion* 58 Supplement (1978): S108–16, at S116.

[5] Karl Rahner, *Foundations of Christian Faith: An Introduction to the Idea of Christianity* (New York: Seabury Press, 1978), 53.

[6] See Colin E. Gunton, *The One, the Three and the Many: God, Creation, and the Culture of Modernity* (Cambridge, UK: Cambridge University Press, 1993), 56–58; see also

while also based on Scripture, read within the tradition of the church, has continued to recognize the importance of natural theology.

Natural Theology

Based on reason rather than revelation, natural theology presumes a certain kinship or analogy between the world of our experience and the divine. The ancient Greeks were the first to move beyond the imagery of their cultural myths to inquire into the logos hidden within them. They sought to identify the ultimate principle (*archē*) of all that is. For Plato, that principle was nous or intellect eternally contemplating the forms. He used the term "theology" for critical discourse about the gods.[7] Aristotle's God was a self-enclosed deity, described as pure thought thinking itself. Neither creator nor personal, it was a spiritual being, pure and changeless, an eternal cosmological cause or prime mover, posited to explain the world's motion but without contact with it.[8] Plotinus's first principle was the transcendent, unchangeable "One," an absolute unity of being and nonbeing. Through its emanations, the One was the source of the world but not its creator. These notions of the divine were more in the nature of philosophical principles—immutable, impersonal, transcendent—not a God who might reach out in love and relationship.

Christian natural theology distinguishes between nature (what things are) and creation (their origin in God). While theologians in the classical tradition—Augustine, Anselm of Canterbury, and Bonaventure—integrated natural theology into the history of salvation,[9] for Aquinas, God's existence was primarily (but not exclusively) a philosophical question. Most influential was his summarizing the various arguments for God's existence. His famous "Five Ways" (*Quinque Via*), arguing from motion, efficient causality, contingency,

---

Robert Barron's essay, "The Christian Humanism of Karol Wojtyla and Thomas Aquinas," in *Bridging the Great Divine: Musings of a Post-Liberal, Post-Conservative Evangelical Catholic* (Lanham, MD: Rowman & Littlefield Publishers, 2004).

[7] Walter Kasper, *The God of Jesus Christ* (London/New York: Continuum, 2012), 72.

[8] See Alexander Sissel Kohanski, *The Greek Mode of Thought in Western Philosophy* (Rutherford, NJ: Fairleigh Dickinson University Press, 1984), 66–70; cf. Aristotle's Metaphysics 1072 a. 24.

[9] Kasper, *The God of Jesus Christ*, 73.

perfection, and design or teleology, are not so much "proofs" in the scientific sense in that they are not demonstrative for those who do not accept their premises but rather arguments which have a certain cogency.

It was Aquinas's third argument, from possibility or necessity, most often identified as the argument from contingency, which represents his most profound insight. He reasoned that all things in nature are observed to be generated and corrupted and thus are able to be and not to be. But it is impossible for these things always to be, since that which is possible not to be at some time is not. His conclusion is that there must be something whose existence is necessary, to avoid an infinite regress, and so he postulates the existence of a being whose *nature* is *to be*, a necessary being that does not receive existence, like contingent beings, but gives it to others. This is what we speak of as God.[10]

Thus, in the thought of Aquinas, God is ineffable, not a being like others beings. As he says in his *De Potentia*, "God is neither a species nor an individual, nor is there difference in him. Nor can he be defined, since every definition is taken from the genus and species."[11] In grammatical terms, God is not object but verb, pure act, *ipsum esse subsistens*, pure subsistent being, the condition for the possibility of the contingent beings we know.

> The being of God, since it is not received into anything, but is pure being, is not limited to any particular mode of a perfection of being, but contains all being within itself: and thus as being taken in its widest sense can extend to an infinity of things, so the divine being is infinite: and hence it is clear that his might or active power is infinite.[12]

Etienne Gilson used the word "aseity" to describe this unique way of existing in virtue of its own nature, by itself (*a se*), without cause.[13] All other beings are beings only by participation. God is not *a* being

---

[10] Aquinas, *Summa Theologica* I, q. 2, a. 3.

[11] Aquinas, *De Potentia Dei* 7.2.

[12] Ibid., 1.2.

[13] Etienne Gilson, *The Spirit of Medieval Philosophy* (New York: Charles Scribner's Sons, 1940).

but pure *Being;* in God existence and essence, God's being and God's whatness (quiddity), are the same.

Protestant theology, more heavily influenced by Augustine's doctrine of original sin and its corrosive effect on human nature and its faculties, is reluctant to place much emphasis on what reason can accomplish on its own. Knowledge of God is through "Scripture alone," as we have seen. An extreme case of this is Karl Barth. Concerned always to defend the transcendence of God and what he calls the "sovereignty of grace," Barth rejected the Catholic principle of the analogy of being (*analogia entis*). Appearing first in late scholasticism, perhaps in the work of the commentator on St. Thomas, Tommaso de Vio, later Cardinal Cajetan (1469–1534), and then in Francisco Suárez,[14] the analogy of being sees a certain commonality or analogy between the beings of the world and Being itself. Created beings are being only in a derivative, secondary sense. It is this analogy or commonality that enables human intelligence to move from "the things God has made" (Rom 1:20) to their ultimate cause, making possible metaphysics and natural theology, even if we remain dependent on revelation to know who God is.

At the beginning of his *Church Dogmatics,* Barth described this Catholic principle as the invention of the Antichrist, arguing that all other reasons for not becoming Catholic are "shortsighted and lacking in seriousness."[15] God is to be known only by faith in God's revelation. But in rejecting the *analogia entis* as well as any kind of natural theology, in either its liberal Protestant or its Roman Catholic form, Barth opened a vast chasm between nature and grace, the divine and the human.

The Augustinian/Franciscan tradition, without subscribing to a Barthian chasm between nature and grace, is less intellectualist in its epistemology than the Thomistic—it is more "voluntarist," stressing the role of the will in knowing. Sin in the world has its effect. One must love the true and good in order to know it. Joseph Ratzinger/Pope Benedict XVI is very much in this tradition. He writes that

[14] Thomas F. O'Meara, *Erich Przywara, SJ: His Theology and His World* (Notre Dame, IN: University of Notre Dame Press, 2002), 74.

[15] Karl Barth, *Church Dogmatics,* vol. 1, pt. 1, *The Doctrine of the Word of God,* ed. G.W. Bromiley and T. F. Torrance (Edinburgh: T & T Clark, 1936), x.

Augustine's epistemology is deeper than that of Aquinas, for "it is well aware that the organ by which God can be seen cannot be a non-historical *'ratio naturalis'* which just does not exist, but only the *ratio pura*, i.e., *purificata* or, as Augustine expresses it echoing the gospel, the *cor purum* ('Blessed are the pure in heart, for they shall see God')."[16] In his *Jesus of Nazareth*, Ratzinger comments that the organ for seeing God is the heart.[17] Or as Robert Neelly Bellah says in reflecting on thinkers as diverse as Charles Taylor, Václav Havel, and Paul Tillich, "I am quite sure that God is not a thing, and so not something that can be proved or disproved. God is not a theory and the way to God is through a living relationship, not theorizing."[18]

Rahner's theological anthropology, based on his transcendental method, can also be considered a natural theology, one that moves beyond modernity's secular rationality with its distrust of traditional arguments for the existence of God. Turning to experience, Rahner finds the absolute disclosed against the transcendental horizon of human consciousness. Because God remains mystery, we can only experience God indirectly in certain transcendent experiences that take us beyond ourselves. He says that the experience of God "constitutes . . . the ultimate depths and the radical essence of *every* spiritual and personal experience (of love, faithfulness, hope, and so on), and thereby precisely constitutes also the ultimate unity and totality of experience, in which the person as spiritual possesses himself and is made over to himself."[19]

In other words, we come to grasp God's existence by reasoning beyond the world of our experience but also by discovering our orientation toward goodness, truth, and beauty disclosed in the structure of our consciousness. This experience is more than knowledge of God obtained from so-called proofs; though it often remains un-

---

[16] Joseph Ratzinger, "The Dignity of the Human Person, Commentary on *Gaudium et Spes*," in *Commentary on the Documents of Vatican II*, ed. Herbert Vorgrimler, vol. 5 (New York: Herder and Herder, 1969), 155.

[17] Benedict XVI, *Jesus of Nazareth*, pt. 1 (New York: Doubleday, 2007), 92.

[18] Robert N. Bellah, "The Rules of Engagement: Communion in a Scientific Age," *Commonweal* 135 (September 12, 2008): 20.

[19] Karl Rahner, "The Experience of God Today," in *Theological Investigations*, vol. 11 (New York: Seabury Press, 1974), 154.

recognized for what it is, it is an experience of God, whether accepted or denied, which for some meets only with incomprehension.[20] John Haught explores how the transcendent is disclosed in experiences of depth, future, freedom, beauty, and truth. Using Whitehead, he argues that the "senses give us only a very abstract and narrow range of the universe. They are inadequate to mediate the full complexity—and beauty—of the world in which we are organically situated."[21]

God in the Hebrew Scriptures

If Jewish monotheism sees God as transcendent, its God is also personal, a God who wants to be in relationship, a God who is close and involved in Israel's history. This God calls Abram out of Ur of the Chaldeans, promises to make him the father of a great people, and gives his barren wife a son. When his descendants are oppressed in the land of Egypt, he raises up Moses to lead them out of bondage, entering into a covenant relationship with them on Mount Sinai, and under Joshua brings them into the Promised Land. When they betray the covenant and fall into idolatry, he sends prophets to call them back to faithfulness, sometimes using the metaphor of the husband of an unfaithful wife, and promises a future intervention in the life of the people and the nation, revealing his salvation. This is a God constantly reaching out to humankind, so beautifully portrayed in Michelangelo's "The Creation of Adam."

The idea that the God of the Old Testament was a wrathful God of law and judgment while the God of Jesus was a God of love and compassion is as old as the early second-century priest Marcion, though unfortunately one still hears it today. Marcion wanted to reject the Old Testament as no longer necessary for Christians and tried to reduce the New Testament to the Gospel of Luke and the letters of Paul. His teachings were ultimately rejected by the church and contributed to the formation of the Christian canon.

[20] Ibid., 149–55.
[21] John F. Haught, *What Is God: How to Think about the Divine* (New York: Paulist Press, 1986), 85.

Jesus, God's Only Son

God's desire to be in relationship with a people is continued in the story of Jesus. The Christian understanding of God cannot be separated from Christology; the neoscholastic approach started with the thesis *De Deo Uno* (*On the One God*), then moved to a second thesis, *De Deo Trino* (*On the Triune God*). The primary sources for a Christian understanding of God remain the Scriptures, both the Old and New Testaments. Jesus' knowledge of God was learned in his home and nourished by the Scriptures of his people. Similarly, the first Christians were all Jews; their God was also the God of Israel, but they came to know God more intimately through the teachings, life, death, and resurrection of Jesus. The Synoptic Gospels show Jesus as one completely dedicated to the God he calls Abba, Father, contrary to the Jewish practice of his day, and referring to himself as son. The report of his virginal conception through the Holy Spirit (Matt 1:20) suggests that his real father is God (Luke 1:35).

Jesus proclaims the coming of the kingdom of God and scandalizes some of the religious leaders of the Jewish community by announcing the forgiveness of sins, clearly a divine prerogative. In Mark, the evil spirits recognize Jesus as the "Holy One of God" (Mark 1:24) or "Son of God" (Mark 3:11). Luke especially emphasizes the importance of prayer in Jesus' life. The Gospel of John, with its high Christology, consistently emphasizes Jesus' union with God in action and affection, describing him as the Word become flesh (John 1:14), the one who has come down from heaven (John 3:13), using several times the divine formula "I AM" (John 8:28, 58; 13:19).

While an earlier Christology dismissed high Christology as a late biblical development, such a position is no longer tenable.[22] Already in Paul's time, the early Christians, mostly Jews, made Jesus the object of the prayer and worship ordinarily reserved for God. Larry Hurtado speaks of the "binitarian" character of their worship, showing Jesus as the recipient of devotion "in ways that can be likened to the worship of a deity."[23] High Christology is also present in Paul's letters.

---

[22] See Terrence W. Tilley, *The Disciples' Jesus: Christology as Reconciling Practice* (Maryknoll, NY: Orbis Books, 2008), 59–66.

[23] Larry W. Hurtado, *Lord Jesus Christ: Devotion to Jesus in Earliest Christianity* (Grand Rapids, MI: William B. Eerdmans, 2003), 135.

In Philippians 2:6-11, Paul cites a pre-Pauline hymn that speaks of Jesus as being "in the form of God" before emptying himself and taking on the form of a slave; the hymn goes on to say that he is the object of cosmic worship that includes the heaven, the earth, and the netherworld. Michael Cook says that it would be hard to find a more strongly worded, concrete expression of Jesus' divinity.[24] A similar exchange can be found in 2 Corinthians 8:9, which says that Jesus for your sake "became poor although he was rich, so that by his poverty you might become rich."

Paul also recognizes the "one Lord, Jesus Christ" as having a role in creation (1 Cor 8:6; cf. Col 1:15-16). Also, part of the Jesus' story is that Jesus, empowered by the Spirit, pours out the Spirit on his own. Therefore the God that Jesus reveals to us is incipiently trinitarian; to talk about God is to speak of God as Father, Son, and Holy Spirit.

The Holy Spirit

The Spirit of God or Holy Spirit, more affect than object or even subject, personifies God's creative presence. According to Brian Daley, "The Spirit of God, the Spirit sent by Christ, is surely much more difficult for the faithful reader of Scripture to characterize and identify; the Spirit does the work of God but seems to lack a "face"—a *prosōpon*; the Spirit is a gift, a force, but seems not to have the individual concreteness that Greek philosophy referred to by the term *hypostasis*."[25]

The Spirit hovers over the waters at creation (Gen 1:2) and inspires the prophets; it will rest upon the messiah (Isa 11:2; 61:1) and be poured out on all humankind in the messianic age (Ezek 36:27; Joel 3:1-2). Jesus is conceived by the Holy Spirit; the Spirit descends on him at his baptism (Mark 1:10), leads him into the desert (Luke 4:1), and empowers his ministry, especially as presented in Luke's Gospel. The Spirit is poured forth on the disciples at Pentecost (Acts 2:2-4)

---

[24] Michael L. Cook, *Trinitarian Christology* (New York: Paulist Press, 2010), 50.

[25] Brian E. Daley, "The Unexpected God: How Christian Faith Discovers the Holy Spirit," Duquesne University 7th Annual Holy Spirit Lecture and Colloquium (September 23, 2011), 23, http://www.duq.edu/Documents/liberalarts/_pdf/337535c%20 Holy%20Spirit%20Colloquium%20Lecture%20Booklet%2010.12WEB.pdf.

and guides the disciples and the leaders of the community in the work of evangelization and founding churches.

The presence and activity of the Spirit is evident throughout Paul's letters, though Paul's pneumatological language still seems to be developing. He does not clearly distinguish between Christ and the Spirit, speaking of "the Spirit of God" or the "Spirit of Christ" or simply "the Spirit." The risen Christ has become "a life-giving spirit" (1 Cor 15:45). To be "in Christ" is to have new life "in the Spirit," enabling us to know God's love poured into our hearts (Rom 5:5), to confess Jesus as Lord (1 Cor 12:3), and to call on God as *Abba* (Rom 8:15; Gal 4:6). The Spirit unites those baptized into one body, breaking down divisions (1 Cor 12:13). God is present and active in the church, described by Paul as a "dwelling place of God in the Spirit" (Eph 2:22).

The Spirit scrutinizes the depths of God (1 Cor 2:10), teaches the disciples to understand the gifts of God (1 Cor 2:12-13), leads or guides them (Rom 8:14; Gal 5:18), intercedes for the members of the church and helps them pray (Rom 8:26-27). Hans Küng speaks of the continuing charismatic structure of the church, in which the Spirit pours out a diversity of gifts and ministries (1 Cor 12:4-6).[26] In John, the Spirit is "the personal presence of Jesus in the Christian while Jesus is with the Father."[27] Jesus speaks of the "Advocate, the holy Spirit that the Father will send in my name" who will "teach you everything and remind you of all that I told you" (John 14:26), the Spirit who Jesus will send from the Father to testify to himself (John 15:26). The divinity of the Spirit, "the Lord, the Giver of Life, Who proceeds from the Father, Who with the Father and the Son is worshiped and glorified," was defined by the First Council of Constantinople (381).

Unfortunately, pneumatology has been largely neglected in the theology of the West, especially in comparison to that of the East. Yves Congar notes that although the Holy Spirit has been very much alive in Catholicism since the Counter-Reformation and after the French Revolution, it was not much present in its ecclesiology. It was lacking

---

[26] Hans Küng, *The Church* (New York: Sheed and Ward, 1967), 179–91.
[27] Raymond E. Brown, *The Gospel According to John (xiii–xxi)* (Garden City, NY: Doubleday, 1970), 1139.

in Bellarmine's teaching about the church. Petavius was famous for developing the personal relationship between the righteous soul and the Holy Spirit, but his theology lacks an ecclesiological extension. And Möhler provided a radical pneumatological ecclesiology in his early *Die Einheit* (1825), "but he later refused to prepare a new edition of this work, and what was preserved of his teaching is taken from his later book *Symbolic* (1832), with its resolutely Christological ecclesiology, in which the Church is seen as a 'continued incarnation.' This idea dominated the Roman school throughout the nineteenth century." [28] Perhaps the Western neglect of the Spirit accounts in part for the success of Pentecostalism in the twentieth century. But if pneumatology has been neglected in the West, Kilian McDonnell emphasizes the inseparability of Christology and pneumatology, recalling Irenaeus's image of the "two hands of the Father." [29] Christology cannot be replaced by pneumatology.

The Trinity

The doctrine of the Trinity is not to be found explicitly in the New Testament, but it is at the heart of Christian faith, even though it remains mystery. It cannot be reasoned to but comes from God's free self-disclosure in the mystery of salvation, thus from revelation. The doctrine of the Trinity reveals a self-giving God who is love, even if the majority of Christians have failed to integrate this mystery into their understanding of their faith; as Rahner has said, Christians in their practical life are "almost mere 'monotheists.' " [30]

Theologians are accustomed to distinguishing between the "economic Trinity," God's self-manifestation in history as Father, Son, and Spirit, and the "immanent Trinity," God *in se*, in the divine inner life. The distinction goes back to the early centuries. Early heresies, variously known as Monarchianism, Modalism, or Sabellianism, collapsed

---

[28] Yves Congar, *I Believe in the Holy Spirit*, pt. 1, *The Canonical Scriptures* (New York: Crossroad, 1997), 154–55.

[29] Kilian McDonnell, "A Trinitarian Theology of the Holy Spirit?" *Theological Studies* 46 (1985): 204–6; cf. Irenaeus, *Against the Heresies* 5.1.3.

[30] Karl Rahner, *The Trinity* (New York: Herder and Herder, 1970), 10.

the distinction between the immanent Trinity into the economic. In contrast to an authentic trinitarian theology, they saw God as one person who appeared in different modes or periods. Rahner insisted on the inseparability of the immanent Trinity from the economic.[31] The roots of the doctrine are clearly present in Jesus' self-identification as the "son," in the Gospel titles Son of God and Lord, in his promise of the Spirit, in the triadic formulas common in the New Testament, and in the trinitarian rule of faith evident in the church's baptismal practice and developing creeds.

Trinitarian Formulas

One finds both binitarian and trinitarian patterns in early Christian prayer and worship.[32] The New Testament offers a multitude of trinitarian formulas, evidence of the early Christians' awareness of God's salvific work taking place through Christ and in the Spirit. As early as 1 Corinthians, Paul speaks of the church's rich diversity of gifts and ministries in trinitarian terms: "There are different kinds of spiritual gifts [*charismata*] but the same Spirit; there are different forms of service [*diakonia*] but the same Lord; there are different workings but the same God who produces all of them in everyone" (1 Cor 12:4-6). The Second letter to the Corinthians concludes with a trinitarian blessing still used in the liturgy: "The grace of the Lord Jesus Christ and the love of God and the fellowship [*koinōnia*] of the holy Spirit be with all of you" (2 Cor 13:13).

Paul's understanding of salvation as the work of Father, Son, and Spirit is continued in Ephesians, most probably a Deutero-Pauline work. The author celebrates God's plan of salvation, choosing us in Christ (1:3-6), accomplishing our redemption through Christ's blood (1:7-10), and sealing us with the promised Holy Spirit as the pledge of our eschatological inheritance (1:13-14). Other passages refer to God's salvation in Christ through the Spirit in trinitarian form (2 Cor 1:21-22; Eph 4:4-6; John 14:25; 16:12-15). Though the early church seems to have baptized simply in the name of Jesus (Acts 2:38; 8:12,

---

[31] Ibid., 21.

[32] See Catherine LaCugna, *God for Us: The Trinity and Christian Life* (San Francisco: Harper SanFrancisco, 1991), 22.

16; 10:48; 19:5), the full trinitarian formula occurs at the end of Matthew when Jesus instructs the eleven disciples to baptize "in the name of the Father, and of the Son, and of the holy Spirit" (Matt 28:19).

The Doctrine of the Trinity

The development of the church's two most important creeds, the Apostles' Creed and the Nicene-Constantinopolitan Creed, are structured in terms of a trinitarian pattern. The Apostles' Creed developed out of the baptismal practice of the Roman church toward the end of the second century. The person being baptized was asked three times to profess faith in God the Father Almighty, in Christ Jesus the Son of God, and in the Holy Spirit. Two early versions of the present Apostles' Creed are extent, one in Latin from Rufinus (404), the other in Greek from Marcellus (340).[33] The eucharistic prayer of the *Apostolic Tradition*, attributed to Hippolytus of Rome, has a trinitarian structure and concludes with a doxology addressed to the Father "through your Child Jesus Christ, through whom [be] glory and honor to you, Father and Son with the Holy Spirit, in your holy church, both now and to the ages of ages. Amen."[34]

The creed of the Council of Nicaea (325) was formulated to refute Arius, who taught that God's being was unique, indivisible, unable to be shared, reducing Jesus to a demigod or creature. This typically Greek understanding of the divine nature amounted to a Hellenization of Christianity. Nicaea adopted the phrase, *homoousios*, of the same being or substance or "consubstantial," to describe Jesus as fully divine, "true God from true God." The creed of Nicaea was completed by the Council of Constantinople (381), which affirmed the divinity of the Spirit as we have seen. It also added the verse about belief "in one, holy, catholic and apostolic church."[35]

---

[33] See Thomas P. Rausch, *I Believe in God: A Reflection on the Apostles' Creed* (Collegeville, MN: Liturgical Press, 2008).

[34] Paul F. Bradshaw, Maxwell E. Johnson, and L. Edward Phillips, *The Apostolic Tradition: A Commentary*, Hermeneia: A Critical and Historical Commentary on the Bible (Minneapolis, MN: Fortress Press, 2002), 40; they postulate a composite text dating from the mid-second to the mid-fourth century, 14, 46–48.

[35] See Norman P. Tanner, ed., *Decrees of the Ecumenical Councils*, vol. 1, *Nicaea I to Lateran V* (London and Washington, DC: Sheed and Ward and Georgetown University Press, 1990), 24.

Irenaeus, Tertullian, and Origen helped formulate the doctrine of the Trinity. Irenaeus (d. c. 202) stressed the eternal existence of the Son and the Spirit, the "two hands of God," in the struggle against Gnosticism, with its theories of emanations or a secondary God (*deuteros theos*), though he did tend to subordinate the Son and Spirit to the Father. Tertullian (c. 160–225) introduced the words "trinity" (*trinitas*) and "person" (*persona*) for a distinction of persons but not of substance (*substantia*) in the Godhead. Stressing the inseparability of the immanent from the economic Trinity, he was able to preserve the monarchy of the Father as well as the distinction of the Son and Spirit. Seeing the Father, Son, and Spirit in terms of their relations, individual centers of action with specific roles in the history of salvation, his thought pointed to "relationality as an essential characteristic of what it is to be God."[36]

Origen (c. 185–254), whose theology was much informed by Platonism, stressed the transcendent, ungenerated, purely spiritual view of the divine. He spoke of Father, Son, and Spirit as three hypostases and seems to have been the first to use the word *homoousios* in speaking of the Son's relation to the Father. To illustrate the mystery of the unbegotten Father eternally begetting the Son, he used the analogy of the operation of the intellect, comparing the generation of the Son to an eternal act of the Father's will, an intellectual metaphor that would play an important role in the theology of the West.[37] His comprehensive view saw reality as God's free creation, coming from God and returning to God through the Son in the Spirit.[38] Like Irenaeus, both Tertullian and Origen shared to various degrees in a subordinationist interpretation of the relation of the Son and the Spirit to the Father.

Most helpful in resolving the church's emerging trinitarian language in a way that respected both the unity and the distinction in

---

[36] Anthony J. Godzieba, "The Trinitarian Mystery of God: A 'Theological Theology,' " in *Systematic Theology: Roman Catholic Perspectives*, ed. Francis Schüssler Fiorenza and John P. Galvin (Minneapolis, MN: Fortress Press, 2011), 159. For what follows I am relying on Kasper, *The God of Jesus Christ*, and LaCugna, *God for Us*, in addition to Godzieba.

[37] Edmund J. Fortman, *The Triune God: A Historical Study of the Doctrine of the Trinity* (Philadelphia, PA: Westminster Press, 1972), 56.

[38] Kasper, *The God of Jesus Christ*, 256.

God was the work of the Cappadocians: Basil of Caesarea (c. 330–379), Gregory of Nazianzus (330–389), and Basil's brother Gregory of Nyssa (335–394). The Council of Nicaea had used the terms *ousia*, being, and *hypostasis*, concrete individual embodiment of this common being, interchangeably, as did Athanasius up to 369. The Cappadocian fathers clarified the traditional language used for how Father, Son, and Spirit were related, distinguishing the terms and speaking of the mystery of God in terms of relations.

Basil's solution was to use *ousia* for what was common and *hypostasis* for what was proper to each. He argued that each hypostasis was distinguished by its proper characteristic, paternity for the Father, sonship for the Son, and sanctification for the Spirit. He also argued that "unbegottenness" is a proper characteristic of the hypostasis of the Father but not of God's *ousia*, while begottenness is a proper characteristic of the Son. Gregory of Nazianzus was apparently the first to use the phrase, one nature and three hypostases, also using *prosōpa* (persons) along with hypostases. He stated that "Father" designates a relation between the Father and the Son; it does not designate a substance or an activity. Gregory of Nyssa, like Basil, said that the Son and the Spirit are distinguished not by their essence (*ousia*) or nature (*physis*), but again, by their relations toward one another. Finally, all three Cappadocians affirmed the divinity of the Spirit, helping the church come to a language capable of expressing its faith in the triune God: Father, Son, and Spirit. As Godzieba says, their treatises and letters "represent the concluding moves in a series of contentious debates that lasted for more than a half century after Nicaea."[39]

The term *perichōrēsis*, first used by Gregory of Nazianzus to refer to the mutual interdependence of the two natures in Christ, was introduced into trinitarian language by John of Damascus (c. 675–749) to indicate the interpenetration or inherence of the three divine persons in each other. In other words, though each has a distinctive mission, each is present in and to the other two, without "mixture or confusion" (Augustine). In Latin, *perichōrēsis* became *circumsessio* or more often *circuminsessio*. The doctrine is important because speaking

---

[39] Godzieba, "The Trinitarian Mystery of God," 173–77, at 177.

of the mutual indwelling or *perichōrēsis* "of the three persons obviates both tritheism and modalism."[40]

It is perhaps helpful to see these christological controversies leading ultimately to the Council of Chalcedon in 451 as an ongoing controversy over theological language. Were the distinctions in the Godhead—Father, Son, and Spirit—real or merely modalities of God's manifestation in the work of salvation? Were the Son and the Spirit subordinate to the Father or equal? How was the unity of God to be affirmed without denying the distinction of persons? And how was the Spirit to be understood?

For example, Basil assumed the Stoic understanding of *ousia* as something general, not limited to a particular entity, while *hypostasis* was often translated in the Latin West by the word *substantia* or "substance." But three hypostases suggested to Western ears three substances, thus three Gods. Aquinas later introduced the term subsistence in place of substance, meaning the subject that stands under the nature of substance; thus in regards to the Trinity, the one divine nature or substance is "possessed" by three subjects or "exists in three relatively distinct modes of subsistence."[41] Another problem was that the term *persona* for distinctions in the Godhead was translated by the Greek *prosōpon*, meaning a mask as used on the stage, hence a mere appearance, which, of course, was problematic. It sounded like modalism, an issue not fully resolved until the Second Council of Constantinople (553) took hypostasis and person as synonyms.

These language issues were not insignificant, because what was at stake was the full mystery of God's revealing presence in Jesus as well as the divine nature. Theologian Catherine LaCugna sees the heart of the trinitarian doctrine in the definition of person in terms of origin: the Father unbegotten, the Son begotten from the Father, the Spirit proceeding from the Father, arguing that *"what a person is in itself or by itself cannot be determined."*[42] Persons are essentially interpersonal, intersubjective, and relational.

---

[40] Kasper, *The God of Jesus Christ*, 284.

[41] Ibid., 281.

[42] LaCugna, *God for Us*, 69, italics in original.

Latin theology after Augustine located divine relationality in the intradivine sphere; Greek theology identified the Father as the origin and ground of all relationality, the Father who moves beyond self toward Son and Spirit and toward the world. Whether our preference is for one of the other or some combination of the two approaches, the doctrine of the Trinity, in one form or another, is the *sine qua non* for preserving the essentially relational character of God, the relational nature of human existence, and the interdependent quality of the entire universe.[43]

Today some theologians remain uncomfortable in using the term "person," as though it referred to three independent subjectivities, that is, person in the modern sense. Gerald O'Collins resists theologizing on the basis of the modern concept of the person. Still, he says that in the Trinity one consciousness subsists in a threefold way, shared by all three persons, "mutually distinct only in and through their relations of origins."[44] Some prefer "three modes of being" (Barth) or there "distinct manners of subsisting" (Rahner).

In spite of our speaking of an immanent as well as an economic Trinity, God remains mystery. The three persons in God are not to be understood as individuals in our modern sense. But with these cautions noted, we must say that the God revealed in salvation history, and the God whose inner life we express in trinitarian language, is indeed personal. This God far surpasses or realizes in a preeminent way what the concept of person means for us, that is to say, freedom, transcendence, openness to others and another, the capacity for love.

The Filioque

The churches of the East and those of the West have long been divided about how to describe the procession of the Holy Spirit. The Creed of the Council of Constantinople (381) taught that the Spirit

---

[43] Ibid., 289; Joseph Ratzinger argues that a nontrinitarian monotheism could not meet Aristotle's objection about the inability of eternity to enter into relationship with time because of its very nature; Ratzinger, *The Feast of Faith* (San Francisco: Ignatius Press, 1986), 20–21.

[44] Gerald O'Collins, *The Tripersonal God: Understanding and Interpreting the Trinity* (New York: Paulist Press, 1999), 178.

proceeds "from the Father," as did the churches of the East. Some Latin theologians spoke of a "double procession," among them Ambrose, Jerome, and Augustine. The phrase *"qui ex Patre Filioque procedit"* (who proceeds from the Father and the Son) was first introduced into a translation of the Creed by the Third Council of Toledo in 589, a local council in Spain. The West sought to stress that from the perspective of the *oikonomia*, the Spirit is the Spirit of both the Father and the Son. As LaCugna says, "It is impossible to think or speak of the Spirit except as the Spirit-of. The Holy Spirit is the Spirit of God, Spirit of Christ, Spirit of the Christian community."[45]

The concern of the East was to emphasize the monarchy of the Father as origin and source of the Spirit. Several popes out of respect for the East resisted efforts to introduce the formula; eventually it was adopted in Rome in 1014. The Western usage, rejected by the East from the beginning, was condemned by Patriarch Photius of Constantinople in 867. The *filioque* has remained a source of division between East and West ever since, largely because it was added to the creed without the consent of the East, though it is also true as Michael Cook observes that "the East does not understand the Holy Spirit as the bond of love between the Father and the Son."[46]

A number of theologians have suggested dropping the *filioque* or interpreting it in the context of the common Creed of 381. Walter Kasper suggests that if Catholics could emphasize that the Spirit *principaliter* emanates from the Father (monarchy), the East might better address the relationship between the Son and the Spirit, with the implication of a relational trinitarian ontology so important for a *communio*-ecclesiology. The Catholic Church, after thorough pastoral preparation, could use the original wording of the Creed in its liturgy for the sake of unity and peace, without renouncing what it intends to affirm and without either side attempting to impose its language on the other.[47] The *Catechism of the Catholic Church* states: "This legitimate complementarity, provided it does not become rigid, does not affect the identity of faith in the reality of the same mystery con-

---

[45] LaCugna, *God for Us*, 298.

[46] Michael Cook, *Trinitarian Christology: The Power that Sets Us Free* (New York: Paulist Press, 2010), 20.

[47] Walter Kasper, *That They May All Be One: The Call to Unity Today* (London: Burns and Oates, 2004), 112–15.

fessed" (no. 248). The doctrine of the Trinity means that God is not an abstract first principle, a totally transcendent other, but personal and intersubjective, revealed in God's salvific work. Relationality is at the very heart of the mystery of the divine.

God in Contemporary Thought

Sallie McFague has popularized a number of models for conceiving the divine mystery, among them, the monarchical model, the world as God's body, and God as mother, lover, or friend.[48] Adapting her work and that of others somewhat, I'd like to suggest some contemporary models, some of which are often uncritically operative in the way people imagine God today, others that seek to incorporate new insights and sensibilities.

The Cosmic Architect

This model takes its origin from the seventeenth-century scientific revolution. It imagines God as the impersonal divine architect who like a clockmaker creates the universe and gives its laws and then lets it run according to those laws. This is a deist concept of a God who gives order and purpose to creation but remains distant from it, unengaged with creatures. Originating in England, deism spread to Germany and the United States through the work of Voltaire. Generally hostile to revealed religion, it privileges the "laws of nature." Jesus is seen as an exemplary moral teacher, not the Word incarnate. Popular with many scientists, this God is unlike the God of the Bible who is present and active in history.

Moralistic Therapeutic Deism

In their book *Soul Searching*, Christian Smith and Melinda Lundquist Denton profile a popular variant of deism, a subjective image of God that emerges from their research on the spiritual and religious lives of US teenagers. They also suggest that this variant may be the "new

---

[48] Sallie McFague, *Models of God: Theology for an Ecological, Nuclear Age* (Philadelphia, PA: Fortress Press, 1987).

mainstream American religious faith for our culturally post-Christian, individualistic, mass-consumer society." Calling it Moralistic Therapeutic Deism, its God creates and orders the world, wants people to be nice and fair to each other as taught in the Bible and most world religions, and does not need to be particularly involved in one's life, except when needed. The goal of life is to be happy and feel good about oneself, and good people go to heaven when they die.[49] The authors find that "religious languages and vocabularies of commitment, duty, faithfulness, obedience, calling, obligation, accountability, and ties to the past are nearly completely absent" from the discourse of their subjects.[50] This is a God who "is always there for me," but makes no demands and remains at a safe distance, a God who does not challenge either the individual or the social, cultural, or political order.

As Smith says in a subsequent article, Moralistic Therapeutic Deism is different from traditional deism in that its God is normally distant from human affairs but can intervene when called on to solve problems: "This is not primarily a saving God of grace and forgiveness, or a Trinitarian God whose Son lived as Jesus of Nazareth and whose Spirit lives daily in human hearts. . . . This is not the God of Matthew Tindal and Thomas Paine [traditional deists], but rather their God who has gotten a serious 'makeover' by Leo Buscaglia, Oprah Winfrey, and *Self* Magazine. Times change. So must God, it seems."[51]

The Divine Monarch

One of McFague's models, the model of God as divine monarch, has its origins in medieval Christian thought, with its emphasis on God's omnipotence, and in the Reformation (especially Calvin's) insistence on God's sovereignty. Many see it as describing the natural

[49] Christian Smith and Melinda Lundquist Denton, *Soul Searching: The Religious and Spiritual Lives of American Teenagers* (New York: Oxford University Press, 2005), 162–63.

[50] Ibid., 262.

[51] Christian Smith, "Moralistic Therapeutic Deism," in *Passing on the Faith: Transforming Traditions for the Next Generations of Jews, Christians, and Muslims*, ed. James L. Heft (New York: Fordham University Press, 2006), 65.

relationship between God and the world.[52] Based on a fundamentalist reading of the Bible (particularly the Old Testament) and a premodern worldview, it imagines God as an absolute king ruling over creation, intervening when necessary, sometimes through miracles, which it understands as a divine suspension of the laws of nature to accomplish some end. Without an adequate theology of secondary causality, it has difficulty explaining human freedom and tends to attribute natural disasters to God's will, thus making God the author of evil.

This model has been implicit in the recent warnings of a famous TV evangelist that God will send an earthquake or tidal wave to punish a city known as a home for sinners. McFague argues that this strongly transcendent model sees the world as empty of God's presence; its God lacks concern for the cosmos, for the nonhuman, and governs by domination, encouraging a passivity on the part of humans.[53] Nor can it account for the role of chance in the evolutionary process. As Elizabeth Johnson says, "Prior to knowledge of evolution the idea of the Creator went hand-in-glove with the model of God as a monarch ruling his realm."[54]

A Dialectical God

Largely a product of twentieth-century liberal Protestant theology, with its respect for God's transcendence, this model tends to restrict God's agency to the realm of human subjectivity. God's activity can never be identified with historical acts, doctrine, or even with ordinary human experience but should be seen rather as occurring in revelatory moments that mark an encounter with the divine mystery. Typical of this approach would be Emil Brunner, Rudolf Bultmann, and the early Karl Barth. They stress God as absolute mystery whose self-disclosure can never be identified with the merely human words of the Bible or Christian proclamation, but sometimes a moment of encounter takes place through these means. As Barth says, "God's Word is not a thing to be described, nor is it a concept to be defined.

---

[52] McFague, *Models of God*, 63.

[53] Ibid., 65–69.

[54] Elizabeth A. Johnson, *Ask the Beasts: Darwin and the God of Love* (London: Bloomsbury, 2014), 155.

It is neither a content nor an idea. It is not 'a truth,' not even the very highest truth. It is the truth because it is God's person speaking. . . . It is not something objective."[55] This view of divine presence has been characterized as "actualist."

In his diagnosis of neoorthodoxy, the name by which dialectical theology was widely known, Langdon Gilkey argued that it "more and more tended, almost against its will, to locate the 'place' of the Word not so much objectively in scripture as subjectively in our own personal experience, in the encounter of faith with God through the scriptural Word, in the challenge of the kerygma (the gospel proclaimed) to our existential self-understanding and authenticity."[56]

Panentheism

From the Greek "all in God," panentheism differs from pantheism by seeing God as present in all the cosmos, pervading and animating it yet still distinct from it, thus maintaining the divine transcendence. But it has been differently understood. McFague sees the world as God's body, a metaphor that has resonance with the Christian tradition which speaks of Christ's eucharistic body and the church as the body of Christ. Though her metaphor comes close to pantheism, she does not reduce God to the world, just as our spirits are not completely identified with our bodies.

Such an approach means "a view of the God-world relationship in which all things have their origins in God and nothing exists outside God, though this does not mean that God is reduced to these things." The world as God's body may be poorly cared for or ravaged in spite of God's care for it, but with this "metaphor of the universe as the self-expression of God—God's incarnation—the notions of vulnerability, shared responsibility and risk are inevitable."[57] She maintains that without personal agential metaphors such as, among others, God as mother, lover, and friend, the metaphor of the world as God's body would be pantheistic.[58]

---

[55] Karl Barth, *Church Dogmatics*, 1.1, p. 155.

[56] Langdon Gilkey, *Naming the Whirlwind: The Renewal of God-Language* (Indianapolis, IN and New York: Bobbs-Merrill, 1969), 97.

[57] McFague, *Models of God*, 72.

[58] Ibid., 71–72.

Elizabeth Johnson takes a different approach. She seeks to broaden theology beyond its anthropocentric focus, showing that Christian faith is not inherently antiecological. She sees "the natural world," the community of plants and animals and their habitats, as pervaded with the "absolute presence" of the living God. In other words, nature in all its diversity and beauty becomes a place of encounter with God, moving Catholic theology beyond the neoscholastic dichotomy between nature and grace, the natural and the supernatural.[59] For a philosophical foundation she appeals to Aquinas, who in speaking of God's personal presence to all creatures, God's immanence to creation, rules out any thought of nature as godless.[60]

Social Trinitarianism

Some contemporary theologians have seen in the relationality at the heart of the divine a model for a more egalitarian human community. Jürgen Moltmann suggests that monotheism has too often been used to justify monarchical, hierarchical, and patriarchal systems of relationship in government, society, and church. Holding that monotheism is monarchism, he argues that the notion of a divine monarchy becomes the justification for earthly domination. Against this he turns to the Cappadocian fathers and the theologians of the East to emphasize a social doctrine of the Trinity: "We have said that it is not the monarchy of a ruler that corresponds to the triune God; it is the community of men and women, without privileges and without subjugation. The three divine Persons have everything in common, except for their personal characteristics."[61] Pentecostal theologian Miroslav Volf has further developed Moltmann's thought.[62]

Catherine LaCugna notes that feminist and liberation theologians like Patricia Wilson-Kastner and Leonardo Boff find the theology of *perichōrēsis* attractive because, rejecting the monarchy of the Father, it grounds the equality of persons in the doctrine of God as three equal

---

[59] Johnson, *Ask the Beasts*, 2–5.

[60] Ibid., 143–44.

[61] Jürgen Moltmann, *The Trinity and the Kingdom: The Doctrine of God* (San Francisco: Harper & Row, 1981), 192–98, at 198.

[62] Miroslav Volf, "'The Trinity Is Our Social Program': The Doctrine of the Trinity and the Shape of Social Engagement," *Modern Theology* 14 (1998): 403–23.

persons,[63] though as Karen Kilby argues, they tend to make the three divine persons separate centers of will and self-consciousness.[64]

A Kenotic God

A frequently heard argument today against the existence of God is the problem of evil. How could an all-powerful, good God permit the suffering and injustice that is so evident today? Why did God not intervene to end the Holocaust or any of the other genocides that so scarred the twentieth century? Implicit in this argument is the traditional notion of the divine omnipotence that ends up making God the author of evil or at least complicit in its continued existence.

Some theologians today, reflecting the kenotic image of Christ who "emptied" himself, giving up equality with God to take on the form of a slave (Phil 2:6-7), offer a model of a self-emptying or self-restricting God who creates by "letting-be, by making room, and by withdrawing himself."[65] They describe a self-effacing God who in creating pours out on finite creatures a share in the divine being, showing the dependence of the creature on the creator. This is a God whose "unobtrusive and self-absenting mode of being invites the world to swell forth continually, through immense epochs of temporal duration and experimentation, into an always free and open future, and to do so in the relatively autonomous mode of 'self-creation' that science has discerned in cosmic, biological, and cultural evolution."[66] For McFague, the world as God's body means that the pain and suffering of creation also affects God, whose inclusive, radical love is the way of the cross. Similarly, for Johann Baptist Metz, this God is revealed

[63] LaCugna, *God for Us*, 272–78; see also Patricia Wilson-Kastner, *Faith, Feminism, and the Christ* (Philadelphia, PA: Fortress Press, 1983), 131–33; Leonardo Boff, *Trinity and Society* (Maryknoll, NY: Orbis Books), 129–30.

[64] Karen Kilby, "Perichoresis and Projection: Problems with Social Doctrines of the Trinity," *New Blackfriars* 81, no. 957 (2000): 432–45.

[65] Jürgen Moltmann, *God in Creation* (San Francisco: Harper & Row, 1985), 88; see also David N. Power, *Love without Calculation: A Reflection on Divine Kenosis* (New York: Crossroad, 2005).

[66] John F. Haught, *God after Darwin: A Theology of Evolution* (Boulder, CO: Westview Press, 2008), 58; see also Johnson, *Ask the Beasts*, 158.

in hiddenness, negativity, and the cross.[67] Such a God cannot "fix" everything—tragedy, disasters, and genocides—for the world has its own causality.

This does not mean a powerless God but one who chooses to act in a nondominative way, a God who rejects violence or coercion, all signs of the demonic, but who calls and inspires and becomes vulnerable, even a God who suffers with us. According to Edward Schillebeeckx, "By creating human beings with their own finite and free will, God voluntarily renounces power. That makes God to a high degree 'dependent' on human beings and thus vulnerable."[68] Karl Rahner says that this self-emptying of God is the primary phenomenon given by faith: God as self-giving fullness who goes out of himself and can do this as freedom because God "is defined in Scripture as love."[69] The creation of a world of freedom implies a self-limitation of the divine power, or as Pope John Paul II said, "In a certain sense one could say that confronted with our human freedom God decided to make himself 'impotent.'"[70] In his 1998 encyclical *Fides et Ratio*, he wrote that from the vantage point of the passion of the incarnate Son of God, "the prime commitment of theology is seen to be the understanding of God's *kenosis*, a grand and mysterious truth for the human mind, which finds it inconceivable that suffering and death can express a love which gives itself and seeks nothing in return" (no. 93).

One finds a similar kenotic view in Elizabeth Johnson's evolutionary perspective. The God she describes is not a God who intervenes in the world to accomplish the divine purpose but a God who works in and through natural causes, including those chance events that allow novelty to emerge. Attributing such a view to Aquinas, she writes: "At every moment divine agency will be physically undetectable. It is not a quantifiable property like mass or energy, not an additional factor in the equations, not an element that can be discovered among the forces of the universe at all. But in and through the

[67] Johann Baptist Metz, *The Emergent Church: The Future of Christianity in a Post-Bourgeois World* (New York: Crossroad, 1981).

[68] Edward Schillebeeckx, *Church: The Human Story of God* (New York: Crossroad, 1990), 90.

[69] Rahner, *Foundations of Christian Faith*, 222.

[70] John Paul II, *Crossing the Threshold of Hope*, ed. Vittorio Messori (New York: Random House, 1994), 61.

creativity of nature, the boundless love of the Creator Spirit is bringing the world to birth."[71]

Conclusion

The mythological deities of the ancients, with their demand for blood sacrifice, were conceived in the image and likeness of humanity. The psalmist speaks of them with sarcasm: "I need no bullock from your house, no goats from your fields. . . . Do I eat the flesh of bulls or drink the blood of goats?" (Ps 50:9, 13). How different was the God of Israel, who created humanity in the divine image and likeness (Gen 1:26)! This God was transcendent, incomprehensible, the holy ground and source of all being.

But God's transcendence is not completely beyond reach. Human intelligence, itself transcendent, intuits God's existence from the things God has made and finds the absolute implicated as the horizon of its own questioning and search for truth; it comes to recognize in the biblical story God's free self-disclosure as Father, Son, and Spirit. Reason tells us that God is; revelation tells us who God is and what God is like.

God is also immanent, closer to us than we are to ourselves (Augustine).[72] The natural world in all its glory reflects the presence of the divine. The biblical metanarrative continually shows this God reaching out in love to humanity, entering into covenant relationship, and taking on flesh in the person of Jesus to proclaim the divine nearness, sanctifying us in the Holy Spirit, drawing us into the divine life. Thus a Christian understanding of God cannot be divorced from the doctrines of Christology and soteriology. These doctrines mediate an understanding of the divine mystery; Christians know God through Jesus.

God's activity does not circumvent the laws of the material universe; rather the "laws of nature" represent a limited, scientific concept which fails to recognize God's ability to act through the events

---

[71] Elizabeth A. Johnson, *Quest for the Living God: Mapping Frontiers in the Theology of God* (New York and London: Continuum, 2007), 193.

[72] Augustine, *Confessions* 2.6.11.

of the world, thus not a supernaturalism but a higher viewpoint that recognizes God's mysterious presence within the natural world. Recognizing that the invisible God is always disclosed to us through created realities and symbols, and especially through the humanity of the man Jesus, mediation is a key concept within the Catholic tradition. Perhaps most suggestive of the divine mystery are those theologians who envision God's agency as a kenotic rejection of coercion and violence, a God who works in and through natural causes, even though chance events to embrace creation in love.

The doctrine of the Trinity is rooted in the relation of Jesus to the one he called Abba and in the prayer and worship of the church as early as Paul. More difficult to conceptualize was the Spirit, present in the experience of the early Christians more as force or affect than object. The doctrine of the Trinity developed out of the baptismal confession of God as Father, Son and Spirit, the *lex orandi* which became the *lex credendi* and was eventually formulated in its creeds as the church sought to safeguard its christological faith. The doctrine affirms that relationality and mission are at the very heart of the mystery of God, a God who, as Pope Benedict XVI has written, is both reason, *Logos*, and love.[73]

For Further Reading

Buckley, Michael J. *At the Origins of Modern Atheism.* New Haven, CT and London: Yale University Press, 1987.

Congar, Yves. *I Believe in the Holy Spirit: The Complete Three Volume Work in One Volume.* Part One: The Canonical Scriptures. New York: Crossroad, 1997.

Doran, Robert M. *The Trinity in History: A Theology of the Divine Mission.* Toronto, Buffalo NY: University of Toronto Press, 2012.

Gilkey, Langdon. *Naming the Whirlwind: The Renewal of God-Language.* Indianapolis and New York: Bobbs-Merrill, 1969.

---

[73] Benedict XVI, Encyclical Letter *Deus Caritas Est*, no. 10, http://w2.vatican.va/content/benedict-xvi/en/encyclicals/documents/hf_ben-xvi_enc_20051225_deus-caritas-est.html.

Johnson Elizabeth A. *Quest for the Living God: Mapping Frontiers in the Theology of God.* London: Continuum, 2007.

Kasper, Walter. *The God of Jesus Christ.* New York: T & T Clark International, 2012.

Kaufman, Gordon. *God the Problem.* Cambridge, MA: Harvard University Press, 1972.

Kelly, J. N. D. *Early Christian Doctrines,* 5th ed. New York: Continuum, 2003.

LaCugna, Catherine Mowry. *God for Us: The Trinity and Christian Life.* San Francisco: HarperSanFrancisco, 1991.

Marion, Jean-Luc. *God without Being.* Chicago: University of Chicago Press, 1991.

McFague, Sallie. *Models of God: Theology for an Ecological, Nuclear Age.* Philadelphia, PA: Fortress Press, 1987.

Moltmann, Jürgen. *The Trinity and the Kingdom: The Doctrine of God.* San Francisco: Harper & Row, 1981.

Murray, John Courtney. *The Problem of God: Yesterday and Today.* New Haven, CT: Yale University Press, 1964.

O'Collins, Gerald. *The Tripersonal God: Understanding and Interpreting the Trinity.* New York: Paulist Press, 1999.

Prestige, George L. *God in Patristic Thought.* London: SPCK, 1959.

Rahner, Karl. *Foundations of Christian Faith: An Introduction to the Idea of Christianity.* New York: Seabury Press, 1978.

———. *The Trinity.* New York: Herder and Herder, 1970.

———."Thomas Aquinas on the Incomprehensibility of God." *Journal of Religion* 58 Supplement (1978): S108-16.

Chapter 4

Jesus the Christ

Nothing has impacted Christology more than the rediscovery of the historical Jesus. As Elizabeth Johnson has pointed out, for centuries Catholic Christology focused on the miraculous birth and death of Jesus but paid little attention to his life and ministry. Think, for example, of the rosary, with its three sets of mysteries, the Joyful, the Sorrowful, and the Glorious, which go from the annunciation, the birth, and the finding of Jesus in the temple, then to the events of the passion, then to the Easter mysteries and the assumption and coronation of Mary as Queen of Heaven. Pope John Paul II implicitly acknowledged this in adding the "Luminous Mysteries."[1]

One sees this same pattern in the church's creeds and too often in official church documents, for example, in Pope John Paul II's encyclical *Redemptor Hominis* and in the *Catechism of the Catholic Church*. Missing is Jesus' preaching about the reign of God which was at the heart of his mission. Johnson suggests that we try to understand the reign of God in urban images taken from life in the United States, or Central America, or in images from Palestine or South Africa under Apartheid.[2]

---

[1] The Luminous Mysteries are as follows: The Baptism of the Lord, the Wedding at Cana, the Proclamation of the Kingdom of God, the Transfiguration, and the Institution of the Eucharist.

[2] Elizabeth A. Johnson, *Consider Jesus: Waves of Renewal in Christology* (New York: Paulist Press, 1990), 52.

The traditional approach, from the incarnation to the birth of Jesus heralded by the angelic chorus, has been called a Christology "from above," or descending Christology. A more historically conscious Christology begins "from below," with the story of Jesus' life, ministry, and fate, thus an ascending Christology. It then moves on to consider the later christological reflection of the church. In this chapter we will review the three searches for the historical Jesus, his life and ministry, the mystery of his resurrection, and some contemporary approaches to Christology and soteriology.[3]

Discovering the Historical Jesus

There have been three different "quests" for the historical Jesus. The first quest began with Hermann Samuel Reimarus (1694–1768), a professor of Oriental languages in Hamburg, Germany. Reimarus was not really a theologian or a person of faith. But he had noticed an important difference between the Jesus of history and the Jesus proclaimed by the church and concluded that the message and intention of Jesus was different from that of his disciples and the early church.[4] What followed was a host of *Leben Jesu* books. Influenced by the Enlightenment and often hostile to Christianity, these lives of Jesus attempted to free Jesus from his Jewish religious background and the faith of the church so as to discover the "real" Jesus. But most succeeded only in presenting a Jesus fashioned according to the ideal image of their authors. Jesus became an ethical teacher, a friend of the poor and social reformer, a preacher of morality, the ideal human being, or simply a character of fiction.

The *coup de grâce* to the first quest, sometimes called the liberal quest, came when Albert Schweitzer (1875–1965) pointed out that Jesus was not a modern man at all, as the Enlightenment scholars had presupposed, but was "a stranger and an enigma," an apoca-

---

[3] For a more detailed treatment see my *Who Is Jesus? An Introduction to Christology* (Collegeville, MN: Liturgical Press, 2003).

[4] Reimarus's work was called *Von dem Zwecke Jesu und seiner Junger. Noch ein Fragment des Wolfenbuttelschen Ungenannten*, published by Gotthold Ephraim Lessing; see *Reimarus: Fragments*, ed. Charles H. Talbert (Philadelphia, PA: Fortress Press, 1970).

lyptic preacher convinced that the end was near.[5] But for all its shortcomings, the first quest did lead to some advances in biblical scholarship.

A new quest was launched by New Testament scholar Ernst Käsemann in a lecture at Marburg in 1953 titled, "The Problem of the Historical Jesus."[6] Käsemann called for a new quest, free of the rationalist, secular presuppositions of the first quest and using the new methods of historical-critical scholarship developed in the interim. This new quest recognized that the gospels, while not histories in the strict sense, did contain more history than had previously been acknowledged. Second, it rejected myth, meaning that the church's preaching must be rooted in the historical Jesus. Finally, the new quest did not ignore the kerygma or preaching of Jesus or the early church but took the kerygma fully into account. The result of Käsemann's programmatic lecture was a flood of new Jesus books, both Protestant and Catholic, focused on the historical Jesus. Still, many of the authors of these works remained half liberal in their presuppositions—skeptical of the miraculous, the eschatological, or even the resurrection—and so remained a product of modernity.

A "third quest" began in the early 1980s when scholars began moving beyond the literary disciplines of the second quest to emphasize more critical historical and social studies focused on the world of Jesus and the Judaism of his day.[7] Second Temple studies and ancient sources such as the first-century Jewish historian Josephus placed Jesus in his Palestinian Jewish context, while social studies uncovered the social, cultural, and anthropological dimensions of Palestinian or Galilean Jewish life, including the religious milieu, family structure, position of women, impact of Roman domination, and economic and tax structure. Understanding the social climate within which Jesus preached often brings new insights into the depths

---

[5] Albert Schweitzer, *The Quest of the Historical Jesus: A Critical Study of Its Progress from Reimarus to Wrede* (London: Adam & Charles Black, 1963), 398.

[6] Ernst Käsemann, *Essays on New Testament Themes* (Philadelphia, PA: Fortress Press, 1982), 15–47.

[7] See Ben Witherington, III, *The Jesus Quest: The Third Search for the Jew of Nazareth* (Downers Grove, IL: InterVarsity Press, 1997).

of his message. Especially worthy of mention is John P. Meier's four-volume work, *A Marginal Jew*.[8]

The various "quests" for the historical Jesus raise the question of the relationship between faith and history. Scholarship overly influenced by the Enlightenment tends to dismiss faith in favor of a more "scientific" historical approach. But a reconstructed historical Jesus can never be the living Jesus of Christian faith. Walter Kasper argues that a purely historical approach cannot give us the full story of Jesus as it cannot deal with the mystery of his resurrection. Therefore he argues for a Christology of "complementarity" that gives us both the historical Jesus and risen Christ; it takes the faith of the church as the primary access to the mystery of Jesus the Christ, with historical-critical scholarship as a "relatively autonomous" criterion against which the church's language must measure itself.[9]

The Reign of God

In his *Antiquities of the Jews* (93–94), the Jewish historian Josephus refers several times to the story of Jesus. The most important reference, minus several later Christian interpolations, reads as follows:

> At this time there appeared Jesus, a wise man. For he was a doer of startling deeds, a teacher of people who receive the truth with pleasure. And he gained a following among many Jews and among many of Gentile origin. And when Pilate, because of an accusation made by the leading men among us, condemned him to the cross, those who had loved him previously did not cease to do so. And up until this very day the tribe of Christians (named after him) had not died out. (18.3.3)

Jesus was more than an itinerant preacher; he was part of the religious community of Israel, familiar with the prophets who preceded

---

[8] John P. Meier, *A Marginal Jew: Rethinking the Historical Jesus*, vol. 1, *The Roots of the Problem and the Person* (New York: Doubleday, 1991); vol. 2, *Mentor, Message, and Miracles* (New York: Doubleday, 1994); vol. 3, *Companions and Competitors* (New York: Doubleday, 2001); vol. 4, *Law and Love* (New Haven, CT: Yale University Press, 2009).

[9] Walter Kasper, *Jesus the Christ* (New York: Paulist Press, 1976), 35; see also Michael L. Cook, *Justice, Jesus, and the Jews: A Proposal for Jewish-Christian Relations* (Collegeville, MN: Liturgical Press, 2003), 13–20.

him and with Jewish hope.[10] The author of the Fourth Gospel suggests that he was originally a part of John the Baptist's group of disciples but later moved out on his own, establishing his own movement, describing his disciples as members of a new family who hear the Word of God and do it (cf. Mark 3:33-35). At the center of his movement was a group called "the Twelve," symbolic of the twelve tribes of Israel and his movement as the new or eschatological Israel.

The Kingdom of God

The mission of Jesus was to proclaim the kingdom or reign of God. The metaphor of the kingdom, rooted in the Old Testament idea of the kingship of Yahweh, dominated his preaching and is present in virtually all levels of the New Testament tradition. The Greek for "kingdom of God" (*basileia tou theou*) is better translated as "reign" or "rule" of God; it is not a place but an event, God's saving power breaking into history in a new way (I will use both terms, depending on the context).

To receive the kingdom demands a conversion of life, or *metanoia* (Mark 1:15); one must welcome it like a little child (Matt 18:3). Hans Küng describes it as "a radical decision for God."[11] The reign of God cannot be reduced to a purely religious matter; while it did not mean restoring Israel from Roman occupation, it would be a mistake to conclude that the words of Jesus had nothing to do with the world and society.[12] The original Beatitudes addressed the poor and needy in Israel; later they were reshaped to characterize the qualities and virtues of the disciples. Jesus reached out to the poor and the marginal, healed the sick, exorcised those bound by destructive spirits, reconciled those who were estranged, and proclaimed the forgiveness of sins. The third quest's emphasis on social context has led to a deeper appreciation of Jesus' preaching. He "enacted" the kingdom; it was already being realized in his ministry.[13]

---

[10] See, for example, Amy-Jill Levine, *The Misunderstood Jew: The Church and the Scandal of the Jewish Jesus* (San Francisco: HarperOne, 2006).

[11] Hans Küng, *The Church* (New York: Sheed and Ward, 1967), 52.

[12] Gerhard Lohfink, *Jesus of Nazareth: What He Wanted, Who He Was* (Collegeville, MN: Liturgical Press, 2012), 53.

[13] The term is from Elizabeth Johnson, *Consider Jesus*, 54.

But Jesus also taught his disciples to pray for the coming of the kingdom in the Lord's Prayer (Matt 6:10) and spoke of the Son of Man coming in judgment (Matt 25:31-46; Luke 12:8-9). The parables of the kingdom describe it as present, hidden, growing, looking forward to a fullness or completion; the farmer and the seed, the weeds and the wheat, the mustard seed, the yeast kneaded in the flour, and the net cast into the sea (Matt 13:1-53) bring to light both the present and future aspects of God's reign. The resurrection of Jesus adds a new dimension to the kingdom—life beyond the grave. Thus the reign of God refers to God's power, justice, compassion, and transforming grace, to the fullness of God's salvation. In the words of St. Paul, "[T]he kingdom of God is not food and drink but righteousness and peace and joy in the Holy Spirit" (Rom 14:17).

Contemporary Expressions of the Reign

If the fullness of the reign of God remains mystery, contemporary theology seeks to find ways to express Jesus' vision in language accessible to men and women of today. Some stress God's action in the world and in our lives; others stress that the grace of the kingdom is mediated through compassionate service of others; some view it from the perspective of liberation theology, while still others see the fullness of the reign as involving not just the human but also the cosmic, all creation.

Thus Michael Cook sees the "kingdom of God" as Jesus' comprehensive term for the blessings of salvation, pointing to the divine activity at the center of human life, while "faith" is his existential term for salvation insofar as it denotes the human response of openness, acceptance, and commitment to his preaching. The mission of Jesus and that of his disciples is fundamentally the same—to embody that most fundamental value Jesus embodied, union with the divine.[14] Edward Schillebeeckx contrasts John the Baptist's warning of a coming judgment with Jesus' good news that God was present within human history and active in our own lives; he argues that God's grace

---

[14] Michael Cook, *The Jesus of Faith: A Study in Christology* (New York: Paulist Press, 1981), 56–57.

is mediated by human beings caring for one another.[15] Albert Nolan says that the kingdom Jesus believed in "was a kingdom of love and service, a kingdom of human brotherhood." His preaching revealed God as a God of compassion. For it is precisely human compassion that "releases God's power in the world, the only power that can bring about the miracle of the kingdom."[16]

From the perspective of liberation theology, Jon Sobrino describes Jesus as calling others to a radical discipleship that would place them at the disposal of the kingdom or reign of God. Borrowing an image from Ignacio Ellacuría, he challenges those who would be disciples to take the crucified peoples of the world down from the cross. Elisabeth Schüssler Fiorenza argues that the rule of God is being realized wherever people are being healed, set free from oppression or dehumanizing powers systems, and made whole.[17] For Terrence Tilley, the reign of God is a realm of human flourishing. Christians like those in the Jesus movement continue the practices of the reign of God—healing, exorcising, sharing table fellowship, forgiving, and teaching, not just in regard to individuals but by working to transform society—though Tilley is careful to add that bringing about the reign is God's work, not our own.[18]

Reacting against any tendency to make the coming of the kingdom the work of human beings, Pope Benedict XVI insists that the coming of the kingdom remains God's work; he says that "the new proximity of the Kingdom of which Jesus speaks . . . is to be found in Jesus himself. Through Jesus presence' and action, God has here and now entered actively into history in a wholly new way . . . [for] in Jesus it is God who draws near to us."[19] For Elizabeth Johnson, the reign of God or fullness of God's salvation affects not just human beings but creation itself. She states,

---

[15] Edward Schillebeeckx, *Jesus: An Experiment in Christology* (New York: Seabury Press, 1979), 153.

[16] Albert Nolan, *Jesus Before Christianity* (Maryknoll, NY: Orbis Books, 1978), 84.

[17] Elisabeth Schüssler Fiorenza, *In Memory of Her: A Feminist Reconstruction of Christian Origins* (New York: Crossroad, 1994), 123.

[18] Terrence Tilley, *The Disciples' Jesus: Christology as Reconciling Practice* (Maryknoll, NY: Orbis Books, 2008), 244–48.

[19] Benedict XVI, *Jesus of Nazareth: From the Baptism in the Jordan to the Transfiguration* (New York: Doubleday, 2007), 60–61.

This extraordinary biblical symbol evokes the final age when the Spirit will be poured out, when creation will be made whole, when the Spirit-filled servant of God will appear to bring forth justice to the nations, when justice will dwell in the land, when there will be no more war, when the lion will lie down with the lamb, when justice and peace shall kiss—in other words, when God's will is finally done on earth as it is in heaven and the well-being and salvation of every human person and of all creation is secured.[20]

Death and Resurrection

Jesus' ministry, presuming the authority to interpret the law and challenging the religious authorities of his day, occasioned opposition on the part of the Jewish leadership of Jerusalem, while any rumor of messianic pretensions of his concern to gather Israel[21] would have been of concern to the Roman governor. But a number of scholars today point to Jesus' action in cleansing the temple, told in all four gospels, as the cause that led the Jewish authorities to conspire with the Romans against him.[22] More than an act of outraged piety for commercial traffic in the temple, Jesus' action in driving out the coin changers, buyers, and sellers of the small birds and animals used for sacrifice was effectively to close down the temple cult, symbolizing that its time was over. This was a prophetic action, intolerable to the high priests, and they conspired with the civil authorities to do away with him.[23]

[20] Johnson, *Consider Jesus*, 75.

[21] See Lohfink, *Jesus of Nazareth*, 59–71.

[22] N. T. Wright, *Jesus and the Victory of God* (Minneapolis, MN: Fortress Press, 1996), 405; Raymond E. Brown, *The Death of the Messiah*, vol. 1 (New York: Doubleday, 1994), 460; Lohfink, *Jesus of Nazareth*, 251.

[23] Michael Cook sees the temple action as linked to the entry into Jerusalem and Last Supper, unified around YHWH's restorative blessings; he argues that Jesus did not intend to establish a new community, replacing the old, but only to create a "sub-society" around the Twelve that would continue to embody in ritual and service the covenantal ideals. See Cook, *Justice, Jesus, and the Jews: A Proposal for Jewish-Christian Relations* (Collegeville, MN: Liturgical Press, 2003), 96–100.

Death of Jesus

Delivering him to the Roman procurator, Pontius Pilate, Jesus was condemned to capital punishment, the excruciating death of crucifixion reserved for slaves, pirates, and enemies of the Roman state. Schillebeeckx eloquently describes what he calls Jesus' "*Abba* experience," facing the apparent failure of his mission, desertion by his friends, and a painful death, while still trusting in the one in whom his life was centered, his "*Abba*" or Father.[24] And God did not abandon him.

Nevertheless his death was a shattering blow to his disciples. In the post-Easter tradition, they sought various themes in the Jewish Scriptures to make sense of his death. The prophetic tradition contributed the image of the rejected prophet. From the Wisdom tradition came the image of the suffering just one, persecuted by the wicked but looking to God for vindication (Wis 2:12-21). Neither of these attached, at least initially, any salvific significance to the death of Jesus. Another theme—present in the pre-Pauline tradition, in the cup words in the Last Supper accounts, in the "ransom for many" passages in Mark 10:45, and in 1 Peter 2:21-24 and 1 Timothy 2:6—sees Jesus' death as a redemptive sacrifice "for us" or "for our sins" or "for all." Finally, there is the theme of the stone rejected by the builder (Mark 12:10-11; Acts 4:11; 1 Pet 2:7).

Is there any justification for the Christian tradition's linking Jesus' death with his mission? Schillebeeckx argues that Jesus himself saw his death as in some way "part and parcel of the salvation-offered-by-God, as a historical consequence of his caring and loving service and solidarity with people."[25] His words at the Last Supper about not drinking again the fruit of the vine "until the day when I drink it new in the kingdom of God" (Mark 14:25; cf. Luke 22:16-18), accepted by most commentators as historical, evidences his belief in a renewed fellowship with his disciples in the kingdom after his death. Jesus died because he was human, and therefore mortal. His preaching was seen as a threat by the civil and religious leaders of his time and led to his death. Still, from a theological perspective, he came

---

[24] Schillebeeckx, *Jesus*, 256–71; see also Kasper, *Jesus the Christ*, 120.
[25] Schillebeeckx, *Jesus*, 310.

not to offer his life as an atoning sacrifice but to proclaim the nearness or reign of God.

The Resurrection

The resurrection stands at the center of the New Testament; without it Jesus would be only another failed messiah. Though presumed throughout the New Testament, the Easter tradition—predating the New Testament—appears in two different forms. The Easter kerygma, short formulaic statements that God raised Jesus from the dead and that there are witnesses (Luke 24:34; Acts 2:32; 3:15; 5:31; 10:40; Rom 10:9; 1 Cor 15:3-7), is the earlier form. The second form, the Easter stories, are later, and they come in two kinds: the discovery of the empty tomb and the appearances to the disciples. For example, the original ending of Mark had only one story, the women at the tomb (Mark 16:1-8). Rather than historical narratives, these dramatic stories are constructed to help others come to Easter faith, teaching that they can recognize the risen Jesus in the breaking of the bread or Eucharist (Luke 24:31, 35), that the disciples have authority to teach, baptize, and forgive sins (Matt 28:19-20; John 20:23), that one does not have to see to believe (John 20:29), and that Peter has pastoral authority as shepherd (John 21:15-17).

The precise nature of the disciples' "Easter experience" remains mysterious. The appearance stories report fear, nonrecognition, disbelief; some think they are seeing a ghost, while Mary Magdalene who loved him mistakes him for the gardener. All of this suggests something nonobjectifiable about the experience. Furthermore, Jesus appeared to those who had followed him and loved him, or, as in the case of Saul of Tarsus, who were genuinely (even if wrongly) seeking God; he did not appear to his enemies. Neither a purely subjective experience nor an objective one (in the sense of something accessible to all), the Easter appearances represent an eschatological event, a real event but one in which Christ's risen existence breaks into space and time. Dermot Lane speaks of it as a "transforming experience" in which those who followed Jesus came to recognize him in a different way.[26] Walter Kasper says that Jesus, while now with God, is

---

[26] Dermot Lane, *The Reality of Jesus* (New York: Paulist Press, 1975), 61.

also with us in a new, divine way.[27] Schillebeeckx describes it as "the experience of grace and mercy, the result of which was that they were received back into a present fellowship with Jesus and confessed him to be their definitive salvation."[28] The resurrection is God's vindication of Jesus' life and ministry, revealing that God's love is stronger than death. The resurrection of Jesus foreshadows the *eschaton*, the fullness of salvation when he returns in glory.

As the early Christians sought to give voice to their experience of Jesus, they drew on the mythopoeic language of the Jewish Scriptures. They called Jesus prophet, Messiah, Son of David, Son of Man, Son of God, Lord, Word, Wisdom, and occasionally even God. Later, as the church grew out of its Jewish matrix, they adapted the more philosophical language of the Greco-Roman world in which the church was now living.

New Testament Christologies

New Testament Christology can be organized or presented in various ways. An earlier approach focused on christological titles. Another approach analyzes Christology from the perspective of different New Testament authors. Some scholars outline different christological types. Schillebeeckx suggests four: Parousia, Divine-man, Wisdom, and Easter Christologies.[29] Roger Haight offers five: Last Adam, Son of God, Spirit, Wisdom, and Logos.[30] Feminist scholars tend to privilege Wisdom Christology, which is less dependent on masculine metaphors.[31] Here I would like to consider first four christological types: Easter, Son of God, Wisdom, and Preexistence, then look more closely at Paul, the gospels, and John. But first a word of caution. While an earlier scholarship presumed that early Christologies were all "low," and "high" Christologies that proclaimed Christ's

---

[27] Kasper, *Jesus the Christ*, 151.

[28] Schillebeeckx, *Jesus*, 381.

[29] Ibid., 401–38.

[30] Roger Haight, *Jesus Symbol of God* (Maryknoll, NY: Orbis Books, 1999), 155–78.

[31] Elizabeth Johnson, *She Who Is: The Mystery of God in Feminist Theological Discourse* (New York: Crossroad, 1992), 94–98; Elisabeth Schüssler Fiorenza, *Jesus: Miriam's Child, Sophia's Prophet* (New York: Continuum, 1994).

divinity or preexistence, as, for example, the Christology one finds in the Gospel of John, developed only later, scholars today recognize the presence of some early high Christologies.

Christological Types

Easter Christologies, most of them very early, come in two types. Parousia Christologies, sometimes called *maranatha* or Second Coming Christologies, come from the early Aramaic-speaking Palestinian communities. They look forward to Christ's imminent return (Acts 3:19-21). Schillebeeckx traces them to the early Q community, but variants can be found in Paul and Mark. Exaltation Christology sees Jesus as constituted Messiah, Lord, and Son of God after his resurrection (Rom 1:3-4) or exaltation from the dead (Acts 5:30-31) and still present to the community as Lord.

Son of God Christologies see Jesus as Son of God even during his ministry, though the title does not necessarily imply divinity. It can mean anything from Son of David (2 Sam 7:14; Ps 2:7), the just one (Sir 4:10; Wis 2:16-20), or an angel (Job 1:6; 2:1), to Son of God by nature, depending on its context. Wisdom Christologies in Paul and John, building on the Old Testament Wisdom tradition, see Jesus as the Wisdom of God, active in creation, coming into the world with a mission as we have seen. Preexistence Christology is present in Paul, also reflective of the Wisdom tradition, and can be found throughout the Gospel of John.

Paul

Paul's most characteristic way of referring to Jesus is "Lord Jesus Christ," an expression combining Jesus' personal name, thought to mean "Yahweh saves," with the Greek *kyrios*, "Lord," and the Greek translation of the Hebrew *mashiah*, "anointed" or "messiah." Jesus may have been recognized as Messiah even during his historical ministry, as is suggested by Peter's confession (Mark 8:27-29). But the title *kyrios*, Lord, used by early Christian communities even before Paul, is far more significant.

According to Larry Hurtado, among others, there is evidence that Jesus was the recipient of devotion normally reserved for God from very early in the Christian movement (30–50 CE) as we saw earlier. He says that the use of "Lord" goes back to the earliest circle of Jewish Christians who used the Aramaic *MarYah* as a substitute for the divine name which out of reverence they would not pronounce. Similarly, for Greek-speaking Jews, *kyrios*, or "Lord," was the word used in the Septuagint to translate the Tetragrammaton, the four Hebrew letters that correspond to the holy name Yahweh. Paul can include the invocation *Marana tha* (1 Cor 16:22), "Our Lord, come," in Aramaic without translating it.[32] In other words, Lord, whether in Aramaic or in Greek, was a title used for God.

Hurtado also offers evidence of a "binitarian pattern" of devotion and worship that appears in Pauline Christianity. Jesus was the object of devotional practices that can only be understood as cultic worship, devotion characteristically reserved for God. Jesus and God were addressed by prayers and invoked in benediction, including the *Marana tha*. Neophytes were baptized in the name of Jesus; he was confessed as Lord, praised in songs, some of them possibly pre-Pauline, and honored as present in the Eucharist.[33]

There is also evidence of a preexistence Christology in Paul, particularly in the pre-Pauline Philippians hymn (2:6-11; cf. 2 Cor 8:9) and in Christ being seen as having a role in creation (1 Cor 8:6; cf. Col 1:5-16)—both traditions reflective of the Wisdom tradition. He also sees the Risen Jesus as having an eschatological role; he is the last or new Adam, the "firstfruits" of the resurrection of the dead to whom everything will be subjected so that God may be all in all (1 Cor 15:21-28). For Paul, the Wisdom of God is Jesus himself (1 Cor 2:7). It is difficult to overlook the cosmic significance that Christ plays in Paul (and in early hymns like Philippians 2:6-11) from the beginning to the end of creation.

---

[32] Larry Hurtado, *Lord Jesus Christ: Devotion to Jesus in Earliest Christianity* (Grand Rapids, MI: William B. Eerdmans, 2003), 108–11; see also Joseph A. Fitzmyer, "*Kyrios* and *Maranatha* and their Aramaic Background," in *To Advance the Gospel: New Testament Studies* (New York: Crossroad, 1981), 222.

[33] Hurtado, *Lord Jesus Christ*, 135–49.

The Synoptics

Mark's Gospel sees Jesus as both Messiah and suffering Son of Man, though his root metaphor is Son of God,[34] in a functional rather than metaphysical sense.[35] Jesus received this title at his baptism. Yet there are epiphanic moments when Mark seems to suggest his awareness of Jesus' identity that goes beyond what he is able to express (Mark 6:45-52; cf. Job 9:8-11).

For Matthew, Jesus is an authoritative teacher and the new Moses. His true identity is no longer hidden. With Luke, he includes the tradition of Jesus' virginal conception (Matt 1:20), showing that Jesus is God's son in a unique way. Jesus frequently refers to God as "my Father" (sixteen times), three times refers to himself as "the Son," once in the so-called "bolt from the Johannine sky," a tradition shared with Luke in which he says, "No one knows the Son except the Father and no one knows the Father except the Son and anyone to whom the Son chooses to reveal him" (Matt 11:27; Luke 10:22), and once he refers to the Son of Man coming "in his Father's glory" (Matt 16:27). Thus Jesus is the Son who operates in union with the Father. When Peter confesses Jesus as Messiah and "the Son of the living God," Jesus attributes this knowledge to divine revelation (Matt 16:16-17). Even those who scoff at Jesus on the cross do so as "the Son of God" (Matt 27:40, 43).

Luke's Christology is difficult to categorize. While he consistently refers to Jesus as Lord, the disciples do not confess him as Son of God during his ministry. Roger Haight sees in Luke a two-stage Christology, a narrative Christology beginning with Jesus' conception as God's Son by the power of the Spirit that empowers him in his ministry; in his second volume, the Acts of the Apostles, the exalted Jesus pours out the Spirit on the disciples, but the question of preexistence or incarnation is never raised.[36] Still, the metaphor of Jesus as Son of God, dependent as he is on Mark's Gospel, is not missing. In the words of Marinus de Jonge, Jesus "is the Son of God, in his own way;

---

[34] Michael L. Cook, *Christology as Narrative Quest* (Collegeville, MN: Liturgical Press, 1997), 93.

[35] Haight, *Jesus Symbol of God*, 161.

[36] Ibid., 163–66.

then as God's representative on earth, now as the living Lord of the church."[37]

John

John's Christology is clearly the highest in the New Testament. Again echoing Wisdom theology, though with the divine Logos (Word) substituted for *Hokhmah* (Wisdom), the Prologue, an early Christian hymn, tells the story of the Word of God who was with God from the beginning. The Word that was God is active in creation, coming into the world, and became flesh, whose glory as the only begotten Son of the Father we have seen (John 1:1-14).

But Johannine Christology is not limited to the Prologue. The author represents Jesus as recognized as Messiah (John 1:41) and Son of God (John 1:49) from the beginning. Jesus speaks openly of himself as the Son (John 3:16, 17; 5:20, 21; 6:40; 14:13), proclaims his divine origin (John 3:13; 8:42) and unity with the Father (10:30, 38; 14:9), and repeatedly uses the divine formula "I AM" (*egō eimi*), several times in the absolute sense, without the predicate, as "When you lift up the Son of Man, then you will realize that I AM" (John 8:28). Raymond Brown argues that this "absolute use . . . has the effect of portraying Jesus as divine with (pre)existence as his identity, even as the Greek OT understood the God of Israel."[38] The climax to John's Christology can be seen in the confession of the doubting Thomas at the end of the gospel, "My Lord and my God" (John 20:28), one of the few times that *Theos* (God) is predicated of Jesus (cf. John 1:1; Heb 1:8-9).[39]

Classical Christologies

One of the challenges that faced the growing church was Gnosticism, a syncretistic religious movement that may have preceded

---

[37] Marinus de Jonge, *Christology in Context: The Earliest Christian Response to Jesus* (Philadelphia, PA: Westminster Press, 1988), 105.

[38] Raymond E. Brown, *An Introduction to New Testament Christology* (New York: Paulist Press, 1994), 139.

[39] Brown analyzes other possible examples in his *Introduction*, 185–95.

Christianity but certainly drew on Christian sources and symbols, particularly evident in the later apocryphal gospels. Gnostic teachers offered salvation through a secret knowledge available only to the initiated. Greek in inspiration, Gnosticism was dualistic, privileging spirit over matter, the eternal over the temporal, and the immutable over the changing. As the church began to move beyond the mythopoeic language of its origins in Judaism and incorporate the language of the Greco-Roman world in which it now found itself, this more abstract, philosophical language proved to be both helpful and a threat.

Docetism, a christological expression of Gnosticism, found the idea of the divine taking on flesh with all its nastiness and mutability incomprehensible. Hence the Docetists (from the Greek *dokeō*, to seem) denied that Jesus was truly human; he only "seemed" to be human or to have died, and as Ignatius of Antioch protested, they could not admit that the Eucharist was really the flesh of the Savior.[40] Similarly, others influenced by Gnosticism and Middle Platonism saw the divine Word as a lesser emanation from the divine source, a mediator between the ineffable God and the world of becoming and change. Such was the position of Arius (256–336), a priest of Alexandria; he argued that the being (*ousia*) of God was unique, transcendent, unable to be shared. The Logos, created out of nothing, had a beginning in time.[41] Thus the Word was a creature. Something of a propagandist, Arius popularized his teachings with little jingles such as "there was a time when he was not" which helped spread his teachings throughout the Empire.

As we saw in chapter 1, two early catechetical schools, the school of Alexandria founded in 195 by Clement of Alexandria, and that of Antioch, thought to have been founded by Lucian of Antioch in about 200, were caught up in these controversies. Looking to its great teacher Origen, Alexandria stressed the divinity of the Logos joined to the person of Jesus. Antioch, always concerned to affirm the full humanity of Jesus against those who challenged it, insisted on his "two natures," human and divine, joined by a substantial (hypostatic)

---

[40] Ignatius of Antioch, *Ephesians* 7; *Trallians* 9; *Smyrnaeans* 1–3.
[41] See J. N. D. Kelly, *Early Christian Doctrines* (London: Adam and Charles Black, 1958), 225–30.

union. Their different approaches have been characterized as word-flesh (Alexandria) and word-man (Antioch) theologies. To bring peace to the empire, the emperor Constantine brought some 318 bishops together at Nicaea in Turkey in 325. The Council condemned several Arian propositions and in its creed taught that Jesus is "God from God, light from light, true God from true God, begotten not made, consubstantial (*homoousion*) with the Father." It thus affirmed the divinity of Jesus but was less clear on his humanity and on the Holy Spirit.

What followed in the long process of "receiving" the council were further controversies and a number of subsequent councils as the two sides sought a language that would do justice to the church's faith in Jesus as both human and divine. Athanasius (296–373) saw clearly that if Christ was not truly divine he could not bestow immortality on humankind. The Cappadocians supplied the language of one *ousia*, three *hypostases* to describe unity of being and diverse characteristics (paternity, sonship, sanctification) within the Godhead. Finally, consequent to Pope Leo's request for a general council, some six hundred bishops (or five hundred, depending on the account) gathered at Chalcedon on the Bosporus in 451. Using the creed of Nicaea, the two letters of Cyril of Alexandria, the letter or "tome" of Pope Leo, and the confession of faith of Flavian, archbishop of Constantinople, the bishops produced a confession of faith that sought to address the concerns of both schools. In part it read:

> We all with one voice teach the confession of one and the same Son, our Lord Jesus Christ: the same perfect in divinity and perfect in humanity; the same truly God and truly man, of a rational soul and a body; consubstantial with the Father as regards his divinity, and the same consubstantial with us as regards his humanity; like us in all respects except for sin; begotten before the ages from the Father as regards his divinity, and in the last days the same for us and for our salvation from Mary, the virgin God-bearer, as regards his humanity; one and the same Christ, Son, Lord, only-begotten, acknowledged in two natures which undergo no confusion, no change, no division, no separation; at no point was the difference between the natures taken away through union, but rather the property of both natures is preserved and comes together into a single person and a single subsistent being; he is not parted or

divided into two persons, but is one and the same only-begotten Son, God, Word, Lord Jesus Christ.[42]

In adopting the language of "two natures" without division or separation, Chalcedon met the Antiochian concern for the full humanity of Jesus. It addressed the Alexandrian concern for the union of Jesus with the divine Logos by using Flavian's expression, "one *prosopōn* and one *hypostasis*," one person and one subsistent being, to describe Jesus confessed as truly God and truly man.

Chalcedon did not answer all the christological questions. But in many ways it represents a classic standard of the church's faith. It did not Hellenize Christian faith, as some have argued. The Christian concept of God still was highly colored by Greek ideas of the divine impassibility and transcendence. Nevertheless, Christian theology, in seeing the existing individual *hypostasis*/substance as most real, moved Western culture beyond a Greek emphasis on universal ontological nature toward thinking in terms of persons.[43] Relationality is at the very heart of the divine mystery.

Contemporary Christologies

It is not possible here to survey adequately the many contemporary Christologies. I propose to look at soteriology, the doctrine of salvation from a contemporary perspective, and then review several christological types, specifically incarnational, pluralist, and praxis Christologies. The last two have been particularly influenced by the recent emphasis on the historical Jesus and the increasing emphasis on dialogue with the great world religions.

Soteriology

Edward Schillebeeckx has written that Christianity did not begin with a doctrine but with an experience of redemption and liberation for those who encountered Christ, which became a message passed

---

[42] Norman P. Tanner, ed., *Decrees of the Ecumenical Councils*, vol. 1 (Washington, DC: Georgetown University Press, 1990), 86.

[43] Kasper, *Jesus the Christ*, 177.

on to others.[44] So how did Jesus bring redemption or salvation? The traditional answer for Catholics is that he died for our sins; a Protestant answer might be that he paid the price for our sins, taking God's wrath on himself. What Elizabeth A. Johnson calls the "dazzling variety" of metaphors used by the New Testament authors to describe the work of Jesus coalesced in Western theology into the idea of an exchange, a sacrifice offered by Christ to win grace and reconciliation for humankind.[45] Under the influence of Augustine and especially Anselm of Canterbury (1033–1109), this hardened into the theology of satisfaction or "penal substitution," while Eastern theology has long placed primacy on the incarnation and its transformation of the human—the idea of divinization (*theosis*).

In his *Cur Deus Homo?* (Why God Became Man) Anselm argued that God became man in Jesus because only an infinite being could make satisfaction for an infinite offense against God's justice, the result of Adam's sin. Thus the incarnation is subordinated to the need for redemption. Abelard (d. 1142), a contemporary of Anselm, offered an alternative view; the incarnation was not to make a payment; it was purely an act of love, teaching the law of love by example.[46] Jesus' salvific work was revelational and exemplary. Early church fathers like Irenaeus and Origen related salvation to the renewal of all creation, bringing it through Christ to a fullness in the Creator.[47]

Anselm's theology, virtually canonized by evangelical Christianity, fails on a number of grounds. It focuses on the death of Jesus rather than on his whole life and preaching. It reduces the mystery of salvation to the atonement, reconciling humankind to God after the Fall. It represents a soteriology "from above," from God's point of view, so to speak. As Rahner says, it "introduces the metaphysically impossible idea of a transformation of God."[48] From a pastoral perspective,

---

[44] Edward Schillebeeckx, *Interim Report on the Books* Jesus & Christ (New York: Crossroad, 1982), 7.

[45] See her excellent article, "Jesus and Salvation," *Catholic Theological Society of America: Proceedings* 49 (1994): 3.

[46] See Richard W. Southern, *Saint Anselm: A Portrait in a Landscape* (Cambridge, UK: Cambridge University Press, 1990), 210.

[47] See Brian E. Daley, *The Hope of the Early Church: A Handbook of Patristic Eschatology* (Cambridge, UK: Cambridge University Press, 1991), 29, 58.

[48] Karl Rahner, "The Universality of Salvation," in *Theological Investigations*, vol. 16 (New York: Seabury Press, 1979), 208.

its emphasis on God's justice and wrath has obscured the divine love and mercy. Ratzinger calls it a "perfectly logical divine-cum-human legal system . . . that can make the image of God appear in a sinister light."[49]

But can we say that Jesus in some way accomplished our salvation? The Christology of the New Testament affirms in multiple ways that Jesus mediates our salvation, that he is God's salvation. Some contemporary Christologies reduce Christ's role to that of a revealer. Others (for example, Karl Rahner) see the incarnation as opening the human to a participation in the divine life, the transforming love of God as Father, Son, and Spirit. It is participating in this trinitarian love that saves us. Michael Cook stresses the central, soteriological meaning of the resurrection as "the constitutive cause of salvation for the whole of creation," even if there are other mediations of saving grace or the Spirit.[50] As the Alpha and the Omega (Rev 22:13), the salvation the risen Jesus brings embraces not just the resurrection of the body but justice for the victims of history and the cosmos itself, as we will see later in the chapter on eschatology.

Incarnational Christologies

The first type refers to Christologies framed within the church's dogmatic tradition, specifically its creeds, based on the incarnation of the Logos. They are more traditional. In Roger Haight's terms, they represent a Logos Christology. This is what they have in common. Beyond that, they will develop their Christologies in light of their own methods and concerns. We will consider briefly Karl Rahner, Walter Kasper, and Pope Benedict XVI.

With his enormous bibliography, it is difficult to identify Rahner's Christology with a specific work. Certainly his *Foundations of Christian Faith* comes closest to a systematic presentation of his thought in this regard.[51] While Rahner presumes the biblical tradition, most of his

---

[49] Joseph Ratzinger, *Introduction to Christianity* (New York: Herder and Herder, 1971), 174.

[50] Michael L. Cook, *Trinitarian Christology: The Power that Sets Us Free* (New York: Paulist Press, 2010), 7.

[51] Karl Rahner, *Foundations of Christian Faith: An Introduction to the Idea of Christianity* (New York: Seabury Press, 1978), 176–321.

work was done before the modern biblical movement began to bear fruit in the Catholic Church, with the result that there is little emphasis on the historical Jesus in his work. He acknowledges that ascending and descending Christologies are intermingled. Rahner's Christology stresses the unity of Jesus of Nazareth with the eternal Logos or Word.

Situating his transcendental Christology within an evolutionary worldview and his theological anthropology, Rahner sees the transcendental self-communication of God to humankind as a process that reaches its goal and climax in the person of Jesus. "The Son" is absolutely identified with the Father. The incarnation means that in God's assuming human nature as God's own, that nature realizes the point toward which it is always moving in virtue of its essence. It is the highest instantiation of that union with God toward which each person is moving in virtue of the transcendent structure of the human person, though that movement is always dependent on human freedom. In other words, in Jesus, the human person's openness to God and God's fullness come together.

For Rahner, creation and incarnation are not two separate acts but different moments or phases in one process. The resurrection, understood as an ontologically unique event, vindicates Jesus' life and foreshadows our own hope; it manifests Jesus as the absolute savior.[52] As Elizabeth Johnson says, paraphrasing Rahner, "The statement of God's Incarnation—of God's becoming material—is the most basic statement of Christology."[53] According to Gerhard Lohfink, Jesus as the Logos of God is "the final and ultimate word spoken by God, the Word in which God has spoken God's self totally and without exception."[54]

For Rahner, Christ is also present in non-Christian religions through the Spirit, mediating God's self-communication and the possibility of salvation. Thus Rahner seeks to integrate two different concerns in his Christology, God's universal salvific will and Jesus Christ as the final prophet and absolute savior who offers salvation

---

[52] Karl Rahner, ed., *Sacramentum Mundi*, vol. 3 (New York: Herder and Herder, 1969), 204.

[53] Elizabeth Johnson, *Ask the Beasts: Darwin and the God of Love* (New York: Bloomsbury, 2014), 197.

[54] Gerhard Lohfink, *No Irrelevant Jesus: On Jesus and the Church Today* (Collegeville, MN: Liturgical Press, 2014), 3.

as a participation in the divine life. He argues that Anselm's understanding of Jesus' death as a sacrificial expiation has never been endorsed by the extraordinary magisterium.

Walter Kasper's *Jesus the Christ* also takes seriously the Christ of the Christian tradition. He argues that a Christian is compelled to become a metaphysician on account of his or her faith.[55] Thus he proposes a Christology of complementarity, based on the earthly Jesus and the faith of the church, using historical research as a relatively autonomous criterion to measure the church's belief, thus the earthly Jesus and the exalted Christ.[56] His use of historical-critical research is extensive, providing considerable insight into the Jesus of the ministry. Particularly interesting is his juxtaposing the approaches of Karl Barth and Karl Rahner. For Barth, the God-world relation is understood within Christology; thus Christian theology becomes the hermeneutical principle for understanding all of reality. For Rahner, Christology lies within the God-world relationship, which means that theological exposition or construction needs to take into account the relation between Christianity, culture, politics, and, we might add, science and history.[57] In other words, from a Catholic perspective, Christian theology, including Christology, is concerned with an understanding of reality in its widest sense, recognizing the different kind of knowledge that comes from faith and science. As the Catholic tradition continues to stress, faith and reason, or science and theology, are complementary.

Perhaps the most traditional approach is Joseph Ratzinger/Pope Benedict XVI's Christology. While respecting the historical-critical method, he constantly stresses its limits. In his 1968 *Introduction to Christianity*, he begins his Christology not from the Jesus of history but from the Apostles' Creed, in christological terms, "from above." In his *Jesus of Nazareth*, he wants to show that the Jesus of the gospels is the real, "historical" Jesus "in the strict sense of the word."[58] His final volume, on the infancy narratives, concludes that "Matthew is

[55] Kasper, *Jesus the Christ*, 21.

[56] Ibid., 35.

[57] Ibid., 21.

[58] Benedict XVI, *Jesus of Nazareth: From the Baptism in the Jordan to the Transfiguration*, xxii.

recounting real history, theologically thought through and inter-preted."[59] Thus critical historical Jesus research plays a much less prominent role. Benedict takes the unity of the Bible as a given, and leaves room for meanings that may go beyond "the precise sense the words were intended to convey at their time and place of origin."[60] This is what biblical scholars refer to as the fuller sense. He rightly insists that Scripture must be read within the living tradition of Israel or the church.

Benedict's own perspective is markedly Johannine. Jesus' preach-ing is about the mystery of his person, including his preaching of the reign of God. He rejects regnocentric or secular-utopian interpreta-tions of the kingdom which make its coming the work of human beings rather than of God. The kingdom is an eschatological, not a this-worldly reality; Jesus is the kingdom of God in person. He argues that the absolute "I AM" sayings in John come from Jesus himself, as well as the passage in Mark 6:50 where Jesus comes walking on the water and says, "It is I" (in the Greek, *egō eimi*)[61] and says that the disciples in various ways were able to sense even during his life the presence of the living God.[62]

Pluralist Christologies

Vatican II's recognition that God's truth can be in some ways re-flected in other religions (NA 2) and its teaching on the universal availability of God's grace has resulted in the rethinking of some Christologies in light of the dialogue with other religions. Edward Schillebeeckx and Roger Haight argue that Jesus is not the efficient cause of salvation but rather its revealer or exemplary cause. Salva-tion is seen not as something Jesus accomplished. Rather, he serves as a revealer or model of the way to the Father. Their Christology is also a soteriology.

---

[59] Benedict XVI, *Jesus of Nazareth: The Infancy Narratives* (New York: Image, 2012), 119.

[60] Ibid., xix.

[61] Ibid., 352–54.

[62] Ibid,. 302.

JeSuS AS
MAM

Schillebeeckx is reluctant to talk about Jesus as the universal redeemer; for Schillebeeckx, he is so only "insofar as what happened
in Jesus is continued in his disciples. Without a relationship to a redemptive and liberative practice of Christians, the redemption
brought about at one time by Jesus is suspended in a purely speculative, vacuous atmosphere."[63] Still, Schillebeeckx finds in the early
Q tradition "an implicit identification between Kingdom and Jesus,
and this on the lips of Jesus himself."[64] He sees Jesus' "Abba experience" as paradigmatic of his unity with the one he calls Father. He
identifies Jesus not as the God-man as in his earlier works but as the
eschatological prophet who proclaims God's final and definitive
intervention in human history.

Haight, starting with a Christology from below, develops a "Spirit
Christology"; he sees Jesus not as the incarnate Word but as a "symbol
of God" which both is and is not what it symbolizes. Jesus is not a
divine figure in the sense of patristic theology, "of the same substance
of the Father," but like others, Haight "recognizes God's saving action
through him and God's presence and power in him."[65] He speaks of
"uncentering the resurrection,"[66] not denying it but objecting to the
view that the resurrection is in some way the center of Christian faith.
Jesus himself remains the center, Jesus in his pre-Easter life, not his
resurrection. But his view overlooks the significance of Jesus as a
person as well as his significance for all creation. Haight asks, how
did Jesus save? "As revealer Jesus preached and actually mediated
in his ministry the kingdom of God. This means that Jesus is an invitation to look for this process going on within the whole of human
life and history. Movements aimed at advancing justice, reconciliation, and peace in the world, at resisting social suffering, have a
sacrality marked with religious depth."[67]

---

[63] Edward Schillebeeckx, "The Religious and Human Ecumene," in *The Future of
Liberation Theology: Essays in Honor of Gustavo Gutiérrez*, ed. Marc H. Ellis and Otto
Maduro (Maryknoll, NY: Orbis Books, 1989), 185.

[64] Ted Schoof, ed., *The Schillebeeckx Case* (New York: Paulist Press, 1984), 62.

[65] Roger Haight, *The Future of Christology* (New York: Continuum, 2007), 47–52, at
52.

[66] Haight, *Jesus Symbol of God*, 149.

[67] Haight, *The Future of Christology*, 71; Paul Lakeland's approach is similar. He sees
Christ as God's presence in history, drawing all humans to himself, not as someone
offering a blood sacrifice to ransom us from sins; see Lakeland, *Church: Living Communion, Engaging Theology* (Collegeville, MN: Liturgical Press, 2009), 54–55.

For Paul Knitter, Jesus' divinity consists in his total responsiveness and transparency to the Spirit of God; he is "truly" divine and "truly" savior but not unique in this sense or the only one of whom this is true. Thus he is not the universal savior or the only one who reveals the deepest truth about ourselves and our world. Nor does he "fix" anything. He is a manifestation or "enfleshment" of Ultimate Reality or Ultimate Truth, but Buddha, Muhammad, and others can be so also. Knitter sees the resurrection of Jesus as a powerful symbol or myth but not as something true in its historical facticity or in the raising of his physical body. The risen Christ is an expression of the universal presence and power of the divine in all religions. His uniqueness is to be found in his preferential identification with the oppressed.[68]

Praxis Christologies

A number of contemporary Christologies have been shaped by the rediscovery of Jesus' preaching of the reign of God, among them the works of Johann Baptist Metz, Jon Sobrino, and Terrence Tilley. For them the key to Christology lies in praxis, what Metz calls "the primacy of praxis."[69] "Metz's christological thesis is that one only knows Christ by imitating him."[70] He seeks to lead others to imitate the Christ of the ministry. While some find his Christology underdeveloped, his concern is to address those who live on the margins of society, turning their attention to the "dangerous memory" of Christ's death and resurrection and to his God who is revealed in suffering. His concern for praxis has resulted in the characterization of his work as a "political" theology, though he does not mean a politics of ideologies and parties:

> What we need in the long run is a new form of political life and new political structures. Only when that arrives will there be any

---

[68] Paul F. Knitter, *Without Buddha I Could Not Be a Christian* (Oxford: Oneworld, 2009), 125–29.

[69] Johannes Baptist Metz, *Followers of Christ: Perspectives on Religious Life* (New York: Paulist Press, 1978), 40.

[70] Bruce T. Morrill, *Anamnesis as Dangerous Memory* (Collegeville, MN: Liturgical Press, 2000), 34; see also Johann Baptist Metz, *Faith in History and Society: Toward a Practical Fundamental Theology* (New York: Seabury Press, 1980), 52.

humane cultures at all in the future. In this sense, "politics" is actually the new name for culture and in this sense, too, any theology
which tries to reflect on Christian tradition in the context of world
problems and to bring about the process of transference between
the kingdom of God and society is a "political theology."[71]

Writing from the perspective of liberation theology, Jon Sobrino
also roots Christology in praxis. His approach is similar to that of
Metz. His starting point is bipolar; the historical Jesus in the context
of the present situation in Latin America, for the following of Jesus
"cannot be any automatic process of imitation which pays no heed
at all to our own concrete situation and bypasses political, anthropological, and socio-economic analysis."[72] He considers Jesus' preaching
of the kingdom of God as the "most all-embracing theological concept." The kingdom does not evolve, it "breaks in."[73] Like Metz, he
adapts an apocalyptic perspective for understanding the resurrection;
it foreshadows not just our own resurrection but "looks forward to
the vindication of God's justice."[74]

In his later works, Sobrino emphasizes practice as foundational to
Christology. Christian discipleship involves a "messianic practice."
It means taking the crucified peoples down from the cross, rescuing
the victims of this world just as God rescued the crucified Jesus.
Discipleship necessarily has a political dimension, working to transform structures. Just as Jesus' liberating actions were "signs" and
"powers" of the kingdom, generating hope in its possibility, so these
partial resurrections generate hope in God's giving life to all the
crucified.[75]

---

[71] Metz, *Faith in History and Society*, 102; see also Morrill, *Anamnesis as Dangerous Memory*, 34–40.

[72] Jon Sobrino, *Christology at the Crossroads* (Maryknoll, NY: Orbis Books, 1978), 12; see also Michael L. Cook, "Jesus from the Other Side of History: Christology in Latin America," *Theological Studies* 44, no. 2 (1982): 258–87.

[73] Sobrino, *Christology at the Crossroads*, 37.

[74] Ibid., 243.

[75] Jon Sobrino, *Christ the Liberator: A View from the Victims* (Maryknoll, NY: Orbis Books, 2001), 47–49; see also Kevin F. Burke and Robert Lassalle-Klein, *Love that Produces Hope: The Thought of Ignacio Ellacuría* (Collegeville, MN: Liturgical Press, 2006).

Terrence Tilley also develops a Christology that begins not in theory but in practice. Rejecting "from above" or "from below" approaches as well as attempts to reconstruct the historical Jesus, he focuses on Jesus as he was remembered by his disciples. Faith is neither merely belief nor merely trust; it means "living in and living out the reign of God by engaging in reconciling practices."[76] Doctrine is secondary. The reign of God is understood as a reign of human flourishing. Christology is done by engaging in those reconciling practices of the Jesus movement: exorcising, healing, teaching, and welcoming others to table fellowship after the example of Jesus. Even if only God can bring about God's reign, the Jesus movement freed people not only from their mental or physical illnesses but also from having to participate in a sociopolitical system that marginalized them by construing them as dirty and dangerous. Thus there is a communal dimension to engaging in reconciling practice, for example, working for an effective health-care system. "In sum, healing in general and exorcism in particular reestablished the relationship of those who had been excluded by the larger community; it was a reconciling practice."[77]

From a doctrinal perspective, Tilley sees Jesus' two natures not as two comparable items but as a natural harmony, wanting and willing what the infinite God wants and wills; "this man, the first among equals, is also the divine agent, unconfusedly, unalterably, indivisibly, inseparably."[78] In Jesus, God's ways and those of humans are aligned. This means for Tilley that one may not have to be baptized to be a member of Jesus' movement, for the Christian movement is neither christocentric nor ecclesiocentric, but theocentric; promoting the reign of God is always first. A similar "regnocentric" approach can be found in the work of Elizabeth Johnson and Peter Phan.[79]

---

[76] Terrence W. Tilley, *The Disciples' Jesus: Christology as Reconciling Practice* (Maryknoll, NY: Orbis Books, 2008), 252.

[77] Ibid., 146.

[78] Ibid., 227.

[79] See Elizabeth Johnson, *Consider Jesus*, 52; Peter C. Phan, *In Our Own Tongues: Perspectives from Asia on Mission and Inculturation* (Maryknoll, NY: Orbis Books, 2003), 40–41.

Conclusion

The relatively brief public ministry of Jesus of Nazareth needs to be centered in the Jewish tradition out of which he came. At the center of his ministry is the kingdom or reign of God, pointing to God's salvific presence at the heart of the world and in our lives. But his preaching was seen as a challenge both by the Jewish authorities and the Roman occupiers of Judea.

Scattered by his terrible death, Jesus' disciples were gathered together again by their Easter experience which transformed them into effective witnesses and evangelists who began the church's christological reflection. The resurrection revealed God's saving grace in its fullness. The controversies of the first four centuries led to a classic standard of the church's christological faith in Chalcedon's confession of Jesus as truly God and truly man, without bringing to an end efforts to more adequately express the mystery of Jesus.

The rediscovery of the historical Jesus has led to an outpouring of works on Christology, both systematic and historical-critical. Incarnational Christologies seek to explain Jesus' story in light of the church's official teaching and its creeds. Pluralist approaches rethink Christology in light of dialogue with other religions. Some authors adopt an exclusively regnocentric position, redefining the mission of the church as regnocentric rather than Christocentric. Praxis Christologies focus more on Jesus' preaching of the reign of God; they emphasize the socially engaged nature of Christian discipleship, while doctrines are seen as less important. Others, like Pope Benedict, continue to stress the eschatological nature of the kingdom; it is God's work, not that of human beings.

It is important to recognize the social and political dimensions of Jesus' preaching without turning it into an ideology for human betterment or social change. Christology cannot ignore the ministry of Jesus. While Pope Benedict has raised some important cautions, it remains true that Jesus reveals that a relationship with God demands a proper relationship with others, one characterized by justice, love, and service.

As Francis Sullivan has argued, "mainstream" Catholic theology recognizes that both non-Christian religions and transcendent values such as justice, fraternity, solidarity with the poor, peace, and compassion, can serve as mediations of grace and salvation for people who do not share a Christian faith.[80] At the same time, Catholic theology recognizes that through love and compassionate service of others, we ourselves can mediate God's saving grace or, perhaps better expressed, allow God's grace to work through us.

For Further Reading

Benedict XVI. *Jesus of Nazareth: From the Baptism in the Jordan to the Transfiguration*. New York: Doubleday, 2007.

———. *Jesus of Nazareth: Holy Week; From the Entrance into Jerusalem to the Resurrection*. San Francisco: Ignatius Press, 2011.

———. *Jesus of Nazareth: The Infancy Narratives*. New York: Image, 2012.

Brown, Raymond E. *An Introduction to New Testament Christology*. New York: Paulist Press, 1994.

Cook, Michael L. *Trinitarian Christology: The Power That Sets Us Free*. New York: Paulist Press, 2010.

Grillmeier, Alois. *Christ in Christian Tradition*. 2 Volumes. Atlanta: John Knox, 1975–1987.

Haight, Roger. *The Future of Christology*. New York: Continuum, 2007.

———. *Jesus Symbol of God*. Maryknoll, NY: Orbis Books, 1999.

Hurtado, Larry. *Lord Jesus Christ: Devotion to Jesus in Earliest Christianity*. Grand Rapids, MI: William B. Eerdmans, 2003.

Johnson, Elizabeth A. *Consider Jesus: Waves of Renewal in Christology*. New York: Crossroad, 1990.

Kasper, Walter. *Jesus the Christ*. New York: Paulist Press, 1976.

Lassalle-Klein, Robert. "Jesus of Galilee and the Crucified People: The Contextual Christology of Jon Sobrino and Ignacio Ellacuría." *Theological Studies* 70 (2009): 347–76.

Lohfink, Gerhard. *Jesus of Nazareth: What He Wanted, Who He Was*. Collegeville, MN: Liturgical Press, 2012.

---

[80] Francis A. Sullivan, *Salvation Outside the Church* (New York: Paulist Press, 1992), 181.

Meier, John P. *A Marginal Jew: Rethinking the Historical Jesus.* Vol. 1, *The Roots of the Problem and the Person.* New York: Doubleday, 1991; Vol. 2, *Mentor, Message, and Miracles.* New York: Doubleday, 1994; Vol. 3, *Companions and Competitors.* New York: Doubleday, 2001; Vol. 4, *Law and Love.* New Haven, CT: Yale University Press, 2009.

Metz, Johannes Baptist. *Followers of Christ: The Religious Life and the Church.* New York: Paulist Press, 1978.

Rausch, Thomas P. *Who Is Jesus? An Introduction to Christology.* Collegeville, MN: Liturgical Press, 2003.

Schillebeeckx, Edward. *Jesus: An Experiment in Christology.* New York: Seabury Press, 1979.

Tilley, Terrence W. *The Disciples' Jesus: Christology as Reconciling Practice.* Maryknoll, NY: Orbis Books, 2008.

Wiley, Tatha. *Thinking of Christ: Proclamation, Explanation, Meaning.* New York: Continuum, 2003.

Witherington III, Ben. *The Jesus Quest: The Third Search for the Jew of Nazareth.* Downers Grove, IL: InterVarsity Press, 1997.

Wright, N. T. *Jesus and the Victory of God.* Minneapolis, MN: Fortress Press, 1996.

———. *The New Testament and the People of God.* Minneapolis, MN: Fortress Press, 1992.

Chapter 5

Revelation and Faith

In the beginning was the Word,
and the Word was with God,
and the Word was God.

(John 1:1)

The word *logos* in Greek, appearing in the opening sentence of the
Gospel of John, means both reason and word, thus language, communication, meaning. It does not mean the beginning for God, who
of course has no beginning, but that before time began, God's primordial act was to break the silence of the eternal night, to communicate, to speak a creative word that brings forth light in the darkness,
the sky, the earth and sea, plants and living creatures of every kind,
and man and woman created in the divine image (Gen 1:1-27). Even
more, God's Word through whom all these things came to be was
coming into the world and became flesh and made his dwelling
among us (John 1:1-14). God's movement is always outward, to share
and create, to reveal. The doctrine of the Trinity reveals that relationship, speech, and *Logos* are present in God.[1]

The New Testament word for revelation is *apocalypsis*, which means
to uncover, to remove a veil, to disclose, hence to reveal. The Judeo-
Christian tradition presumes God's revelation; so does Islam which
is based on it. The very word Bible, *ta biblia* in Greek, means the books,

---

[1] Joseph Ratzinger, *The Feast of Faith* (San Francisco: Ignatius Press, 1986), 25.

which of course contain words. But how does revelation take place? How do we encounter God's free self-disclosure that reveals but does not take away the mystery of the divine? Theology speaks of two kinds of revelation, a general revelation accessible to all and special revelation, taking place in salvation history and reaching its fullness in Jesus.

General Revelation

Sometimes called natural revelation, general revelation refers to the knowledge of God's existence available to all people. Scripture points to a knowledge of God from the design and government of the natural world. The psalmist proclaims, "The heavens declare the glory of God; the sky proclaims the builder's craft. One day to the next conveys that message; one night to the next imparts that knowledge" (Ps 19:1-3). The Wisdom literature, sometimes characterized as a creation theology, recognizes God's self-communication through nature (Job 12:7-9), even in the personification of Lady Wisdom (Prov 8).

St. Paul, influenced by Wisdom theology, taught that the wicked have no excuse for their refusal to acknowledge God, "For what can be known about God is evident to them, because God made it evident to them. Ever since the creation of the world, his invisible attributes of eternal power and divinity have been able to be understood and perceived in what he has made. As a result they have no excuse" (Rom 1:19-20). As Calvin writes in his *Institutes* (1.3.1), "There is within the human mind, and indeed by natural instinct, an awareness of divinity. To prevent anyone from taking refuge in the pretense of ignorance, God himself has implanted in all men a certain understanding of his divine majesty."

The Catholic Church has continued to teach that God's existence can be known from the work of creation. According to Vatican I (1869–1870), "The Church, holds and teaches that God, the first principle and last end of all things, can be known with certainty from the created world by the natural light of human reason."[2] Similarly,

---

[2] Vatican I, *Dei Filius* 2; Cf. DS 3004.

Vatican II's *Gaudium et Spes*, the Pastoral Constitution on the Church in the Modern World, affirmed that "all believers of whatever religion always hear [God's] revealing voice in the discourse of creatures. When God is forgotten, however, the creature itself grows unintelligible" (GS 36).

But knowledge of God's existence is more than an intuition from the beauty or complexity of nature, and it cannot be reduced to the conclusion to a rational argument. As Karl Rahner has shown in his theological anthropology, the infinite is disclosed as the horizon against which every act of human knowing takes place. "Man is a transcendent being insofar as all of his knowledge and all of his conscious activity is grounded in a pre-apprehension (*Vorgriff*) of 'being' as such, in an unthematic but ever-present knowledge of the infinity of reality."[3] Without experiencing in some way the infinite, we would never grasp the finite. We experience the transcendent reach of human understanding in the experience of questioning, in moving beyond the concrete things we know to ask about the things we cannot experience, about where being came from, about justice for all those who suffer without redress, about a life beyond death.

This experience of transcendence and sense for the infinite, even if unthematic, points to the inadequacy of the disjunction between the natural and the supernatural, presumed by neoscholasticism and Enlightenment thinking. Gordon Kaufman rejects what he calls the mythology of the metaphysical-cosmological dualism found both in the Bible and in Western religious thought, dividing reality into "earth" and "heaven." This dualism makes it seem as though God were somehow "out there," beyond the realities of our experience.[4] He argues that it is our experience of limit, of finitude or radical contingency that is the justification for God language.[5]

---

[3] Karl Rahner, *Foundations of Christian Faith: An Introduction to the Idea of Christianity* (New York: Seabury Press, 1978), 33.

[4] Gordon D. Kaufman, "On the Meaning of 'God': Transcendence without Mythology," in *Transcendence*, ed. Herbert W. Richardson and Donald R. Cutler (Boston: Beacon Press, 1969), 115.

[5] Ibid., 120–23.

Thus both the natural world as well as the experience of transcendence revealed in human knowing testify to God's existence, even if the divine nature remains unknown, for God remains incomprehensible mystery. The Second Vatican Council recognized that other religions often reflect a ray of that Truth that enlightens all men and women and so regards them with sincere reverence (NA 2). John Haught argues, with reference to Paul Tillich and Schubert Ogden, special revelation has meaning only if we have experienced an openness to the encompassing presence of the mystery of God's being, giving us reason to seek truth and the good life. In this sense, he says that all the great religions are concerned at least implicitly with revelation.[6]

Conservative evangelical theology recognizes a general revelation but usually holds that because of sin it does not afford human beings the reliable knowledge of God and the things of the spirit necessary for salvation.[7]

Special Revelation

Beyond general revelation, God has chosen to enter into relationship with humanity, first with Israel and then with all people through the story of Jesus who came among us to reveal the Father. This "history of salvation" is called special revelation. As Hans Küng beautifully says, "Where others perceived only infinite silence, Israel heard a voice."[8]

Salvation History

The biblical story of creation shows God's creative work taking place through the divine word. The story of the Fall in Genesis 3 describes a lost intimacy of the man and woman with God who was accustomed to visit them "in the breezy time of the day" (Gen 3:8).

---

[6] John F. Haught, *Mystery and Promise: A Theology of Revelation* (Collegeville, MN: Liturgical Press, 1993), 51–54.

[7] Harold Lindsell, *The Battle for the Bible* (Grand Rapids, MI: Zondervan, 1976), 29.

[8] Hans Küng, *Does God Exist? An Answer for Today* (Garden City, NY: Doubleday, 1980), 634.

In spite of human sinfulness which brings with it violence, alienation, and fratricide, threatening God's creation itself in the story of the Great Flood, God continues to seek a relationship with human beings.

He calls Abram out of Ur of the Chaldeans and leads him into the land of Canaan, establishing a covenant with him, changing his name to Abraham and promising that he will become the father of a people numerous as the stars of the sky and the sands on the seashore. When Abraham's descendants migrate to Egypt in a time of famine, God leads them forth again under Moses and establishes a covenant with them on Mount Sinai, promising a relationship of mutuality. There is a strong moral dimension to Israel's experience of God, who commands them, "Be holy, for I, the LORD, your God, am holy" (Lev 19:2). The very expression of the covenant is a moral code, the Decalogue or Ten Commandments (Exod 20:2-17; Deut 5:6-21), outlining what it means to live in covenant relationship with Yahweh. God's people too were to be holy, set apart, a priestly people.

God leads this covenanted people into the land of promise, helping them overcome their enemies, giving them a nation and a king. When they violate his covenant, he promises not to abandon them, speaking his word to them through prophetic figures like Elijah, Isaiah, Jeremiah, and a host of others. Various images or symbols promise a future salvation, include a coming Davidic king or messiah, a Day of the Lord when Yahweh will judge Israel and the nations, bringing justice for the poor and the oppressed, a renewed covenant or even a new covenant, writing the Law upon their hearts. In those days, God's salvation will be extended to all the nations—it will mean the resurrection of the dead.

The New Testament tells the story of how in the fullness of time, God once more sends the Word to God's people, this time the Word become flesh, God's only begotten Son. In his brief ministry Jesus healed the sick, drove out evil spirits, proclaimed the forgiveness of sins and the poor blest, and gathered disciples who shared in his ministry. Jesus showed them the way to the God he called "Abba," Father. When his challenge to the religious and political authorities of the day led to his public execution, his death on a cross, God raised him up to glory, where from the Father's right hand he poured forth his Spirit upon his disciples, his church. This, in short, is the biblical story of salvation history, the story of a God who wants to be in relationship with a people.

Dei Verbum

The best Catholic statement on revelation is Vatican II's *Dei Verbum*, the Dogmatic Constitution on Divine Revelation. It would be difficult to deny that post-Reformation Catholicism tended to neglect the place of Scripture in the life of the church. Nervous about the Protestant error of "private interpretation," official Catholicism was reluctant to put the Bible in the hands of the faithful; instead, young Catholics grew up reading "Bible stories" in beautifully illustrated books, but they didn't read the Bible itself. During the long period in which Catholic theology was dominated by neoscholasticism, the Bible was used as a source for "proof texts," but not for theology; the highest authority was magisterial teaching. But that began to change with the publication of *Divino Afflante Spiritu* (1943), the encyclical of Pope Pius XII giving Catholic scholars the green light to use modern historical-critical biblical disciplines in their work.

Dei Verbum restored the Bible to its proper place in Catholic theology and life. The constitution argued that the church has always venerated the Sacred Scriptures just as she venerates the body of the Lord in the liturgy, and that the Scriptures, together with sacred tradition, constitute the supreme rule of faith (DV 21). It emphasizes that God's plan of revelation is realized "by deeds and words having an inner unity: the deeds wrought by God in the history of salvation manifest and confirm the teachings and realities signified by the words, while the words proclaim the deeds and clarify the mystery contained in them" (DV 2). In this way the constitution sought to move beyond the salvation history theology, so popular in the 1940s and 1950s, which identified God's revelation with God's mighty acts in history rather than with the biblical narratives. It also avoids the doctrine of biblical inerrancy, so important to conservative Protestants. Inerrancy claims that the Bible is without error, infallible in all its affirmations, even those in the areas of history or science. While the tradition has always recognized the Scriptures as trustworthy or true, expressing this in various ways, the concept of "inerrancy" is relatively late, appearing in English only as late as the nineteenth century. It is a confessional doctrine, not one found in Scripture. Instead, *Dei Verbum* asserts that "the books of Scripture must be acknowledged as teaching solidly, faithfully and without error that truth which God wanted put into sacred writings for the sake of salvation" (DV 11). A carefully qualified affirmation.

Dei Verbum argues for an inner unity between events and the interpretation, preaching, or rereading of these events in the story of Israel or later in light of Christ by prophets, apostles, and evangelists.[9] The 1993 statement of the Pontifical Biblical Commission, *The Interpretation of the Bible in the Church*, further develops how this takes place, speaking of re-reading (*re-lectures*) of earlier biblical texts, developing new aspects of meaning which gives the Bible an inner unity (3.A.1), thus "actualizing" the biblical text within the living tradition of the church and its liturgy (4).[10]

In regards to revelation, *Dei Verbum* said that "the words proclaim the deeds and clarify the mystery contained in them," while the deepest truth about God and salvation shines out "in Christ who is both the mediator and the fullness of all revelation" (DV 2). It is important to notice that the constitution is placing revelation not primarily in a text but in the interpretation of the tradition and sees revelation reaching its fullness in Christ who perfected revelation in his words and deeds, especially through his death, resurrection, and sending of the Spirit (DV 4). In other words, for the Second Vatican Council, revelation is personal rather than propositional, trinitarian in form, and christological in realization.

The Transmission of Revelation

The constitution then addresses how God's revelation is handed on to subsequent generations, from the preaching of the apostles, to the apostolic men who committed the message of salvation to writing,

---

[9] Walter Brueggemann sees this as "cross-examining" the tradition in his *Theology of the Old Testament* (Minneapolis, MN: Fortress Press, 1997), 317–25.

[10] Pontifical Biblical Commission, *The Interpretation of the Bible in the Church*; see also the PBC's *The Jewish People and Their Sacred Scriptures in the Christian Bible* (2002), which recognizes this rereading of earlier texts as common practice in Judaism (2.A.2).

and to the bishops whom the apostles left as their successors with "the authority to teach in their own place" (no. 7). What God has revealed is expressed in inspired books and in the tradition that comes from the apostles, as well as in the church's teaching, life, worship, and faith, what is referred to as the *sensus fidei*, the sense of faith of the church. This tradition develops in the church with the help of the Spirit and there is a growth in understanding what has been handed down. "This happens through the contemplation and study made by believers, who treasure these things in their hearts (see Luke, 2:19, 51) through a penetrating understanding of the spiritual realities which they experience, and through the preaching of those who have received through Episcopal succession the sure gift of truth" (DV 8).

Scripture and Tradition

Sacred Scripture and Sacred Tradition form one sacred deposit of the Word of God committed to the church. While the Council of Trent never used the expressions "two sources of revelation," its Decree on Scripture and Apostolic Tradition (April 8, 1546), in saying that "these truths and rules are contained in the written books and unwritten traditions which have come down to us" (DS 1501), could be seen as implying that revelation was fully contained in either Scripture or tradition. This led to the assumption that Trent had taught that there were "two sources" of revelation, a misunderstanding that lasted down to Vatican II. Again stressing the importance of critical interpretation, *Dei Verbum* points to the importance of seeking the intention of the sacred writers, having regard for the "literary forms" they used—whether prophecy, poetry, or some other type of speech—and taking care to read and interpret a text within the whole of Scripture, if its meaning was to be brought to light (DV 12).

Sensus Fidei

If Scripture and tradition witness to revelation, so too does the *sensus fidei*, the sense of the faith or *sensus fidelium*, sense of the faithful. The doctrine of the *sensus fidelium* means that the church is not divided into teachers and taught but is a communion united in the Holy Spirit. The theology of *communio* was implicit in the 2014 International Theological Commission's report, Sensus Fidei *in the Life of the Church.*[11] Reflecting on the sense of faith, both of the individual believer and of the church as a whole, the study noted that the lay faithful play a role in the development of doctrine, sometimes when even bishops and theologians are divided on an issue (no. 72). They contribute also to the development of the church's moral teaching (no. 73). Therefore, in matters of faith, the baptized cannot be passive, and the magisterium needs not only to listen but also to develop "means by which to consult the faithful" (no. 74).

The report also added an ecumenical dimension to its treatment of the *sensus fidei*, answering affirmatively its question of whether separated Christians should be understood as participating in and contributing to the *sensus fidelium* in some manner (no. 86). It also stressed that the *sensus fidei* cannot be reduced to an expression of popular or majority opinion; it needs to be discerned. The most important disposition for participating in the *sensus fidei* is participation in the active life of the church, including prayer, the sacraments, and the Eucharist (no. 89), in addition to listening to the Word of God, openness to reason, and adherence to the magisterium.

Teaching Authority and Infallibility

Dei Verbum stresses that the task of authentically interpreting the Word of God, whether written or handed down, has been entrusted to the church's teaching office which "is not above the word of God, but serves it" (DV 10). Teachings of the ordinary, noninfallible magisterium are to be accepted with a "religious submission of mind and will" (LG 25). Some noninfallible teachings have clearly been in error.[12] But those teachings on faith and morals proclaimed infallibly are owed a "submission of faith." To reject them places one outside the community of faith.

---

[11] International Theological Commission (hereafter ITC), Sensus Fidei *in the Life of the Church* (2014), http://www.vatican.va/roman_curia/congregations/cfaith/cti _documents/rc_cti_20140610_sensus-fidei_en.html.

[12] See J. Robert Dionne, *The Papacy and the Church: A Study of Praxis and Reception in Ecumenical Perspective* (New York: Philosophical Library, 1987); John. T. Noonan, Jr., *A Church that Can and Cannot Change: The Development of Catholic Moral Teaching* (Notre Dame, IN: University of Notre Dame Press, 2005).

According to Vatican I, the church's charism of infallibility was entrusted to the successors of Peter, not to reveal some new doctrine, but that with the assistance of the Holy Spirit they "might religiously guard and faithfully expound the revelation or deposit of faith transmitted by the apostles."[13] In other words, infallibility was not to be understood as a new source of revelation but as a safeguard to the revelation entrusted to the whole church. Vatican II extended the exercise of the "charism of infallibility" to the bishops united with the Roman Pontiff, noting that "to these definitions the assent of the Church can never be wanting, on account of the activity of that same Holy Spirit, by which the whole flock of Christ is preserved and progresses in unity of faith," an implicit reference to the *sensus fidei*, affirming that authority teaches what the whole church believes.

Beyond those teachings proclaimed infallibly by the papal magisterium, Vatican I said: "All those things are to be believed with divine and Catholic faith which are contained in the word of God, written or handed down, and are proposed by the church either by a solemn judgment or by its ordinary and universal magisterium as divinely revealed and to be believed as such" (DS 3011). According to Francis Sullivan, Vatican II went beyond Pius IX and Vatican I by allowing for infallible teaching of the ordinary universal magisterium on matters that are only connected with revelation but not themselves revealed. But Sullivan also points out that there is a real difficulty in determining not only that the bishops of the whole world are agreed, along with the pope, in teaching a particular doctrine but also that what they are proposing is as "to be held definitively."[14]

There are actually very few teachings that have been proclaimed infallibly by the papal magisterium; most theologians agree that only the two Marian definitions, the immaculate conception defined by Pius IX in 1854 and her assumption, defined by Pius XII in 1950, meet the criteria, and in both cases, the popes consulted the church in the

---

[13] Vatican I, *Pastor Aeternus* 4.5, *Decrees of the Ecumenical Councils*, vol. 2: *Trent to Vatican II*, ed. Norman P. Tanner (New York and Washington, DC: Sheed and Ward and Georgetown University Press, 1990), 816.

[14] Francis A. Sullivan, *Creative Fidelity: Weighing and Interpreting Documents of the Magisterium* (New York: Paulist Press, 1996), 103.

persons of the bishops before the definitions.[15] Again, Sullivan makes a very important point concerning teaching authority: "The fact is that, with few exceptions, our Catholic faith is based not on dogmas defined by popes, but on those that have been defined by councils, and on those that have never been formally defined, but are part of the faith which we profess when we participate in the liturgy."[16]

Models of Revelation

How revelation is transmitted in the life of the church does not answer more basic questions about how God's self-disclosure takes place. What is the nature of revelation, and how are church pronouncements about revelation related to revelation itself? Avery Dulles has been interested in these questions since early in his professional career. One of his most successful books was his *Models of Revelation*. He says in the preface that what helped him especially was Michael Polanyi's distinction between tacit and explicit knowing.[17] Here, in order to gain a better understanding of the nature of revelation, I'd like to outline briefly his five models, keeping in mind that the models are not of equal value. While one may prove to be the most insightful, this does not mean that other models might not have helpful perspectives or corrections to offer. We will give special attention to revelation as symbolic mediation.

Revelation as Doctrine

Dulles's first model, also identified as the propositional model, is the most traditional. It tends to reduce God's communication to truths or propositions, giving us information about God and God's dealing with humankind. Dulles offers examples from several well-known

---

[15] Francis A. Sullivan, "Developments in Teaching Authority since Vatican II," *Theological Studies* 73, no. 3 (2012): 586; see also Richard R. Gaillardetz, ed., *When the Magisterium Intervenes: The Magisterium and Theologians in Today's Church* (Collegeville, MN: Liturgical Press, 2012).

[16] Sullivan, *Creative Fidelity*, 86.

[17] Avery Dulles, *Models of Revelation* (New York: Doubleday, 1983), viii; see also his "The Symbolic Structure of Revelation," *Theological Studies* 47, no. 1 (1980): 51–73.

evangelical theologians. Carl Henry states that God is revealed "in the whole canon of Scripture which objectively communicates in propositional-verbal form the content and meaning of all God's revelation,"[18] or again, "God's revelation is rational communication conveyed in intelligible ideas and meaningful words, that is, in conceptual-verbal form."[19] Similarly, Francis Schaeffer says, "God has spoken in a linguistic propositional form, truth concerning himself and truth concerning man, history, and the universe."[20]

For conservative evangelicals and fundamentalists a propositional understanding of revelation is reinforced by the doctrine of biblical inerrancy, meaning that the Bible is true in all its affirmations, including those in the area of history, science, and doctrine. For example, the "Chicago Statement on Biblical Inerrancy" states that "being wholly and verbally God-given, Scripture is without error or fault in all its teaching, no less in what it states about God's acts in creation, about the events of world history, and about its own literary origins under God, than in its witness to God's saving grace in individual lives."[21] Such an approach puts the truth of the biblical word ahead of critical literary evidence, for example, maintaining that the author of 1 Peter was Peter because the letter is attributed to him, in spite of evidence that it was written some decades after Peter's death.

The Catholic Church also tended toward a propositional understanding of revelation prior to Vatican II. While this model, long accepted by both Catholics and Protestants alike, can claim some basis in both Scripture and tradition which treat biblical statements as the Word of God without reservation, it ignores the fact that patristic and medieval commentators also used allegorical and spiritual interpretations that went considerably beyond the literal. Propositions are necessary as a second level of reflection. But a propositional model of revelation tends toward a literalism, reducing what is mysteriously communicated to literal statements or propositional speech.

---

[18] Dulles, *Models of Revelation*, 39; C. F. H. Henry, *God, Revelation, and Authority*, vol. 2 (Waco, TX: Word, 1976), 87.

[19] Henry, *God, Revelation, and Authority*, 12.

[20] Francis Schaeffer, *The God Who Is There* (Chicago: InterVarsity, 1968), 93.

[21] "Chicago Statement on Biblical Inerrancy with Exposition"; http:// www.bible -researcher.com/chicago1.html.

Revelation as History

Dulles's second model, revelation as history, is based on the work of many twentieth-century Protestant theologians who located God's revelation not primarily in words but rather in deeds—in God's mighty acts in history. Among them he names William Temple, G. Ernest Wright, John Baillie, James Barr, and Oscar Cullmann, who saw revelation as an aspect of what was called salvation history. Jean Daniélou developed some of Cullmann's ideas in a more specifically Catholic direction. Wolfhart Pannenberg went further, identifying certain revelatory events such as the Exodus and the resurrection of Jesus and their interpretation with world history. He sees the resurrection as having unsurpassing significance, proleptically revealing the goal of history.

The historical model is pastorally powerful and the theme is strong throughout much of the Bible, though noticeably lacking in the Wisdom literature. But many of the mighty events of God in the Bible—for example, creation, the flood, or the Exodus—do not qualify as history is understood today. Is the Exodus an act of God or a migration of peoples? Such questions make the issue of divine agency a matter of interpretation. As Dulles observes later, underlying this theory is a more naïve doctrine of miracle, with God suspending the laws of nature.[22]

Langdon Gilkey criticizes neoorthodoxy, a movement in Protestant theology against liberal theology after the two world wars, for continuing to use the language of events despite the fact that these events cannot be credibly established by the canons of history. Thus neoorthodoxy remained "at least half secular and naturalistic in its attitudes."[23] Finally, Pannenberg's basing revelation on the resurrection is problematic because the resurrection, while real, is not something that can be historically verified.

Revelation as Inner Experience

The third model, largely a product of liberal theology, sees God as communicating not through created signs but inwardly with each

---

[22] Dulles, *Models of Revelation*, 147.
[23] Langdon Gilkey, *Naming the Whirlwind* (Indianapolis, IN, and New York: Bobbs-Merrill, 1969), 82–83.

believer. Friedrich Schleiermacher and Albrecht Ritschl were influential in the development of this model. George Tyrrell could be considered a Catholic representative. Others could include Evelyn Underhill, C. H. Dodd, and John Hick. All of them, maintaining that God is both transcendent and immanent, reject any dichotomy between natural and revealed religion and tend to collapse special revelation into a general revelation accessible to all. Revelation tells us little about history or eschatology, and differences between religions are not particularly important. What is important is a religious attitude and openness to the divine mystery.

This model helpfully distinguishes between revelation and scientific knowledge, stressing in a rationalist age a different kind of knowing, and it encourages devout life and a respect for mystical experience. Negatively, it shifts emphasis from God's prophetic word to psychology, divorces revelation from doctrine, and "substitutes a natural elitism for the biblical idea of election," restricting revelation and faith to a privileged minority.[24] It remains private.

Revelation as Dialectical Presence

Dialectical theology, or neoorthodoxy, was in many ways a reaction to liberal theology with its stress on revelation as inner experience. Particularly after the horrors of the First World War that brought about a new awareness of sin and the differences between the human and the divine, dialectical theology sought to acknowledge God's presence and action in history and still respect the divine transcendence. Thus it was paradoxical, a succession of affirmations and denials which saw revelation as an encounter with God who remains mystery. It argued that God's truth or revelation could never be objectified, reduced to biblical words, doctrines, or symbols; it could never identified with anything finite, not even the Bible, which in its witness to Christ can only point to revelation. Nor could revelation be identified with the conceptual language of the preacher or the theologian. Revelation takes place in the moment of encounter with the living God.

---

[24] Dulles, *Models of Revelation*, 79.

Foremost among the dialectical theologians were Emil Brunner, Rudolf Bultmann, and especially Karl Barth. For the early Barth, revelation both reveals and conceals: "Revelation in the Bible means the self-unveiling, imparted to men, of the God who by nature cannot be unveiled to men. . . . It is the *Deus revelatus* who is the *Deus absconditus*."[25] The Bible and church preaching are not the Word of God but can become such if and when God chooses to speak through these means, the hidden God who turns toward human beings in Christ. Barth later moved beyond this "actualism" to a more incarnational understanding of God's self-gift in Christ.

Because of their christological emphasis, the dialectical theologians rejected the idea of nature, religious experience, natural theology, or non-Christian religious traditions as mediating God's revelation. This christological emphasis is both a strength and a weakness of the model. Dulles states that their taking the Bible and the theological tradition more seriously than they had been taken since the Reformation "spearheaded a major revival in Protestant systematic theology."[26]

But many critics found their approach lacking inner coherence.[27] They speak of God's acts in history and yet deny that the special events of revelation can be distinguished from ordinary historical events. While identifying revelation with Jesus the Christ, they are not clear on how the Christ of faith is related to the Jesus of history, thus opening the possibility that christological faith in Jesus is no more than a mythologization of the Gospel. It was to prevent this that led Ernst Käsemann in 1953 to call for a new quest for the historical Jesus, one unburdened by the liberal presuppositions of the first quest.[28]

Revelation as New Awareness

Dulles's fifth model, revelation as new awareness, sees revelation as fulfilling the human drive toward greater consciousness. Rather

---

[25] Karl Barth, *Church Dogmatics*, vol. 1, pt. 1, *The Doctrine of the Word of God* (Edinburgh: T & T Clark, 1975), 304.

[26] Dulles, *Models of Revelation*, 93.

[27] Ibid., 94.

[28] Ernst Käsemann, "The Problem of the Historical Jesus," in *Essays on New Testament Themes* (Philadelphia, PA: Fortress Press, 1982), 15–47.

than disclosing God, it opens humans to a new perspective—deeper understanding of the self and the world. Among English-speaking theologians who follow this approach, Dulles names Gregory Baum, Leslie Dewart, Gabriel Moran, Ray L. Hart, and William M. Thompson, with some aspects of it found in Paul Tillich, Karl Rahner, and Teilhard de Chardin.

Karl Rahner saw revelation as a particular instance of a greater phenomenon, namely, that of created reality's self-transcending movement toward greater freedom, though he holds that Christ is the unsurpassable high point of God's self-communication. For Gregory Baum, this new awareness is not information about the divine but rather salvational truth, a new awareness enabling one to see the world in a new light and commit one's self to a new kind of action. For Paul Tillich, revelation involves a manifestation of the holy, making transparent the divine ground in nature or history; he thus correlates revelation with human questioning, speaking to ultimate questions and concerns. Thus for virtually all of them, revelation is not about new knowledge but rather a transformed vision.

Positively, the new awareness model avoids dogmatism; it is compatible with an evolutionist or transformationist understanding of human history and is ecumenical or universalistic in appeal. Negatively, it is difficult to see how it is faithful to Scripture or tradition. It relativizes earlier faith knowledge in light of its fundamental vision and makes ecclesial allegiance difficult. Nor is it obvious that it is able to speak to all believers.

Revelation as Symbolic Mediation

Dulles chooses the concept of symbolic mediation for his own explanation of how revelation happens. Seeing symbol functioning in each of his five models (though in varying degrees), he argues that revelation takes place neither in purely interior experience nor in an unmediated encounter with God. Revelation is always mediated by some symbol, some natural object, historic person, or artistic symbol which is loaded with meaning that is more evoked than explicitly stated, though symbols must always be interpreted.

Symbols speak to our affections as well as to our head. They move us; frequently we "indwell" them. They are "multivalent," with a plurality of meanings. Among the symbols he discusses are light, the sun, the Exodus, Mount Sinai, King David and the Davidic monarchy, temples and icons, the kingdom of God, the cross, the resurrection, and the Eucharist. For a patriot, a national flag is such a symbol. At the heart of this approach is Ricoeur's famous statement that symbol gives rise to thought.[29]

How might we, going beyond Dulles's text, see symbols as mediating revelation? As Schillebeeckx says, revelation and experience are not opposites. "God's revelation follows the course of human experience."[30] The Israelite scribes, prophets, and biblical authors took institutions, events, symbols, and stories from their environments and adapted them, often transforming them in the process to express the religious experience of their communities. A sacred story could be just as revelatory as a prophetic oracle. Thus from Akkadian, Sumerian, and Mesopotamian creation myths the biblical authors behind the Priestly account developed their own story of Yahweh creating simply by the power of the divine word (Gen 1:1-2:4a). From the political or "suzerainty" treaties or covenants of the late second millennium BCE, others developed the symbol of the covenant as expressing Yahweh's election and bond with Israel.

The prophets, in seeking to reassure the people of Israel that God would not abandon them in spite of their sins, spoke of a new intervention of God in the future, using various symbols such as a new Davidic king or messiah, a Day of Judgment, and a renewed or new covenant. From the experience of Jews being martyred for their faith in the persecution of Antiochus IV (c. 215–164 BCE) came the hope for a general resurrection of the dead, when God would raise the just to life. As these stories with their symbols were repeated, reread, and reinterpreted in the tradition, always under the inspiration of the Spirit, they became revelatory, mediating knowledge of God as sovereign creator, binding himself to a special people, promising salvation in the future, even a life beyond the grave, or in more theological terms, they mediated a theology of creation, election, covenant, and eschatology.

---

[29] Paul Ricoeur, *Symbolism of Evil* (Boston: Beacon, 1969), 348.

[30] Edward Schillebeeckx, *Interim Report on the Books* Jesus & Christ (New York: Crossroad, 1982), 11.

Similarly, in the New Testament Jesus' preaching of the kingdom of God, itself with roots in the Hebrew Scriptures, becomes a rich, polyvalent symbol of God's nearness, hiddenness, saving power, concern for the last and the least, and eschatological promise. The cross, an instrument of capital punishment, becomes a symbol of salvation, redemption, and reconciliation with God and one another; it is a symbol of God's love for sinners in sending his only begotten Son and at the same time a symbol of discipleship and Christian life. The Eucharist, Jesus' last meal with his own, developing out of his table-fellowship tradition, becomes a ritual, a sacramental meal, a memorial of his sacrificial death, a communion in his body and blood establishing the church as his body for the world, a sign of the kingdom, and an anticipation of the heavenly banquet. This is to mention only some of the richness contained in these symbols that we continue to reflect on, reread, and celebrate in our ecclesial life today.

Jesus himself, "the fullness of all revelation" (DV 2), illustrates Dulles's point about revelation as symbolic mediation. In his historical ministry, Jesus was not a teacher like Plato or Aristotle whose words could be put down in philosophical treatises. In his preaching, Jesus used aphorisms, told stories and parables, reached out to the marginal, healed the sick, and called the poor blessed. He spoke little about himself, but there was a claim to authority implicit in his proclamation of the forgiveness of sins, challenging the religious authorities, calling on God as Abba, and referring to himself as son. Christianity begins not with a doctrine but with an experience; those who encountered Jesus experienced redemption and liberation.[31]

The evangelists sought to put the church's experience of Jesus into narrative form. Later, the fathers of the church used more formal language—not the mythopoeic language of the Scripture but the more technical, propositional language of Greco-Roman culture in which the church was now living, some of which, in being officially received, became part of the church's doctrinal heritage.

Ongoing Revelation?

The church has traditionally taught that revelation "ceased with the death of the last apostle," a way of affirming that the church

---

[31] Ibid., 7.

expects "no further new public revelation before the glorious manifestation of our Lord Jesus Christ" (DV 4). Dulles notes that Vatican II did not repeat the traditional formula, and that the notion of ongoing revelation, not unknown to the church up to the Middle Ages, was ignored from the sixteenth to the nineteenth centuries when revelation was understood propositionally as an objective deposit of truth. The council, while insisting on the normative character of God's revelation in Christ, recognized that God is not silent in our time (DV 8, 21; SC 7; GS 11). Because of God's active presence in the church and world, a comprehensive doctrine of revelation cannot be limited to biblical times. He points to an eschatological dimension of revelation, evident in those New Testament passages speaking of Christ's manifestation (2 Thess 1:7) and his coming in glory (Heb 9:28; 1 Tim 6:14; Titus 2:13).[32]

Faith

If revelation can be understood as God's initiating a relationship with us by disclosing something of the divine mystery, then faith can be understood as our free response to God's self-disclosure. The Greek *pistis* (Latin *fides*, English "faith") conveys belief, assurance, and trust in another. Pope Francis stresses this personal aspect of faith in his encyclical (originally drafted by Pope Benedict) *Lumen Fidei*: "Faith is our response to a word which engages us personally, to a 'Thou' who calls us by name" (no. 8). The encyclical stresses that faith is first of all a relationship with God; it is an affair of the heart.

For Aquinas, the formal object of faith is the "First Truth" or God, made known to us in the Scripture and teachings of the church.[33] A traditional distinction is made by Aquinas between (a) faith as a personal response to God, entering into a relationship, (b) the act of faith (*fides qua*), and (c) the faith as that which is believed about God as revealed in Christ (*fides quae*). These distinctions stem from

[32] Avery Dulles, "Faith and Revelation," in *Systematic Theology: Roman Catholic Perspectives*, ed. Francis Schüssler Fiorenza and John P. Galvin, 2nd ed. (Minneapolis, MN: Fortress Press, 2011), 88–89.
[33] Aquinas, *Summa Theologica*, IIa–IIae, q. 5, a. 3.

St. Augustine (*de Trinitate* 13.2.5) and bring out both the personal and the intellectual aspects of faith.

Many Catholics with a strong sense of the church's doctrinal tradition tend to favor an intellectual approach to faith. They identify faith with its contents, with what the church teaches. For them faith means to accept or to believe. Young Catholics too often define faith as "believing in things you can't prove," rarely mentioning God or Christ. But faith cannot be reduced to beliefs. Protestants, perhaps as a result of the heritage of Luther and his efforts to find righteousness before God, stress faith as a relationship of trust, confidence, and commitment. Every now and then an evangelical student in the classes I teach will say that faith is a personal relationship with Jesus, or that it means accepting Christ as Lord and Savior. Of course faith has both an intellectual and a personal aspect.[34]

Faith as Act

"Faith as act" is a more personal aspect of faith. It means accepting, trusting, and committing oneself to God and God's love disclosed in Christ; basically it refers to entering into a relationship. This personal dimension of faith predominates in the biblical view. In the Old Testament, Abraham is the symbol of the person of faith. Called by God, he leaves behind the security of home and tribe and sets off into the unknown because God calls him (Gen 12:1-3). For Søren Kierkegaard, Abraham's willingness to sacrifice his beloved son Isaac when asked to do so by God (Gen 22:1-14) makes him the archetype of the person of faith. He argues that this was not something that could be justified by any commitment or ethical standard but only by his response to a profoundly personal call that flowed from his relationship with God.[35] Of course the story is a symbol, not to be interpreted literally.

The Synoptic Gospels especially stress faith as trust in Jesus (or in God's presence in Jesus). In answering a request for healing, Jesus

---

[34] Paul Crowley argues that the *fides qua* and the *fides quae* belong together; faith is a response to a personal call that is lived out by participating in the mission of Jesus, in a mystagogy that leads to a personal experience of God; see Crowley, "Mystagogy and Mission: The Challenge of Nonbelief and the Task of Theology," *Theological Studies* 76, no. 1 (2015): 7–28.

[35] Søren Kierkegaard, *Fear and Trembling*, ed. C. Stephen Evans and Sylvia Walsh (New York: Cambridge University Press, 2006).

repeatedly says, "Your faith has saved you" (Mark 5:34; 10:52; Luke 18:42; Matt 9:29). These are moments when someone opens himself or herself completely to Jesus; it is always a free, total response of a person, a response of trust, belief, and acceptance, what is sometimes referred to as expectant faith. Evangelicals refer to this as a "born again" experience. For some, this can happen in an instance when one moves from indifference or unbelief to commitment and trust; for others it is not so much a moment in time but a gradual deepening of a faith long present, often through times of crises and high points along the way. Some Christians reduce faith to an individualistic experience, even a subjective feeling.

For Catholics, faith has an ecclesial dimension; it is mediated by a community of faith. Gerhard Lohfink stresses that faith must be learned. It means entering into a long history and is mediated in the intimacy of the family; it must grow, be ritually expressed and celebrated, and lay claim to the whole of life.[36] Pope Benedict XVI speaks of faith as having a "we-structure." While a philosophy is the work of an individual thinker, faith comes from hearing the proclaimed word and is thus heard and received in community. In coming to an ecclesial faith we transcend the "I" of the ego.[37]

Faith as Belief

Faith as belief refers to the more intellectual side of faith. It means accepting or believing *what* God has revealed. It is specific. As the author of the Fourth Gospel says, "These things are written that you may [come to believe] that Jesus is the Messiah, the Son of God, and that through this belief you may have life in his name" (John 20:31). But faith is not primarily a collection of truths or doctrines. As we have seen, Vatican II's understanding of revelation is personal, reaching its fullness in the person of Jesus.

The content or primary object of faith is God's love and concern for all persons, revealed in the Old Testament and in the story of

---

[36] Gerhard Lohfink, *No Irrelevant Jesus: On Jesus and the Church Today* (Collegeville, MN: Liturgical Press, 2014), 286–94.

[37] Joseph Ratzinger, *Introduction to Christianity* (New York: Herder and Herder, 1970), 58–59; see also his *Principles of Catholic Theology* (San Francisco: Ignatius Press, 1987), 34–35; *Lumen Fidei*, no. 39.

Jesus. As *Dei Verbum* says, "Through this revelation . . . the invisible God (see Col 1:15; 1 Tim 1:17) out of the abundance of His love speaks to men [and women] as friends (see Exod 33:11; John 15:14-15) and lives among them (see Bar 3:38), so that He may invite and take them into fellowship with Himself" (DV 2). God's love is without limit; it is for all, freely offered, and generously poured out, embracing not just humanity but creation itself.

But God's love, the primary content of faith, is not known immediately. We do not encounter God directly. God's revelation does not take place in some kind of inner experience. Nor does it take place in heavenly visions or come to us in carefully formulated propositions as we have seen. When we look at the history of Israel or the experience of the first Christians, it becomes apparent that revelation takes place in their ordinary experience, in moments of tragedy and hope, in the events of their history and the interpretation of these events by prophetic figures. Revelation is mediated by Scripture, theology, doctrine, sacraments, tradition, and the symbols arising out of reflection by the community of faith on the mysteries from which it lives.

Important as these symbols are, they are derivative, expressed in human language, historically and culturally conditioned, always less than the mystery. Scripture always needs to be interpreted and can be misconstrued. Sacraments can be expressions of an encounter with grace or empty rituals. Tradition is living; the church grows in its understanding of the fullness of divine truth (DV 8). Theologies are many and diverse and not equally insightful. Doctrines can be true and still be capable of more accurate formulation or interpretation. Therefore faith and reason must always work together; the complementarity of faith and reason is fundamental to the Catholic tradition.[38]

We might also mention as symbols, in a more popular sense, the church's catechisms, its charitable works, the stories of the saints, the example of faithful Christians, and the rich traditions of Christian art, spirituality, and mysticism. Symbols are powerful; they work mysteriously on human consciousness to suggest more than we can clearly describe or define.[39] We inhabit symbols and they can trans-

[38] See "Faith and Reason," in chap. 6 of this work, p. 158.
[39] Avery Dulles, *Models of Revelation* (New York: Doubleday, 1983), 131.

form us; they speak to our hearts as well as our heads. They put us in touch with the mystery of God.

Faith and Salvation

Is faith necessary for salvation? The church has always taught its necessity, but faith has been differently understood in the tradition. For centuries, the principle stood firm, *extra ecclesiam nulla salus*, no salvation outside the church. Prior to Augustine, it was applied by some of the fathers, among them Ignatius of Antioch, Irenaeus, Origen, Cyprian of Carthage, and Ambrose, to those who had separated themselves from the church by heresy or schism. John Chrysostom applied it to the Jews with particularly offensive language. Augustine, stressing the necessity of baptism, rejected the possibility of salvation for Jews or pagans, whether they had heard of the Gospel or not. For Augustine, even unbaptized children were damned.

But as Francis Sullivan points out in his classic study, after the discovery of the so-called "New World," populated by millions who had never heard the Gospel or been evangelized, some Dominicans and Jesuits began to question the principle, ultimately concluding "that salvation must be possible, even in the Christian era, through faith in God without explicit faith in Christ."[40] Pope Pius IX proclaimed as late as 1863: "It is a well-known Catholic dogma that no one can be saved outside the Catholic Church" (DS 2867). The pope was particularly concerned with religious indifferentism. Yet he also recognized the possibility of salvation for those outside the church through no fault of their own if they followed the natural law inscribed in their hearts (DS 2865–67).

Vatican II moved the church's tradition forward; in *Lumen Gentium*, the Dogmatic Constitution on the Church, it stated:

> Nor is God far distant from those who in shadows and images seek the unknown God, for it is He who gives to all men life and breath and all things, and as Saviour wills that all men be saved.

[40] Francis A. Sullivan, *Salvation Outside the Church: Tracing the History of the Catholic Response* (New York: Paulist Press, 1992), 98.

> Those also can attain to salvation who through no fault of their own do not know the Gospel of Christ or His Church, yet sincerely seek God and moved by grace strive by their deeds to do His will as it is known to them through the dictates of conscience. Nor does Divine Providence deny the helps necessary for salvation to those who, without blame on their part, have not yet arrived at an explicit knowledge of God and with His grace strive to live a good life. (LG 16)

The council was far from teaching universal salvation. The same paragraph warns of the deceptions of the evil one, who leads some to exchange the truth of God for a lie, serving the creature rather than the Creator. But the council also had a more existential understanding of faith. Rather than limiting it to an explicit christological commitment, it recognizes faith as openness to God's mysterious presence revealed in one's inner life. For those open to that presence, God can enter.

In *Nostra Aetate*, the Declaration on the Relation of the Church to the Non-Christian Religions, the council went further. It acknowledged that there is often found among different peoples a certain perception of a hidden power hovering over the course of things, a recognition of a Supreme Being, even of a Father. These religions seek to answer the questions concerning the meaning of life and the mystery encompassing our existence. The council's response to this seeking was positive: "The Catholic Church rejects nothing that is true and holy in these religions. She regards with sincere reverence those ways of conduct and of life, those precepts and teachings which, though differing in many aspects from the ones she holds and sets forth, nonetheless often reflect a ray of that Truth which enlightens all men" (NA 2). God's revelation is not limited to the Christian tradition; it is at least reflected in other religions.

Pope John Paul II moved Catholic teaching forward in regards to religious pluralism. In his encyclical *Redemptoris Missio*, he acknowledged the Spirit's presence outside of Christianity; he affirmed that the "Spirit's presence and activity affect not only the individuals but also society and history, peoples, cultures and religions" (no. 28), which is to say that the Spirit is mysteriously present in other religions and cultures, even if Jesus remains the one savior of all and so the church must continue to evangelize. Though he did not go so far as to speak of these religions as mediations of saving grace in their own right, he spoke of "participated forms of mediation of different kinds and degrees," acquiring meaning from Christ, the one mediator between God and humankind (no. 5).

Modernity and the Loss of Faith

Christian faith once informed the culture of the West. But today it has largely been dissolved by what has been described as the "acids of modernity." The roots of modernity's secularism go deep. Charles Taylor sees them beginning with the Reformation's emphasis on personal faith and its discomfort with sacraments, priesthood, and the sacred, abolishing the enchanted medieval cosmos, stripping it of its mystery and its narratives of faith and religious practice. The Reformers, especially Calvin, stressed salvation as exclusively God's work. In addition, their elevation of the juridical-penal understanding of salvation, from Augustine and Anselm and then to the Reformers, led eventually toward a humanist alternative to faith. From the Enlightenment came an impersonal universe, with deism and Unitarianism in place of historic Christianity. A personal God had disappeared, leaving an impersonal universe governed by unchanging natural laws. From this perspective, Taylor argues that deism can be seen as a "half-way house" on the road to contemporary atheism.[41]

German idealism further depersonalized the God of Christianity to an alienated personification of spirit, mind, or human intelligence. Hegel (1770–1831) taught that the object of religion was Absolute Being, the product of human consciousness, but consciousness in alienation from itself. As Michael Buckley has written in his seminal study on atheism, "The Hegelian dialectic maintained that art, religion, and philosophy all have the same content, the Absolute, but in art it exists in the immediacy of the sensuous and as an individual object; in religion it exists in the mode of figurative representation (*Vorstellung*) and in acts of worship; and in philosophy it exists in its

---

[41] Charles Taylor, *A Secular Age* (Cambridge, MA: Belknap Press of Harvard University, 2007), 77–79, 270.

own proper form, that of thinking knowledge, as pure thought."[42] For Hegel, belief or faith was in reality a flight from the actual world. The alienation was overcome through what Hegel called the enlightenment of pure insight, when Absolute Reality professed by belief is recognized as "its own thought, something produced from and by consciousness."[43] Insight was both salvation and the end of alienation for Hegel.

If Karl Marx turned Hegel upside down, setting his system on its earthly feet, he did so to a Hegelianism which had already been carried to its own logical conclusion by the critique of Ludwig Feuerbach (1804–1872). Feuerbach adopted Hegel's concept of religion as alienation, naturalizing his Absolute into an objectified projection of human consciousness. Humanity negates itself to create a God. He argued that Hegel's Absolute was humanity's real, unrecognized essence, not as a metaphysical Supreme Being standing over against humanity, but as a projection of human psychology.[44] Thus Feuerbach was the father of both Marx and Freud. God was humanity's own projected need.

The philosopher Friedrich Nietzsche (1844–1900) dramatically called modernity's loss of faith the "death of God," attributing it to a free decision made by those inhabiting the West's increasingly secular culture. In his *Die fröhliche Wissenschaft*, his Madman answers his question, "Where is God?" with a confession, "I tell you. We have killed him—you and I! We are all his murderers."[45] Nietzsche's concern was that modernity, having separated faith from reason and having reduced truth to the scientifically demonstrable, found that God was no longer credible. If any God was left to an increasingly autonomous humanity, it was a comfortable God, domesticated and undemanding.

---

[42] Michael J. Buckley, *At the Origins of Modern Atheism* (New Haven, CT: Yale University Press, 1987), 17–18.

[43] G. W. F. Hegel, *The Phenomonology of Mind* (New York: Harper Torchbooks, 1967), 567.

[44] See Sidney Hook, *From Hegel to Marx* (New York: Columbia University Press, 1994).

[45] Friedrich Nietzsche, *The Gay Science*, ed. Bernard Williams (Cambridge, UK: Cambridge University Press, 2001), no. 125.

The New Atheists

The beginning of the twenty-first century saw the emergence of a group of popular writers known as the "new atheists," foremost among them Richard Dawkins, Sam Harris, and the late Christopher Hitchens. These "new atheists" wrote provocative books with titles such as *God Is not Great: How Religion Poisons Everything* (Hitchens), *The End of Faith: Religion, Terror, and the Future of Reason* (Harris), and *The God Delusion* (Dawkins). While their broad-brush critiques of the Catholic Church too often accurately reflect the church's failings, the arguments they bring forth against the existence of God have little to do with more serious atheist arguments, either philosophical or existential. Their books sold well but lacked real depth.

Richard Dawkins's argument that the notion of God should be treated like any other scientific hypothesis represents a naïve scientism which seeks to submit religious claims to empirical verification, as though God was just another object in the world, albeit a Supreme Being. Similarly, Sam Harris wonders why a book like the Bible, supposedly authored by the Creator of the universe, would not be the richest source of mathematical insight or say something about electricity or DNA. John Haught argues, the "engagement with theology on the part of these 'new atheists' lies at about the same level of reflection on faith that one can find in contemporary creationist and fundamentalist literature."[46]

Far more substantive was a remark of Martin Heidegger cited by Michael Buckley about a "forgetfulness of being" (*Seinvergessenheit*), with, in Buckley's words, its concomitant inability to ask the question of God at the depth "which alone can give any theological sense to the content of the answer."[47] The mystery of being is deep and profound, occasioning questions about the mystery of the divine, for of course, the two are related. Why there is anything at all is the fundamental question. "Forgetfulness of being" means that this fundamental question never gets asked. Still, the denial of God's existence

---

[46] John F. Haught, *God and the New Atheism: A Critical Response to Dawkins, Harris and Hitchens* (Louisville, KY: Westminster John Knox Press, 2008), xi.

[47] Buckley, *At the Origins of Modern Atheism*, 348–49; see Martin Heidegger, *An Introduction to Metaphysics* (New Haven, CT: Yale University Press, 1959), 18–21.

involves more than intellectuals; today it affects millions of ordinary people. Modernity has forgotten its origin in mystery. According to a 2012 Pew Forum study, people with no religious affiliation (not identified with a particular religion, though they may have some spiritual beliefs in a God or "higher power") today make up the third-largest global group, 16 percent, coming after Christians and Muslims and just ahead of Hindus.[48]

Conclusion

God dwells in unapproachable light. Revelation can be seen as the unveiling or self-disclosure of the incomprehensible divine mystery, moving from transcendence into the world of symbols, language, and events. God's existence, known from the beauty of creation and intuited in the experience of transcendence, is evidence of a general revelation, open to all. The Bible tells the story of a special revelation, first to Israel, then with the coming of Jesus, God's Son, to all people through the church. While revelation cannot be restricted to the Bible, Scripture tells us of God's gracious movement toward us.

Unlike early conciliar accounts of revelation, more intellectual and propositional in form, Vatican II's dogmatic constitution *Dei Verbum* adopts a personal view. Revelation occurs through the words of the prophets and reaches its fullness in the person of Jesus. The constitution restores Scripture to its proper place in the life of the church. Jesus did not teach like the Scribes or the Pharisees. His language was simple, aphoristic; he told stories or parables. Symbols were important: the Good Samaritan, the Prodigal Son, the Rich Man and Lazarus, the kingdom of God. Those who encountered him experienced salvation.

Revelation is handed on not as a collection of truths but in the life of the church, in its Scriptures, its tradition, its teachings, and its sacraments and liturgy. Both Scripture and tradition form one deposit of the Word of God, committed to the church. Correct interpretation of Scripture demands sensitivity to literary form and historical con-

---

[48] http://www.pewforum.org/2012/12/18/global-religious-landscape-exec/.

text, providing a clue to the intention and meaning of the biblical authors and taking place under the guidance of the magisterium. Catholicism eschews fundamentalism. Avery Dulles's examination of different models of revelation suggests that revelation is mediated by symbols arising from the ordinary experience of the community of faith, speaking both to the head and to the heart. This is not to deny extraordinary moments, like the resurrection.

Faith has both a personal and an intellectual dimension; it is both act and content. While the church has always insisted that faith is necessary for salvation, faith can be understood more broadly as an openness to God's presence disclosed in the transcendental reach of our knowing and God's love sensed in our hearts. Modernity's pervasive secularism and loss of faith has deep roots in the intellectual history of the West. Heidegger attributes it to a "forgetfulness of being," with its accompanying question about why there is anything at all.

For Further Reading

Bullivant, Stephen. *Faith and Unbelief*. New York: Paulist Press, 2014.

Dulles, Avery. *The Assurance of Things Hoped For: A Theology of Christian Faith*. New York: Oxford University Press, 1994.

———. *Models of Revelation*. New York: Doubleday, 1983.

Gaillardetz, Richard R. *Witness to the Faith: Community, Infallibility, and the Ordinary Magisterium of the Bishops*. New York: Paulist Press, 1992.

Haught, John F. *Mystery and Promise: A Theology of Revelation*. Collegeville, MN: Liturgical Press, 1993.

Latourelle, René. *Theology of Revelation*. Staten Island, NY: Alba House, 1966.

Rahner, Karl. *Foundations of Christian Faith: An Introduction to the Idea of Christianity*. New York: Seabury Press, 1978.

Ratzinger, Joseph. *Introduction to Christianity*. New York: Herder and Herder, 1970.

Schillebeeckx, Edward. *Interim Report on the Books* Jesus *&* Christ. New York: Crossroad, 1982.

Sullivan, Francis A. *Magisterium: Teaching Authority in the Catholic Church.* New York: Paulist Press, 1983.

————. *Salvation Outside the Church: Tracing the History of the Catholic Response.* New York: Paulist Press, 1992.

Chapter 6

Sin, Grace, and the Human Person

We begin our discussion of sin, grace, and the human person, usually called Christian anthropology, with Karl Rahner's turn to the subject. When Rahner (1904–1980) began his studies, Catholic theology was dominated by a traditional neoscholastic realism which saw all knowledge as mediated by the senses. But Rahner's work very early took a "transcendental turn," influenced by his study of Kant and the Transcendental Thomists Pierre Rousselot and Joseph Maréchal, as well as by Martin Heidegger, under whom he had studied at Freiburg. Starting with the subject, his theological anthropology or theological view of humanity reveals the human person as spirit-in-the world, open to the absolute. As he writes in his *Hearers of the Word*, "Man is absolute openness to being in general, or, in a word, . . . man is spirit."[1]

Rahner's anthropology discloses the absolute as the horizon against which human knowing takes place; thus the transcendent God is grasped implicitly but non-thematically in every act of knowing. But this "experience" is different from knowing:

> With regard to this experience of God we must emphasize here above all that it can be so non-thematic, so different from any theology, whether popular or scholarly (whether philosophical or revelational in character) that on the one hand the experience

[1] Karl Rahner, *Hearers of the Word* (New York: Herder and Herder, 1969), 53; see also his *Spirit in the World* (New York: Herder & Herder, 1968).

really is present, yet on the other, under circumstances, the individual concerned may be ignorant of the very word God.[2]

This openness to "absolute being" is the ground of his *potentia oboedientalis*, the human person's capacity to welcome or reject a possible revelation, the ground for Rahner of a Christian philosophy of religion, or as we would say today, fundamental theology.

Thus grace for Rahner is not something "added on" or superimposed. While still gratuitous, grace is revealed in the constitution of the human person as openness to the absolute. Grace is God's free self-communication, for humans are not just open to the infinite but drawn to what is already intuited or grasped non-thematically. "Modern theology has as one of its chief assertions . . . the claim that a purely graceless world or individual has never existed."[3] For Rahner, grace lies prior to freedom as the condition for its possibility in concrete action: "*Self*-communication of the absolutely *holy* God designates a quality sanctifying man prior to his free and good decision."[4]

Rahner's theological anthropology thus sees the structures of human subjectivity as informed by grace a priori. Anthropology is theology and conversely, theology is anthropology. The ground for his vision is the incarnation of the Logos, the hypostatic union of the God-Man Jesus Christ. Christology becomes both the foundation and the elevation of an anthropological theology,[5] while nature and grace are intimately related.

We start with Rahner in this chapter, not to canonize Rahner's thought, but because his theological anthropology reveals the human person as open to the transcendent, while his view that grace and nature, even if the latter is touched by sin, are also profoundly bound

---

[2] Karl Rahner, "Experience of Self and Experience of God," *Theological Investigations*, vol. 13 (New York: Seabury Press, 1975), 123.

[3] Stephen J. Duffy, "Our Hearts of Darkness: Original Sin Revisited," *Theological Studies* 49 (1988): 618.

[4] Karl Rahner, *Foundations of Christian Faith: An Introduction to the Idea of Christianity* (New York: Seabury Press, 1978), 113.

[5] Anton Losinger, *The Anthropological Turn: The Human Orientation of the Theology of Karl Rahner* (New York: Fordham University Press, 2000), 42.

in unity, is profoundly Catholic.[6] In this chapter we will consider the myth of the Fall, original sin, grace, and the relation between sin and grace from Catholic and Protestant perspectives.

The Myth of the Fall

Western theology, particularly as a result of the massive influence of Augustine, has placed great emphasis on the Genesis story of the Fall, with the incarnation as God's response. This is particularly true of Protestant and evangelical theology today, though Catholic theology also fell under the mantle of Augustine. Jansenism in seventeenth-century France, with its emphasis on original sin, human depravity, and unworthiness to receive Holy Communion, is one Catholic example, but there are others.

There is no doctrine of original sin in the Bible. The Genesis creation accounts are concerned with the goodness of God's creation. The first story, from the Priestly editor, repeats over and over, "and God saw how good it was," like a liturgical refrain. The second story, from the Jahwist editor (Gen 2–3), portrays the man and the woman living an idyllic existence in the Garden of Eden, naked and without shame. The "myth of the Fall" in Genesis 3 (remembering that myth means a story from a prescientific culture meant to teach some lesson or truth) is an effort to explain how evil comes into the good world shaped by the creator. It is easy to miss the subtlety of the serpent's temptation; eating the fruit of the tree in the center of the garden leads not to death but to divinization: "No, God knows well that the moment that you eat of it your eyes will be opened and you will be like gods who know what is good and what is bad" (Gen 3:5). Here is the fundamental temptation of human beings, putting themselves first, refusing to acknowledge the creator by becoming gods unto themselves. In Stephen Duffy's words, the man and woman fall "because they are capable of reaching for the stars, seeking divine status and

---

[6] Stephen J. Duffy, "Experience of Grace," in *The Cambridge Companion to Karl Rahner,* ed. Declan Marmion and Mary E. Hines (Cambridge, UK: Cambridge University Press, 2005), 47.

becoming the source of their own meaning."[7] This absolutizing of the self is what Augustine called an *"aversio a Deo,"* a turning from God that lies at the root of all sin.

This overturning of the order of creation has disastrous results. The man and woman no longer enjoy intimacy with God who would visit them in the cool of the evening. Symbolically driven out the garden, they are alienated from nature, the man earning his living by the sweat of his brow, the woman subject to her husband and bringing forth her children in pain and labor. And they are alienated from each other, their sexuality now a source of tension. Or as Pope Francis says in his encyclical *Laudato Sì*, humankind's three fundamental and closely intertwined relationships—with God, the neighbor, and the earth itself—are ruptured due to sin (no. 66). This is not so much God's punishment as it is the result of their refusing to place God first.

The following chapters in Genesis show the results: brother killing brother (Gen 4), the Great Flood or Deluge in which the evil that humans have let loose destroys all but Noah and his family and threatens creation itself, saved only by God's intervention (Gen 6:5–8:22), and the confusing of languages and scattering of the peoples at Babel (Gen 11:1-9), followed by the promise of a blessing for all communities on earth through the descendants of Abraham (Gen 12:1-3).

Paul

While the story of Adam and the sin of the first couple plays little role in the rest of Scripture, Paul returns to it, largely to contrast the first Adam in whom all die with Christ, the "last Adam" who becomes a life-giving spirit, bringing all to life (1 Cor 15:22; 45-47; cf. Rom 5:12-21). But Paul also has a strong sense of the power of sin that touches all of us. In Romans, Paul distinguishes between "sin" (*hamartia*) and "transgression" (*parabasis*) or sometimes "a sin" (*paraptōma*), formal sin or sin in the sense of lawbreaking. He describes Adam, taken as a type, introducing sin (*hamartia*) into the world by his transgression (*parabasis*): "For up to the time of the law, sin was

---

[7] Duffy, "Our Hearts of Darkness," 609.

in the world, though sin is not accounted when there is no law. But death reigned from Adam to Moses, even over those who did not sin after the pattern of the trespass of Adam, who is the type of the one who was to come" (Rom 5:13-14).

What then is the difference between sin and transgression? Transgression is formal sin, the deliberate, conscious violation of a law or precept, refusing to respect the dignity and rights of others. But Paul looks on transgression as the expression, the exteriorization of a much more radical evil, sin, *hamartia*, that deeply rooted egoism by which human beings order everything to themselves rather than to God and to others.[8] Paul is referring to something more existential than transgressions or lawbreaking.

Original Sin

If Paul describes sin as a power in the world from its introduction by Adam, it was Augustine (354–430) who formulated what became the doctrine of original sin. His starting point was Christ as universal savior. He saw all humanity as sinful, even infants prior to baptism. Stephen Duffy sees his theology as seeking a way between a pessimistic Manichean Gnosticism that identified evil with human finitude and a Pelagian optimism that maintained that sin was accidental, purely contingent on free choice. For the dualistic Manicheans, evil was something real, infecting those existing in a finite, material world. For Pelagius (an ascetical teacher from Britain), on the other hand, the person as free could not only avoid sin but also choose it; to sin was voluntary. Thus he rejected infant baptism, now widely practiced. Augustine's own personal experience made him react strongly to Pelagius; his own view mediated between the two; he saw sin as a kind of "second nature," resulting in what Duffy calls the three pivotal points of his doctrine of sin: original perfection, original sin, and original guilt.[9]

For Augustine, creation is good; evil has no ontological status of its own but comes from a privation of good. He saw Adam's sin as

---

[8] Stanislas Lyonnet, "St. Paul: Liberty and Law," *Readings in Biblical Morality*, ed. C. Luke Salm (Englewood Cliffs, NJ: Prentice-Hall, 1967), 69.

[9] Duffy, "Our Hearts of Darkness," 600.

a historical event; it introduced a corruption (*vitium*) which affected all his descendants, a predisposition toward evil that affects our choices and is passed on through generations. His view was based in part on Jerome's Vulgate mistranslation of Roman 5:12 that said sin and death passed to all through Adam "in whom all sinned," rather than "inasmuch as all sinned," and in part on the church's now common practice of baptizing infants, implying that they too needed redemption by Christ. Without baptism, they could not be saved, though later medieval theologians mitigated his harsh views, teaching that unbaptized infants went to limbo, a place of natural happiness but without the joys of the blest.

Augustine's theology was also influenced by his long struggle to amend his life. He was deeply aware of our resistance to the good and how we are shaped by our history and experience, suggesting a limitation to our freedom. His teaching on an inherited original sin was affirmed in 418 by the Synod of Carthage and again in 529 by the Synod of Orange (DS 370–97), and so became Catholic doctrine. Aquinas's approach basically followed Augustine's; he taught that all, deprived of habitual grace, are sinners even prior to any exercise of free will, while concupiscence continues to damage human freedom.

The Sixteenth Century

The Reformers intensified Augustine's thought. For Luther and Calvin, sin is more than the absence of grace; it corrupts human nature precisely in its relation to God, affecting both intellect and will. Both spoke of a total depravity that "contaminates all dimensions of human existence," most of all, reason.[10] According to Calvin, original sin "seems to be a hereditary depravity and corruption of our nature, diffused into all parts of the soul, which first makes us liable to God's wrath, then also brings forth in us those works which Scripture calls 'works of the flesh' [Gal 5:19]."[11] He went so far as to teach that prior to the grace of regeneration, the will, hostile to God, is not free to

---

[10] Ibid., 605.

[11] Calvin, *Institutes* 2.1.8; see *Institutes of the Christian Religion*, ed. John T. McNeill (Philadelphia, PA: Westminster Press, 1960); see also Luther's *Commentary on Rom.* 5.

choose the good and the intellect is spiritually blind; nor can the person cooperate with grace, resulting in his doctrine of double predestination. God determines from eternity who will be saved and who will be condemned.

Trent's teaching on original sin did not go much beyond the teaching of Carthage and Orange, nor did it canonize any particular theology of justification. As Avery Dulles says, "The Council wished to present a coherent Catholic doctrine that would exclude the errors of the Reformers without condemning the positions of any of the recognized Catholic schools."[12] The idea that original sin is transmitted *"propagatione, non imitatione,"* was meant to exclude the Pelagian idea that the damage of original sin is only by imitating Adam's example and also to affirm the importance of infant baptism. But Trent also insisted that the human person freely cooperates with the grace of God (DS 1525; 1554–56). This goes along with a fundamental principle of Catholic theological anthropology; God always respects our freedom.

A Contemporary Approach

How do we understand original sin today? A naïve approach sees it as a corruption affecting our human nature, inclining us to evil in the Catholic view or resulting in total depravity in Reformation theology. Inherited from Adam, the effects of original sin are passed on by generation, almost like a bad gene infecting the human genome.

A more contemporary approach sees original sin as a social concept rooted in the radically social nature of the human person and the social nature of sin itself. The basic truth of the doctrine is that we are all touched by sin, while the freedom that is the expression of our existence as embodied spirit is constricted. Piet Schoonenberg refers to this as the "sin of the world," the social situation into which each of us is born.[13] Roger Haight describes sin as a structure prior to the

---

[12] Avery Dulles, *The Assurance of Things Hoped For: A Theology of Christian Faith* (New York: Oxford University Press, 1994), 48.

[13] Piet Schoonenberg, *Man and Sin: A Theological View* (Notre Dame, IN: University of Notre Dame Press, 1965), 104–5.

exercise of our freedom and one that is actualized by that freedom.[14] Duffy, though sympathetic to Freud's emphasis on unconscious libidinal energies and drives, acknowledges that insights from the social sciences predominate; we are shaped by the greed, pride, inertia, and divisions plaguing human history, making us both "responsible agents but also tragic victims."[15]

Just like grace, sin is mediated socially. The human race emerges from an evolutionary history based on the survival of the fittest, and we have inherited more than traces of the egoism that marks our biological past, with its primary instinct for struggle and survival. Even more, each of us is born into a world in which sin reigns; it is present in our families, our cultures, and our societies. Each of us is shaped by a network of relationships—familial, social, cultural, economic, sexual, and interpersonal—of which we are largely unaware. Our families do not always provide the love and acceptance we so deeply need. Our cultures teach us social roles based on race or class or gender or sexual orientation that prejudice us against those who are different. Our societies institutionalize social and economic inequalities that are profoundly damaging to others. The theologies of liberation have introduced the concept of social sin—the objectification of evil in political and economic structures in ways that systematically disadvantage and oppress others.

Human history is a sad story of violence, war, injustice, and the slaughter of the innocent. Think of the millions of victims in the twentieth century alone. So, like the child in the dysfunctional family, the youth whose violent neighborhood makes him seek safety in a gang, the girl who competes in the destructive gossip of her peers, or the disadvantaged young man whose repressive social situation turns him to violence, we act out, damaging ourselves and others. Our freedom is limited even before we exercise it by forces beyond our control.

The doctrine of original sin is one of the great Christian insights into the mystery of the human. It shows how our freedom to do the

[14] Roger Haight, "Sin and Grace," in *Systematic Theology: Roman Catholic Perspectives*, ed. Francis Schüssler Fiorenza and John P. Galvin (Minneapolis, MN: Fortress Press, 2011), 396.
[15] Duffy, "Original Sin Revisited," 616.

good to which we are drawn is compromised because we are enfleshed in a world so touched by egoism and sin. Original sin is one of the few doctrines for which there is empirical evidence. As Kathleen Norris has said, "If I'm O.K. and you're O.K., and all our friends (nice people and, like us, markedly middle class . . .) are O.K., why is the world definitely not O.K?"[16] The church's teaching on original sin reveals our need for salvation, for God's transforming grace. The church itself should be a different kind of society, mediating that grace, without denying that other societies may have a similar effect. Because we are born into concrete situations both flawed and blessed, we have solidarity not only in sin but also in grace.

Grace

So what is grace? The word "grace" (*charis*, *gratia*) in the New Testament did not have the technical meaning it acquired later in the tradition. In general, it referred to God's salvation bestowed in Christ. More specifically, it was used for God's favor (Rom 1:5; 3:24), goodness (John 1:14), or help (Jas 4:6; Heb 4:16). Pre–Vatican II manuals had a complicated taxonomy of grace—actual and sanctifying, habitual and prevenient, created and uncreated grace. From a post–Vatican II perspective, Jesus' preaching of the kingdom of God means that God's saving grace is present in the world and in our relationships. For modern theology, "a purely graceless world or individual has never existed."[17]

Today, thanks especially to the work of Karl Rahner, grace is understood as God's self-communication, God's gracious, enabling, salvific presence, offering to each a participation in the divine life, though of course God's free offer must also be freely accepted. Because for Rahner God's will to save is universal, grace is universally available; it cannot be limited to the church or its sacraments. Roger Haight notes that Vatican II effected a shift from the an objective, neoscholastic approach to grace to a more personal encounter of the human

---

[16] Kathleen Norris, *Dakota: A Spiritual Geography* (Boston: Houghton Mifflin, 1993), 97–98.

[17] Duffy, "Our Hearts of Darkness," 618.

subject with God's revealing word, arguing that today a theology of grace is to a considerable degree a theology of the Holy Spirit.[18]

Catholic and Protestant Perspectives

Protestant and Catholic theology have viewed the relationship between sin and grace differently. Reformation theology, driven by Luther's soteriological interests, rejected the medieval world with its sacraments, saints, priesthood, and mediating structures, leaving the individual naked and alone before God. The answer was personal faith. At the same time, the Reformation's emphasis on divine transcendence resulted in distancing God from creation, as Charles Taylor has argued.[19] Jesus' great insight about the presence of his Father and the kingdom was blurred. American religious individualism, with its focus on subjective individual experience, has deep roots in the Reformation.[20] Catholic theology, with its emphasis on sacramentality, mediation, and community, results in a more communal expression of Christianity.

These different starting points and accents have resulted in significant differences in Catholic and Protestant theological anthropologies. The Reformers, reacting to certain real abuses in the Catholic Church, too often ended up by turning principles into absolutes, with the result that Protestantism inherited an either/or approach, one that said "faith alone" (*sola fides*), "Scripture alone" (*sola Scriptura*), "grace alone" (*sola gratia*), and "Christ alone" (*solus Christus*). Catholicism has traditionally been characterized by a both/and approach.

It needs to be said that years of ecumenical dialogue have narrowed considerably the gap between Catholic and Protestant positions. Perhaps one of the most significant ecumenical agreements is the 1998 "Joint Declaration on the Doctrine of Justification between Lutherans and Catholics," the crucial issue that led to the break in unity

---

[18] Haight, "Sin and Grace," 378.

[19] Charles Taylor, *A Secular Age* (Cambridge, MA: Belknap Press of Harvard University, 2007), 77–80, 270–80.

[20] Robert Neelly Bellah, "Religion and the Shape of National Culture," *America* 181, no. 3 (July 31, 1999): 9–14.

in the sixteenth century. Also important is the statement, *From Conflict to Communion: Lutheran-Catholic Common Commemoration of the Reformation in 2017*, sponsored by the Lutheran World Federation and the Pontifical Council for Promoting Christian Unity.[21] Because not all Protestant churches have embraced these agreements, particularly those in the evangelical tradition, much of their theology remains informed in varying degrees by these traditional Reformation perspectives. Therefore in the following section we will consider some of these differences, focusing on several key principles of a Roman Catholic theological anthropology, expressing a Catholic view of the human person.

Creation Is Both Flawed and Graced

As we have seen, the doctrine of the Fall tells us that human nature is in some way damaged. Yet Catholicism also recognizes that human nature and indeed creation are also graced, for a gracious God not only sustains us and all creation but also endows us in some mysterious way with a participation in the divine life. While we can separate nature and grace conceptually, there is no nature apart from grace, for creation is ordered and stamped by the incarnation (John 1:3).

While both the Eastern and Western church fathers recognized the damage done to the descendants of Adam and Eve, the theological anthropology of the East, with its emphasis on the incarnation, tends to be more optimistic. The Eastern fathers see creation as elevated and humanity restored, even divinized, because of the Word's assumption of human nature. The Western fathers tended to place more emphasis on redemption, the cross, and the idea of satisfaction for sin, first introduced by Tertullian (c. 160–220); in Roger Haight's words, "Western soteriology leans more on a transaction performed in Jesus." From there it is not far to the substitutionary atonement theology of Augustine and Anselm.[22]

---

[21] Lutheran World Federation and the Catholic Church, "Joint Declaration on the Doctrine of Justification," *Origins* 28, no. 8 (1998); see also *From Conflict to Communion: Lutheran-Catholic Common Commemoration of the Reformation in 2017; Report of the Lutheran/Roman Catholic Commission on Unity* (Leipzig: Evangelische-Verlaganstalt/Bonifatius Verlag Paderborn, 2013).

[22] Roger Haight, *Jesus Symbol of God* (Maryknoll, NY: Orbis Books, 1999), 223.

Augustine's doctrine of original sin was to permanently stamp Western theology. He saw Christ's death as a "propitiation" or "satisfaction" offered to God for the sins of humankind. Anselm of Canterbury (d. 1109), in his powerful work *Cur Deus Homo*? (Why God Became Man?), gave quasi-magisterial status to Augustine's teaching on satisfaction; Christ, the divine Son, alone could make satisfaction for the infinite offense against God's justice, thus restoring the order of creation. Or at least, this is how Anselm has been interpreted in the West. But if human nature was damaged by Adam's sin, it was not totally corrupted, a position that was followed by Aquinas. Like the Eastern fathers, the Catholic tradition has generally placed far more stress on the doctrine of the incarnation than on the redemption.

The perspective of the Reformation was quite different, with significant consequences for Protestant theological anthropology. The Reformation began with Luther's concerns over his own struggle for righteousness before God, with his justification. His discovery of Paul's teaching on justification by faith in his letter to the Romans (cf. 1:17) led to the foundational Reformation doctrine of justification by faith alone (*sola fide*). Catholic theology, following Trent's insistence that we must cooperate with grace and recognizing also the Gospel call to discipleship, conversion of life, and witnessing to the kingdom of God, says faith and works.

Like Augustine, Luther (d. 1546) stressed the damage done to human nature by Adam's sin; in Luther's view, access to God was through grace alone (*sola gratia*), while his suspicion of the medieval church's teaching on the mediation of grace through devotions, sacraments, priests, and saints led him to stress that we are saved through Christ alone (*solo Christo*). Because of Christ, God no longer looks on our sinfulness but sees only the righteousness of Jesus. He taught that our sins are "covered over," but sin itself remains, what the Reformation called "forensic" or declarative justification. A person remains *simul justus et peccator*, both justified and a sinner. Still, Luther also taught that grace transforms the person in the Spirit, just as the heated iron glows because of its union with the fire, and leads to good works. The 2013 *From Conflict to Communion* report moves the dialogue forward; it explains Luther's position by saying "our righteousness is external insofar as it is Christ's righteousness, but it must become our righteousness, that is, internal, by faith in Christ's promise" (no. 112).

Luther's emphasis on the individual's illumination by the interior witness of the Holy Spirit contributed to Protestantism's individualism. While Catholic theology acknowledges that salvation is through Christ alone, it remains always suspicious about a religious individualism that reduces the life of grace to a "personal relationship with Jesus," short of the mediation of the church. It continues to emphasize that both Scripture and tradition witness to Christ who is the mediator and the fullness of all revelation (DV 2).[23] Furthermore, Scripture cannot stand alone; it is always read and interpreted within the living tradition of the church,[24] particularly in its liturgy.

At the same time, unlike fundamentalist Christianity, Catholicism presumes an evolutionary worldview; the human species has emerged from an evolutionary process "red in tooth and claw" and still possesses under a veneer of civility and self-restraint those primitive instincts. In the soul of the lover or the poet lurks that of the hunter who once had to struggle for survival. No one has expressed this better than Annie Dillard, who in her beautiful book *Pilgrim at Tinker Creek* describes the beauty of nature in her home in Virginia's Blue Ridge Mountains, but with a vision that often shifts from the peaceful surface of the creeks and grasses of the meadows to see in the animal kingdom up close violence, horror, and death. In her own words, "Every live thing is a survivor on a kind of extended emergency bivouac" and at the same time something created.[25]

From a theological perspective, the redemption is not some kind of later moment in this evolutionary process, an intervention or transaction on the part of Jesus to set things right as many imagine, but rather a confession that in the incarnation the eternal Word spoken forth in creation realizes perfectly what every person is potentially. We are both flawed and graced, touched by sin but open to God.

---

[23] Second Vatican Council, *Dei Verbum*, chap. 3, "Scripture and Tradition."

[24] Some Protestant theologians also move in this direction; see D. H. Williams, ed., *The Free Church and the Early Church: Bridging the Historical and Theological Divide* (Grand Rapids, MI: William B. Eerdmans, 2002); see also Williams, *Evangelicals and Tradition* (Grand Rapids, MI: Baker Academic, 2005).

[25] Annie Dillard, *Pilgrim at Tinker Creek* (New York: HarperCollins, 1974), 6–7.

Grace Builds on Nature

A corollary of the preceding principle is that grace builds on nature, working through it, elevating and perfecting it. Nature is not something to be transcended; Christianity honors it as the work of God's hands. We discover God not by fleeing the world but by becoming more fully involved in it, while salvation involves becoming more truly human, more open to others and to God.

As Christian theology moved beyond the mythopoeic language of the Bible and into the Greco-Roman world, its greatest christological challenge was not giving expression to the divinity of Jesus but rather insisting that God's Word had truly become a human being, something incomprehensible to the Greek mind. The early church was engaged in a long struggle with Gnosticism and Docetism, reflecting the dualism of Greek thought that privileged spirit over the merely material. Gnosticism could not accept that the divine could take on flesh, with its nasty implications of materiality and corruptibility. It tended to reduce the Johannine Logos or Word to a lesser emanation of the divine as with Arius, leading ultimately to Nicaea's confession that the only Son of God is "one in Being" (*homoousios*) or "consubstantial" with the Father.

Gnosticism was inherently elitist; knowledge (*gnosis*) did not come from experience but was available only to the few through a kind of illumination. Salvation was a matter of escaping the entanglements of human existence, with its implied responsibility for ethical living. Docetism, a variant of Gnosticism, taught that Jesus only "seemed" to have a real human body (in Greek *dokeō* means "to seem"), only seemed to die, and that the bread of the Eucharist could not really be the flesh of our Savior Jesus Christ.[26] Such was the Greek distaste for the world of materiality.

But from the beginning, the biblical creation narrative pronounced nature as good (Gen 1:1-2:4a). The man and woman are created in God's image and likeness (Gen 1:27); thus every human person is sacred, an absolute value, from the unborn child in the womb, the immigrant or homeless person on the streets of our cities, to the prisoner on death row. Catholicism's respect for life is rooted here.

---

[26] Ignatius of Antioch, *To the Smyrnaens*, no. 6.

It sees grace working through Mary, in her conception (the immaculate conception) and in her parents (Saints Joachim and Ann) preparing her to be the mother of God's Son. The humanity of Jesus has long been celebrated in Catholic art and devotion, from the traditional devotion to the Sacred Heart with its roots in the Middle Ages to Pope Benedict XVI's celebration of the image of the pierced side of Christ as an icon of God's love.[27]

Thomas Aquinas spoke of all creation mirroring the goodness of God:

> [God] brought things into being in order that His goodness might be communicated to creatures, and be represented by them; and because His goodness could not be adequately represented by one creature alone, He produced many and diverse creatures, that what was wanting to one in the representation of the divine goodness might be supplied by another. For goodness, which in God is simple and uniform, in creatures is manifold and divided and hence the whole universe together participates in the divine goodness more perfectly, and represents it better than any single creature whatever.[28]

A fascinating book, *The Sexuality of Christ in Renaissance Art and in Modern Oblivion*, shows how during the Renaissance, many works of art focused on the genitalia of Christ, a way of showing that humanity in all its concreteness could be the bearer of the divine.[29] The body is the medium through which spirit expresses itself; we intuit the spirit through sensitivity to body language. We can dispose ourselves to a fruitful reception of God's transforming grace through asceticism, disciplining our sometimes unruly nature (concupiscence). Human love reflects the love of God. Sexuality itself is sacred, even sacramental when expressed within the marriage covenant; it shares in God's gift of bringing forth new life and the love that will sustain it. Society is not some necessary evil, at best to be tolerated, but necessary for full human flourishing. Thus Catholicism's fundamental

---

[27] Benedict XVI, Encyclical Letter *Deus Caritas Est*, no. 12.

[28] Aquinas, *Summa Theologica*, I, q. 47, a. 1.

[29] Leo Steinberg, *The Sexuality of Christ in Renaissance Art and in Modern Oblivion* (Chicago: University of Chicago Press, 1996).

ethos, recognizing the social nature of the human person, is communitarian. Even the saints are still close to us; we are able to ask their intercession through the communion we share with them and with God (the communion of saints).

If grace builds on nature, then our salvation is accomplished not by fleeing from the world as something evil but by living lives of faithful discipleship within it. Recent studies in Christology have rediscovered Jesus' preaching on the kingdom or reign of God, which those in his movement were missioned to proclaim and "enact," healing, reconciling, driving out oppressive spirits (cf. Matt 10:7-8; Luke 10:3-9). The Jesus movement became the church. For Saint Paul, to be "in Christ" means to be in his body, the church. His letters are always to or about churches. As the body of Christ, the church mediates his life in its preaching, teaching, communion, ministry, and worship.

Paul tells us, "Work out your salvation with fear and trembling. For God is the one who, for his good purpose, works in you both to desire and to work" (Phil 2:12b-13). Similarly, in his Spiritual Exercises, St. Ignatius of Loyola invites the retreatant to consider "how God works and labors for me in all creatures upon the face of the earth" (no. 236). From this comes the Jesuit principle of finding God in all things. Each of us must enter into the mystery of our own lives in all their weakness and vulnerability, for it is precisely there that God's grace is to be found. Grace works in us, not in spite of our humanity, but in and through it.

The principle that grace builds on nature has taken on a new complexity for questions about human nature and sexuality for those who find themselves different or "other." If modernity with its optimistic rationalism saw the self as autonomous, from the perspective of postmodernism the self is more fluid, its identity shaped by social location and power relationships. Similarly, feminist thinkers have raised new questions about sexuality and a morality based chiefly on what is given biologically, stressing rather the importance of relationality, embodiment, justice, and lived experience, especially that of women.

If, for example, same-sex attraction is not a "preference" or choice but a given, an orientation determined early in a child's life or even before birth, what then is "nature" for those with such an orientation?

And what is the meaning of "gender" for those children who from their early years identify with the opposite sex and want to express that in the way they dress and live, later choosing a new identity and gender by means of hormone replacement therapy or even surgery? As Susan Ross argues, "From a postmodern perspective, our sexual and gender identities are not stable and essential, as official Catholic teaching holds, but constructed, diverse, and open to ambiguity."[30] Some Catholic ethicists are attempting to rethink the Catholic tradition on some of these difficult questions.[31] Without giving in to the widespread approval of casual sex, they seek to develop a morality that is not physicalist but personalist, focused on relationships and mutuality rather than exclusively on acts.

Grace and Mediation

If grace builds on nature, there are important consequences for how we come to know and experience God. The doctrine of the analogy of being means that while God remains transcendent, there is an analogy, even communion between God's pure, absolute existence and the contingent beings in the world which grounds the possibility of a metaphysical knowledge of God's existence, though personal knowledge of God depends on revelation. When we review the history of Israel and the earliest Christian communities, it becomes evident that it was precisely in the events of their ordinary lives, in encounters both mundane and extraordinary, in tragedy and hope and self-transcendence, in examples of love, compassion, and self-sacrifice that God's grace became transparent and the divine self-disclosure took place, a revelation most fully realized in the person of Jesus.

We do not encounter God directly; God's revelation or self-disclosure is always mediated by some experience in the world, some person, event, story, or natural phenomenon. The community discerns

---

[30] Susan A. Ross, *Anthropology Seeking Light and Beauty* (Collegeville, MN: Liturgical Press, 2012), 70.

[31] In addition to Ross, see Margaret A. Farley, *Just Love: A Framework for Christian Sexual Ethics* (New York: Continuum, 2006); Todd A. Salzman and Michael G. Lawler, *The Sexual Person: Towards a Renewed Catholic Anthropology* (Washington, DC: Georgetown University Press, 2008).

the divine presence and action through persons, events, and things; expresses it in language and story; and eventually formulates its religious teaching in doctrines. Catholicism's appreciation of the capacity of art and symbol to mediate a sense for the sacred and the transcendent is referred to as its sacramental imagination. The artist's ability to evoke transcendent beauty, the expressive power of religious symbol, music and song, light and darkness can create a sense for the sacred, and the love of a spouse can lead one to experience the unconditional love of God.[32] As Aquinas said, God works through secondary causes.[33]

The Reformers insisted that only Scripture could give us knowledge of God. Furthermore, both Luther and Calvin were uncomfortable with the Catholic concept of the mediation of grace through popular devotions and the church's sacramental system, seeing only the abuses in the Christianity of their day. In reaction they put far more emphasis on the transcendence of God and insisted, "Christ alone." Countries influenced by Calvin's theology saw a widespread destruction of religious images, an iconoclasm that led to a "stripping of the altars."[34] A Protestant pastor once told me he wanted to use candles on his communion table but some parishioners objected because "that was Catholic."

The result of this overemphasis on the divine transcendence was what has sometimes been described as a "disenchanting," or secularizing, of nature, pushing the divine presence out of the world. With such a chasm between the human and the divine, nature and grace, it was no big step at all to an atheistic naturalism. Nature became a closed system, without room for the immanent divine presence, particularly as the scientific method was assumed to be the only way to genuine knowledge. Thus for Newton's physics and Darwin's biology, God was no longer a necessary hypothesis.

Catholic theology also recognizes that the saving grace of Christ can be mediated by persons and events as well as by non-Christian

[32] See Andrew Greeley, *The Catholic Imagination* (Berkeley and Los Angeles: University of California Press, 2000).

[33] Aquinas, *Summa Contra Gentiles* 3.71.

[34] See, for example, Eamon Duffy, *The Stripping of the Altars: Traditional Religion in England, c. 1400–c. 1580* (New Haven, CT: Yale University Press, 1993).

religions or even by a commitment to transcendent values such as justice, peace, and service to humanity.[35] The encounter with God is always a mediated experience, as is any experience of reality. Thus while both Protestants and Catholics see Christ as the one mediator between God and creation, Catholics have a broader view of mediation. They recognize that grace of the Lord is mediated through the church, its sacraments, its community, and through people who touch others through their faith, goodness, or compassionate service, opening them to the mystery of God.

Faith and Works

Catholics and Protestants have argued about the relation between faith and works since the Reformation. For Luther, justification by faith is God's answer to persons fearful of God's judgment and unsure about their own righteousness. Justification is by "faith alone," not by any "works." But is human freedom involved in accepting the grace of justification? Luther's position remains somewhat ambiguous. Calvin was clear—because of the damage done by original sin to the will, unable to choose the good, justification is entirely God's work, leading to the doctrine of double predestination. The Council of Trent insisted that while justification is God's work, human freedom is always involved (DS 1525).[36] Some evangelicals and strict Calvinists teach that the grace of justification, once gained, cannot be lost; "Hyper-Calvinism's fifth point is the perseverance of the saints," meaning "once saved, always saved."[37]

Catholic theology continues to insist on the call to discipleship and faithful living in witness to the kingdom of God. As Terence Nichols shows, the New Testament insists on conversion of life and care for one's neighbor. Matthew's Gospel teaches us in the Sermon on the Mount that we must have a higher righteousness, expressed in love, that we will be judged on the basis of our care of the hungry, the

---

[35] Francis A. Sullivan, *Salvation Outside the Church* (New York: Paulist Press, 1992), 181.

[36] Dulles, *Assurance of Things Hoped For*, 49.

[37] See Edwin H. Palmer, *The Five Points of Calvinism* (Grand Rapids, MI: Baker House, 1972).

thirsty, the poor, the sick, and the imprisoned, without saying any-thing about belief or faith (Matt 25:31-36). Luke stresses the impor-tance of repentance and conversion, a *metanoia* manifested not just in words but in deeds. Paul never uses the expression "faith alone." This becomes clear in the letter to the Galatians; his concern was those who tied justification to observance of the Jewish law. He writes that Christians must live with what he calls an "obedience of faith" (Rom 16:2), meaning living in the gifts and fruits of the Spirit, especially love (1 Cor 13:13). But to do this we need a mediator who brings us grace surpassing our natural powers that he variously identifies as the Spirit of God or the Spirit of Christ (Rom 8).[38] Paul also demands conversion of life and moral living, as we see throughout 1 Corin-thians and in his exclamation in Romans 6:1, "Should we persist in sin that grace may abound? Of course not!"

According to evangelical theologian Scot McKnight, "An increasing tension remains among evangelicals about who gets to set the terms: Jesus or Paul. In other words, will we center our gospel teaching and living on 'the kingdom' or 'justification by faith'?"[39] Significantly, the 1998 "Joint Declaration on the Doctrine of Justification between Lutherans and Catholics" found "a consensus in basic truths of the doctrine of justification," in light of which "the remaining differences of language, theological elaboration and emphasis" in the under-standing of justification were deemed acceptable.[40]

God Always Respects Our Freedom

If grace builds on nature, then God always respects our freedom. In the book of Revelation there is a lovely verse in which the risen Jesus says, "Behold, I stand at the door and knock. If anyone hears my voice and opens the door, [then] I will enter his house and dine with him, and he with me" (Rev 3:20). What is suggestive about this is the certain hesitancy it shows on the part of the risen Lord; he does not force his way in; he stands and waits for an invitation; he respects

[38] Terence Nichols, *Death and Afterlife: A Theological Introduction* (Grand Rapids, MI: Brazos Press, 2010), 151–58.
[39] Scot McKnight, "Jesus vs. Paul," *Christianity Today* 54, no. 12 (2010): 26.
[40] Lutheran World Federation and the Catholic Church, "Joint Declaration on the Doctrine of Justification" (1998).

our freedom. This is another basic principle. One finds frequent illustrations of it in Scripture.

In the gospels, Jesus invites others to follow him; he does not force them. The rich man in Mark turns down an invitation to be in Jesus' company and goes away sad, "for he had many possessions" (Mark 10:22). One can see this theme again in the Easter stories. There is a theme of nonrecognition that runs through them. The disciples don't recognize the risen Jesus—they are frightened or think that they are seeing a ghost (Luke 24:37). Thomas wants empirical evidence (John 20:25), while Mary Magdalene, who loved him, mistakes him for the gardener (John 20:15).

These stories suggest a number of things. First, recognizing the risen Jesus is very different from knowing the earthly Jesus. Jesus' presence cannot be objectified. Second, Jesus did not appear to his enemies but to those who loved him, to those who had opened their hearts to him and who had followed him in faith. The others had shut him out; he could not have appeared to them, for their hearts were closed. Third, the experience does not compel the disciples to believe. Like us, they had to be led to faith; Jesus shows them his wounds in John. He asks for something to eat as evidence or breaks bread with them in Luke. But the disciples must still assent to the mystery. In Matthew's description of the appearance of Jesus on the mountain in Galilee, some of the disciples continue to doubt even as others worship him (Matt 28:17). God always respects our freedom.

Today, when more people experience God as absent rather than present and all powerful, perhaps we can gain some insight into the mystery of a God whose apparent weakness in the face of our freedom reflects the sovereign creator's love for the creature. Recent popes have stressed how God respects our human freedom. In his encyclical *Ecclesiam Suam*, Pope Paul VI refers to what he calls the "dialogue of salvation" as an "appeal of love" which leaves us free to accept or reject God's grace (no. 75). Few have expressed this more powerfully than Pope John Paul II, who wrote, "In a certain sense one could say that confronted with our human freedom, God decided to make Himself 'impotent.'"[41] In his *Laudato Sì*, Pope Francis says that "God is intimately present to each being, without impinging on

---

[41] John Paul II, *Crossing the Threshold of Hope*, ed. Vittorio Messori (New York: Random House, 1994), 61.

the autonomy of his creature, and this gives rise to the rightful autonomy of earthly affairs" (no. 80). God's ability to renounce power
for persuasion, so unlike our own, is the ultimate witness to God's
power which is really benevolence rather than control. God who
created us as free beings honors our freedom.

Protestant theology, especially in its Reformed or Calvinist expression, sees a chasm between nature and grace because of sin, as we
saw earlier. The will, corrupted by sin, is unable to choose the good.
Though Catholic theology also has been influenced by its Augustinian heritage, its anthropology has generally remained more optimistic, stressing human freedom, the transcendental reach of reason, and
God's presence within nature and the human. In reaction to the
Reformers, the fathers gathered at the Council of Trent (1545–1563)
insisted that while our justification was always through God's grace
in Jesus, our freedom was always involved; we have to cooperate
with grace.[42]

The implications of this are many. Our destiny remains in our own
hands, so much does God respect our freedom. God does not force
the divine will on us, far less predestine us for salvation or damnation. God is always present, inviting us into a relationship, present
in the midst of the human and empowering us with grace. God cannot
force us to love God any more than we can force another to love us.
Love is always a gift, freely offered and freely received. But we must
open our hearts, cooperate with grace, welcome the divine presence,
and live before God in reverence and awe.

Faith and Reason

Protestant and Catholic religious epistemologies are also different.
Protestant theology, founded on Luther's "rediscovery" of the "gospel" of justification by faith in Romans and Galatians and Calvin's
emphasis on the corruption of the intellect because of sin, teaches

---

[42] See Council of Trent, "Canons Concerning Justification," no. 9; see also the
Catechism of the Catholic Church, 2nd ed. (Vatican City: Liberia Editrice Vaticana, 2000),
no. 2002.

that actual knowledge of God comes only from Scripture.[43] It has always given primacy to the authority of Scripture. Though the Reformers appealed to tradition, including the ecumenical creeds, the writings of the fathers, and the church's worship, recourse to history did not become normative and a doctrine of Scripture as an independent dogmatic locus and infallible rule of faith exclusive of any other authority, including that of the church, developed in subsequent Reformation history.[44]

But for some, the primacy of the Scriptures was short-lived. Under the influence of the Enlightenment, biblical theology was transformed from a normative discipline into a critical one.[45] No longer interpreted within the life of the church, the Bible became just another historical document rather than a revelatory one.[46] The results were too often the alternatives of theological liberalism or a biblical fundamentalism, privileging the biblical word against the evidence of scientific or historical disciplines. Fundamentalist Protestants continue to battle against teaching evolution in the public schools today, long after the infamous 1925 Scopes trial.

Catholicism has long insisted that faith and reason, or as we might say today, theology and science, are complementary and must work in harmony. Aquinas rejected the medieval theory of a "double truth," one of philosophy, another of faith. They are different ways of knowing, with different methodologies and different understandings of what counts as evidence. Science investigates the phenomena of the physical world; it can neither prove nor disprove the truths of faith, though good theology does not discount the data of the sciences. Faith reflects on the incomprehensible God's self-disclosure to the religious community which must be expressed in language faithful

[43] See Erling T. Teigen, "The Clarity of Scripture and Hermeneutical Principles in the Lutheran Confessions," *Concordia Theological Quarterly* 46 (1982): 147–66; Calvin, *Institutes* 2.6.1.

[44] Daniel H. Williams, "Scripture, Tradition, and the Church: Reformation and Post-Reformation," in *The Free Church and the Early Church: Bridging the Historical and Theological Divide*, ed. Daniel H. Williams (Grand Rapids, MI: William B. Eerdmans, 2002), 120–21.

[45] Gerhard Ebeling, *Word and Faith* (Philadelphia, PA: Fortress Press, 1963), 79–97.

[46] See Brevard S. Childs, *Biblical Theology in Crisis* (Philadelphia, PA: Westminster Press, 1970), 102; see also Sandra M. Schneiders, *The Revelatory Text: Interpreting the New Testament as Sacred Scripture* (Collegeville, MN: Liturgical Press, 1999), 22–23.

to Scripture and the church's tradition and at the same time in harmony with scientific and philosophical reason. They are different ways of arriving at truth, which is one.

While Catholic theology recognizes Scripture as a unique source of knowledge of God, it also agrees with Paul that God's invisible power and divinity can be perceived in the things God has made (cf. Rom 1:20). Protestant theology says faith alone, grace alone; it is generally reluctant to speak of a "natural" knowledge of God. But transcendental Thomists like Rahner see the absolute disclosed against the horizon of every act of human understanding, an initial communication of grace. Thus Catholicism says grace and nature as well as faith and reason, even if revelation is needed to know *who* God is.

Pope John Paul II argued in his 1998 encyclical *Fides et Ratio* (no. 44) that faith and reason are complementary forms of wisdom, though there have been unhappy moments when this complementarity has not been respected, as in the case of Galileo, the silencing of various *ressourcement* theologians in the period before Vatican II, or even today.[47] The pope noted that faith and reason are too often at odds today, while philosophical reason itself has been marginalized:

> Other forms of rationality have acquired an ever higher profile, making philosophical learning appear all the more peripheral. These forms of rationality are directed not towards the contemplation of truth and the search for the ultimate goal and meaning of life; but instead, as 'instrumental reason', they are directed—actually or potentially—towards the promotion of utilitarian ends, towards enjoyment or power (no. 47).

Few have stressed the need for faith and reason to work in harmony more than Pope Benedict XVI. In his *Truth and Tolerance*, he wrote, "Reason needs to listen to the great religious traditions if it does not wish to become deaf, blind, and mute concerning the most essential elements of human existence."[48] At the same time, faith needs reason

---

[47] See Richard R. Gaillardetz, ed., *When the Magisterium Intervenes: The Magisterium and Theologians in Today's Church* (Collegeville, MN: Liturgical Press, 2012).

[48] Joseph Ratzinger, *Truth and Tolerance: Christian Belief and World Religions* (San Francisco: Ignatius Press, 2004), 252; see also Ratzinger, *Values in a Time of Upheaval* (San Francisco: Ignatius Press, 2006), 65–66.

if it is not to fall into some kind of fundamentalism. Disassociating reason from faith means that faith itself becomes incredible. Who can believe when faith is seen as irrational? Throughout his career, Benedict has stressed that this synthesis or complementarity of faith and reason is what distinguishes Christianity from other religions.

In his controversial Regensburg lecture, Benedict argued that the Septuagint or Greek translation of the Old Testament represents not just another translation but an important step in the history of revelation which witnesses in the later Wisdom tradition to an inner rapprochement between biblical faith and Greek reason or philosophical inquiry.[49] Even if reason cannot produce faith, the act of faith itself is rational.

Conclusion

Karl Rahner's theological anthropology discloses the human person as already in relation to the absolute. This non-thematic grasp of the transcendent God, implicit in human understanding, shows that grace, God's free self-communication and presence to the human, reveals how nature and grace are bound together rather than the more traditional neoscholastic view of grace as something added on. His transcendental theology takes its point of departure from the incarnation which "is the unique and *highest* instance of the actualization of the essence of human reality," for in the Word becoming flesh human nature gives itself to the mystery of God in an unsurpassable and radical way and so "becomes the nature of God himself." This is how Rahner understands the incarnation.[50]

The myth of the Fall conveys in mythopoeic language the basic truth that sin has been present in the world from the beginning and affects all born into it. Augustine in the fifth century formulated the concept of original sin passed on from Adam through generation, underlining the truth of the devastating effect of the sin of the world and our need for grace. But grace is not absent. Acknowledging that the world is a sinful place, Robert Schreiter writes that "God's grace

---

[49] Benedict XVI, "Faith, Reason and the University," Regensburg Lecture, September 12, 2006.

[50] Rahner, *Foundations of Christian Faith*, 218.

is greater, and God has not left the world but continues to love it and sustain it."[51]

Reformation theology, shaped to a considerable extent by Augustine, traditionally sees human nature as totally depraved because of original sin. Its canonization of Anselm's theory of substitutionary atonement suggests a soteriology that may need to be rethought. Catholic and Orthodox theology has been more optimistic. A more contemporary understanding of original sin sees it as a social concept. We are born into a world bearing the traces of the egoism that characterizes our evolutionary inheritance, while the sin present in our familial, social, cultural, economic, and interpersonal relationships shapes each of us in unforeseen ways and diminishes our freedom.

With different starting points and sensibilities, Catholic and Protestant theological anthropologies have traditionally differed on the relationship between sin and grace. From the perspective of a Catholic anthropology, nature is both flawed and graced; grace builds on nature; faith and reason are compatible; and the stress is on a God who always respects human freedom. Protestant theology generally remains more shaped by its Augustinian heritage. If some of these sensibilities are still discernable, contemporary theology and the ecumenical movement have brought many Catholics and Protestants closer together on these issues, and both traditions remain focused on Christ. And both are challenged by the more fluid concepts of nature, sexual identity, and the self so prevalent in our postmodern age.

For Further Reading

Abraham, Susan, and Elena Procario-Foley, eds. *Frontiers in Catholic Feminist Theology*. Minneapolis, MN: Fortress Press, 2009.

Duffy, Stephen J. *Dynamics of Grace: Perspective in Theological Anthropology*. Collegeville, MN: Liturgical Press, 1993.

———. "Our Hearts of Darkness: Original Sin Revisited." *Theological Studies* 49 (1998): 597–622.

---

[51] Robert Schreiter, "The Repositioning of a Theology of the World," in *The Task of Theology*, ed. Anselm Min (Maryknoll, NY: Orbis Books, 2014), 74.

Dulles, Avery. *The Assurance of Things Hoped For: A Theology of Christian Faith*. New York: Oxford University Press, 1994.

Gonzalez, Michelle A. *Created in God's Image: An Introduction to Feminist Theological Anthropology*. Maryknoll, NY: Orbis Books, 2007.

Haight, Roger. *The Experience and Language of Grace*. New York: Paulist Press, 1979.

Johnson, Elizabeth A. "Jesus and Salvation." *Catholic Theological Society of America: Proceedings* 49 (1994): 1–18.

Lutheran World Federation and the Catholic Church. "Joint Declaration on the Doctrine of Justification." *Origins* 28, no. 8 (1998).

Rahner, Karl. *Foundations of Christian Faith: An Introduction to the Idea of Christianity*. New York: Seabury Press, 1978.

Rondet, Henri. *Original Sin: The Patristic and Theological Background*. Staten Island, NY: Alba House, 1972.

Ross, Susan. *Anthropology: Seeking Light and Beauty*. Collegeville, MN: Liturgical Press, 2012.

Salzman, Todd A., and Michael G. Lawler. *The Sexual Person: Towards a Renewed Catholic Anthropology*. Washington, DC: Georgetown University Press, 2008.

Vandervelde, George. *Original Sin: Two Major Trends in Contemporary Roman Catholic Reinterpretation*. Amsterdam: Rodopi, 1975.

Chapter 7

Mary and the Communion of Saints

The notion of the communion of saints, with its connotation of a shared life of God's people on earth and the saints in heaven, has long played an important role in the Catholic tradition. Added to the Apostles' Creed by the beginning of the fifth century, the early Christians gathered to pray at the tombs of the martyrs, invoked the saints in a litany from at least the time of Pope Gregory the Great (c. 540–604), and sought their patronage by giving their names to their children and their churches. Monks and nuns frequently take religious names in their honor. Foremost among the saints is Mary, the mother of Jesus, who has been invoked in prayer since the third century.

The Concept of Communion

The concept of communion comes from the Greek *koinōnia*, meaning a sharing or participation in something else. Appearing nineteen times in the New Testament, *koinōnia* is generally translated as sharing in, fellowship, or communion (Latin *communio*). Catholics, sensitive to its sacramental or spiritual implications, prefer communion, while evangelicals generally translate it as fellowship.[1] The term is used in the New Testament in a number of contexts.

---

[1] See "Church, Evangelization and the Bonds of *Koinonia*: A Report of the International Consultation between the Catholic Church and the World Evangelical Alliance (1993–2002)," no. 1, http://www.vatican.va/roman_curia/pontifical_councils

First of all, *koinōnia* has the soteriological sense of sharing in the divine life through incorporation into Christ. "God is faithful, and by him you were called to fellowship (*koinōnia*) with his Son, Jesus Christ our Lord" (1 Cor 1:9). Christians become one with Christ through faith (Phlm 6) and through sharing in his sufferings (Phil 3:10; 2 Cor 1:7). Paul concludes 2 Corinthians with a threefold benediction still used in the liturgy: "The grace of the Lord Jesus Christ and the love of God and the fellowship [*koinōnia*] of the holy Spirit be with all of you." The author of 2 Peter uses particularly strong language, asking that through God's promises "you may come to share (*koinōnia*) in the divine nature" (2 Pet 1:4). Thus *koinōnia* means more than simply fellowship; it refers to the believers' share in the divine life, what the fathers of the Eastern churches speak of as a process of divinization (*theosis*).

Second, there is an ecclesial sense to *koinōnia*. Communion in the divine life means a shared life with other disciples. For Paul, to be "in Christ" means that Christians share a common life in grace and the Spirit. Luke uses *koinōnia* to describe the communal life of the primitive community (Acts 2:42). The author of 1 John points to the vertical and horizontal dimensions of the community's life with God and with one another:

> [W]hat we have seen and heard
> we proclaim now to you,
> so that you too may have fellowship with us;
> for our fellowship with the Father
> and with his Son, Jesus Christ. (1 John 1:3; cf. 6, 7)

In Paul there is a sacramental dimension to *koinōnia*. He writes to the community at Corinth that they are baptized into one body, given to drink of one Spirit (1 Cor 12:13), and that by their participation (*koinōnia*) in the body and blood of Christ they themselves become his body (1 Cor 10:16-17). Finally, the Apostles' Creed speaks of the communion of saints, pointing to the communion of the faithful with God and with those who have entered fully into the divine life.

/chrstuni/evangelicals-docs/rc_pc_chrstuni_doc_20111220_report-1993-2002_en .html.

The Communion of Saints

The term "saints" or "holy ones" (*hagioi*) used by Paul for members of his churches (Rom 1:7; Phil 1:1) was soon expanded to refer to those who had finished the race and were with the Lord. The author of Hebrews uses this metaphor; after reviewing the men and women of faith of the Jewish Scriptures he writes, "Since we are surrounded by so great a cloud of witnesses, let us rid ourselves of every burden and sin that clings to us and persevere in running the race that lies before us" (Heb 12:1-2).

From the beginning, Christians honored those who had witnessed to Christ with their blood, the martyrs. They were seen as icons of Christ, following him even to his death. According to Peter Brown, the cult of the saints broke the imaginative boundaries between heaven and earth, the divine and the human, the living and the dead: "The graves of the saints—whether these were the solemn rock tombs of the Jewish patriarchs in the Holy Land or, in Christian circles, tombs, fragments of bodies or, even physical objects that had made contact with these bodies—were privileged places, where the contrasted poles of Heaven and Earth met."[2]

The graves of the martyrs became the objects of pilgrimage, especially on the anniversary of their death, with prayers through the night and the Eucharist celebrated at dawn, followed by a meal, a tradition inherited from pagan funeral rites, not unlike the Mexican *Dia de los Muertos*. "The custom of directly calling upon a martyr for prayer arose, originally as the expression of the private piety of individuals . . . a specific way of invoking the solidarity that existed between pilgrims on earth and those who had been sealed with the victory of Christ."[3] Ambrose popularized the enshrining of relics; they were valued not as a reminder of death but as signs of the martyrs' triumph over death. Augustine, preaching on the feasts of the martyrs, conveyed the idea of one community of those on earth and the martyrs in heaven who prayed for those still on the way.

As the age of martyrs faded into history, Christians honored others whose lives were worthy of imitation. Confessors who had suffered

---

[2] Peter Brown, *The Cult of the Saints: Its Rise and Function in Latin Christianity* (Chicago: University of Chicago Press, 1981), 3.

[3] See Elizabeth A. Johnson, *Friends of God and Prophets: A Feminist Theological Reading of the Communion of Saints* (New York: Continuum, 1998), 77–78.

for the faith, holy men and women, bishops and popes, and those who cared for the sick or the poor were invoked as saints and intercessors, or as Johnson argues, sometimes as companions and fellow disciples.[4] Multiple commemorations contributed to the development of a liturgical calendar with saints' days. Among the saints from the beginning was Mary, the mother of Jesus. The Second Council of Nicaea (787) distinguished the worship and adoration (*latria*) to be given to God alone from the veneration (*dulia*) given to the saints. As local saints proliferated, bishops began to turn to the pope for guidance. By the thirteenth century, naming new saints, "canonizing" them, or adding their names to the canon became the exclusive responsibility of the bishop of Rome.[5]

Communio Sanctorum

According to J. N. D. Kelly, the term originated in the East as *koinōnia ton hagion*. The Latin phrase *communio sanctorum* appears in a commentary by Nicetas of Remesiana (d. 414), who used it to describe the church as the fellowship of holy persons of all ages: "Patriarchs, prophets, martyrs, and all other righteous men [and women] who have lived or are now alive, or shall live in time to come."[6] This vision of the church living, dead, and to come is the more popular understanding. By the fifth century, it can be found in versions of the Apostles' Creed. The idea, however, of those living in communion with Christ as being in communion with the faithful of every age is older than the phrase. In addition to Nicetas, Augustine (d. 430) and Faustus of Riez (452) gave expression to this idea.

A good argument is made that the original version of the phrase *communio sanctorum* referred to the sacraments. The Latin is ambiguous; it could mean either a communion of holy people (masculine form) or the communion of holy things (neuter form), i.e., the sacraments, which is how the equivalent Greek phrase, *koinōnia tōn hagiōn* was understood in the East as early as 388. Many maintain that its

---

[4] Ibid., 80.

[5] Kenneth Woodward, *Making Saints* (New York: Simon & Schuster, 1997).

[6] J. N. D. Kelly, *Early Christian Creeds*, 3rd ed. (New York: Longman, 1972), 388–91, at 391.

original reference in the Apostles' Creed was to the sacraments.[7] The Councils of Vienne (394) and Nimes (396) used it in reference to the Eucharist.

Unfortunately, in the second millennium, the connection between communion in holy things and the communion of saints, or in other words, between the sacraments and the church, was largely lost as people received the Eucharist less frequently and interpreted it in terms of personal devotion. In many Reformation traditions, the practice of regular Sunday Eucharist disappeared. The CDF addressed this sacramental meaning of the communion of saints in a 1992 letter on the church as communion: "The Church is a *Communion of the saints*, to use a traditional expression that is found in Latin versions of the Apostles' Creed from the end of the fourth century. The common visible sharing in the goods of salvation (*the holy things*), and especially in the Eucharist, is the source of the invisible communion among the sharers (*the saints*)."[8]

Mary in the Church

From the second century, the church has honored Mary, the mother of Jesus, a tradition shared today by both Catholic and Orthodox Christians (some evangelicals are showing a new interest in Mary today as well).[9] It is hard to image a Catholic church without a statue of Mary or an Orthodox liturgy that did not include prayer to the most holy Theotokos, Mother of God. But in spite of the important place Mary has in the tradition, the New Testament says more about

---

[7] For example, Avery Dulles, "The Church as Communion," in *New Perspectives on Historical Theology: Essays in Memory of John Meyendorff*, ed. Bradley Nassif (Grand Rapids, MI: William B. Eerdmans, 1996), 126.

[8] CDF, "Letter to the Bishops of the Catholic Church on Some Aspects of the Church Understood as Communion," (1992), no. 6, http://www.vatican.va/roman_curia /congregations/cfaith/documents/rc_con_cfaith_doc_28051992_communionis -notio_en.html.

[9] See Tim Perry, *Mary for Evangelicals: Toward an Understanding of the Mother of Our Lord* (Downers Grove, IL: InterVarsity Academic, 2006); Scot McKnight, *The Real Mary: Why Evangelical Christians Can Embrace the Mother of Jesus* (Brewster, MA: Paraclete Press, 2007).

the faith of the primitive churches than what can be affirmed as simple history.[10]

Scripture

Paul never mentions Mary by name, beyond saying that Jesus was "born of a woman, born under the law" (Gal 4:4). John refers to her only as "the mother of Jesus" in the story of the miracle at Cana and at the crucifixion, where the dying Jesus gives his mother to the Beloved Disciple to be his own (John 20:26-27), this in spite of the fact that John refers to other "Marys" some fifteen times. The point here is the reinterpretation of family relationships in terms of the new family of the disciples (cf. Mark 3:34-35). Mark is ambiguous as to whether or not Mary is to be included among the relatives who consider Jesus to be "out of his mind" (Mark 3:21; cf. 6:4). The virginal conception is mentioned only in the infancy narratives of Luke and Matthew, and there is no confirmation of Luke's report that Jesus and John the Baptist were related. Acts 1:14 places "Mary the mother of Jesus, and his brothers" with the eleven and some other women in the upper room in the days before Pentecost.

Tradition

Nevertheless, the image of Mary continued to develop in the tradition. Some of what became part of the Marian tradition originates in the apocryphal gospels. The *Protoevangelium* or *Gospel of James*, from the mid-second century, tells the story of Mary's birth, presentation in the temple, the names of her parents (Joachim and Anna), and the explanation that the "brothers and sisters of Jesus" were children of Joseph by a previous marriage. Over 150 Greek manuscripts of this text have survived, so it must have been very popular. Stories of Mary's death or "dormition" and assumption into heaven date from the fourth century. Some of this may represent the product of pious imagination wondering about the "hidden years" of the Jesus story.

---

[10] See Raymond E. Brown, et al., eds., *Mary in the New Testament* (Philadelphia, PA/ New York: Fortress Press/Paulist Press, 1978), 8.

From the second century on, the fathers of the church continued to reflect on the person of Mary, usually from a christological perspective. Ignatius of Antioch (d. 110) emphasized that Mary truly carried Jesus in her womb and truly gave him birth to counter Docetist teaching that Jesus was not truly human; he also refers to the virginity of Mary, though this is not really consistent with his anti-Docetist polemic. Justin Martyr (d. 165) and Irenaeus of Lyons (d. 202) develop the parallelism between the virgin Eve and the Virgin Mary, a corollary to Paul's symbolism of Christ as the new Adam. Irenaeus, stressing her active role through her obedience in the work of redemption, associated her with the church, a theme further developed by Tertullian, Hippolytus, and especially Augustine.

As early as the third century (c. 250), there is evidence of Christians asking for Mary's intercession. The *Sub Tuum Praesidium*, a beautiful prayer which addresses Mary as Mother of God (*theotokos*), used by both the Eastern and the Western church, can be traced back to a third-century Greek text:

> We fly to thy patronage,
> O holy Mother of God;
> despise not our petitions
> in our necessities,
> but deliver us always from dangers,
> O glorious and blessed Virgin,
> Amen.

Another form of this prayer appears in the opening petition of the medieval *Memorare*: "Remember O most gracious Virgin Mary, that never was it known that anyone who fled to your protection . . ."

More recent scholarship cannot find any reliable pictures of Christ and his mother in the first two or three centuries of Christian history.[11] The earliest seems to have been representations of the adoration of the Magi, dating from the middle of the third century, very popular in catacomb frescoes and sarcophagus carvings.[12] By the fourth cen-

---

[11] George H. Tavard, *The Thousand Faces of the Virgin Mary* (Collegeville, MN: Liturgical Press, 1996), 65.

[12] Geri Parlby, "The Origins of Marian Arts: The Evolution of Marian Imagery in the Western Church until AD 431," in *Mary: The Complete Resource*, ed. Sarah Jane Boss (Oxford: Oxford University Press, 2007), 120.

tury, the cult of Mary in art and prayer was becoming widespread, especially in the East.[13] In the Middle Ages, the identification of Mary as the new Eve and *theotokos*, along with the emergence of Marian liturgical feasts, gave way to an increasingly popular cult of the person of Mary. She was hailed as Mother of Mercies, Mother of God, and Queen of Heaven. Her intercessory power was emphasized, as was her role in Christ's great work of salvation.

The Reformers objected strongly to this, particularly to any idea that detracted from the idea of Christ as the sole redeemer. Luther objected to hymns such as the *"Salve Regina"* which called Mary "Queen of mercy" and "our life, our sweetness, and our hope."[14] Yet he kept on the wall of his study a crucifix and an image of the virgin and wrote more about Mary than any other Reformer.[15] In post-Reformation history, devotion to Mary and the saints continued to flourish among Catholics, sometimes with excesses, while for Protestants it largely disappeared. For example, Karl Barth wrote in his *Church Dogmatics*, "Where Mary is 'venerated,' . . . there the Church of Christ is not."[16] Not all Protestants would agree with Barth here.

On a recent visit to Germany, I found an icon of the Madonna in Dietrich Bonhoeffer's study in Berlin, and we visited the great Lutheran Frauenkirche or Church of Our Lady in Dresden, rebuilt after its destruction during the Second World War. At the Second Vatican Council, some of the fathers wanted a separate document declaring Mary to be mother of the church and mediatrix of all graces; after a considerable struggle, they voted to include the treatment of Mary as the final chapter of *Lumen Gentium*, the Dogmatic Constitution on the Church, though *Lumen Gentium* 55 implies that she is Mother of the Church in teaching that she is "the mother of the members of Christ."

---

[13] See Stephen Shoemaker, "The Cult of the Virgin in the Fourth Century: A Fresh Look at Some Old and New Sources," in *The Origins of the Cult of the Virgin Mary*, ed. Chris Maunder (London: Burns & Oats, 2008), 72.

[14] Gottfried Maron, "Mary in Protestant Theology," in *Mary in the Churches*, Concilium 168, ed. Hans Küng and Jürgen Moltmann (New York: Seabury Press, 1983), 40–47.

[15] Toivo Harjunpää, "A Lutheran View of Mariology," *America* 117 (1967): 437.

[16] Karl Barth, *Church Dogmatics*, vol. 1, pt. 2, *The Doctrine of the Word of God* (Edinburgh: T & T Clark, 1956), 143.

Popular Religion

Marian piety, if sometimes controversial, remains popular with most Catholics. Much of it falls into the category of popular religion, expressions of faith in the symbols and iconography of a particular people. Popular religion includes hymns and prayers, popular devotions such as Marian novenas, May crownings, the rosary, statues and icons, various domestic rituals, and Marian apparitions. The official church generally sees these expressions of popular piety as helpful inculturations of the faith. Pope Francis has a particular appreciation for popular religion (*religiosidad popular* in the Spanish), with its emphasis on feeling or sentiment which moves the heart. He sees it as a synthesis of faith and culture, thus as a form of theology.[17] As he says in his apostolic exhortation *Evangelii Gaudium*, "We cannot demand that peoples of every continent, in expressing their Christian faith, imitate modes of expression which European nations developed at a particular moment of their history, because the faith cannot be constricted to the limits of understanding and expression of any one culture" (no. 118).

Marian apparitions represent another example of popular piety, for example, those of Our Lady of Guadalupe at Tepeyac (1531), La Salette (1846), Lourdes (1858), and Fatima (1917). Even if judged credible and approved by the church, they remain in the category of private revelation and are not a matter of the church's faith. Karl Rahner sees such visions as moments of grace that overflow into the imagination.[18]

Raymond Brown has sketched the "symbolic trajectory" of Mary's image which remains malleable to different cultural expressions of Christian discipleship. Thus, Mary took on the image of an Egyptian nun for the ascetics of the desert in the early church; in the chivalrous culture of the Middle Ages she became "Our Lady" to the knights, a symbol of chaste love; in the twentieth century, Mary has been honored as part of the "Holy Family," a model of family life; most recently she has been portrayed as an example of the liberated woman in a

[17] See also Jorge Mario Bergoglio, "Religiosidad Popular Como Inculturación de la Fe," in *Testigos de Aparecida*, vol. 2 (Bogota: CELAM, 2009), 281–325, esp. 308–14.

[18] Karl Rahner, *Visions and Prophecies* (London: Burns & Oats, 1963), 55–56; see also "Mary in Visions," chap. 10 in Tavard, *The Thousand Faces of the Virgin Mary*, 171–89.

letter of the American bishops.[19] Andrew Greeley has attributed her popularity at least in part to her ability—given our patriarchal God language—to symbolize feminine aspects of the divine.[20]

The Marian Dogmas

If the church has generally made room for popular religion in its devotional life, its doctrinal tradition is more restrained. There are four Marian dogmas: perpetual virginity, Mother of God, immaculate conception, and assumption into heaven.

Perpetual Virginity

While Luke and Matthew both include the virginal conception of Jesus in their gospels, the idea of the perpetual virginity of Mary developed later in the church. The *Protoevangelium* or *Gospel of James*, dating from the middle of the second century, suggests that Mary remained a virgin in its explanation that the "brothers and sisters of Jesus" mentioned in the gospels are children of Joseph by a previous marriage. As mentioned earlier, church fathers such as Ignatius of Antioch, Justin Martyr, and Irenaeus of Lyons refer to the virginity of Mary, though denying Jesus' birth through sexual intercourse is not really consistent with their polemic against the Docetists who denied the humanity of Jesus. The baptismal creed of the *Apostolic Tradition* attributed to Hippolytus of Rome (c. 215) asks, "Do you believe in Christ Jesus, the son of God, Who was begotten by the Holy Spirit from the Virgin Mary?" Athanasius (d. 373), Epiphanius (d. 404), and Jerome (d. 419) each attest to belief in Mary's perpetual virginity. By the end of the fourth century, Mary's response to the angel, "How can this be, since I have no relations with a man?" (Luke 1:34) was being taken as a vow of virginity.[21] The phrase "born of the

[19] Raymond Brown, *Biblical Reflections on Crises Facing the Church* (New York: Paulist Press, 1975), 106–7.

[20] Andrew Greeley, *The Mary Myth: On the Femininity of God* (New York: Seabury Press, 1977).

[21] Raymond Brown, et al., *Mary in the New Testament*, 278.

Virgin Mary" became part of the creed with the Council of Constantinople (381), while the Second Council of Constantinople (553) referred to Mary as "ever virgin."

What *if* the virginal conception of Jesus was "merely a symbol," as is sometimes alleged? Would that affect our faith? Joseph Ratzinger once addressed this question in his famous *Introduction to Christianity*. With remarkable lucidity he wrote:

> The doctrine of Jesus' divinity would not be affected if Jesus had been the product of a normal human marriage. For the Divine Sonship of which faith speaks is not a biological but an ontological fact, an event not in time but in God's eternity; God is always Father, Son, and Spirit; the conception of Jesus means, not that a new God-the-Son comes into being, but that God as Son in the man Jesus draws the creature man to himself, so that he himself "is" man.[22]

Mother of God

The title *theotokos*, literally "God-bearer" or Mother of God, was clearly christological. Jaroslav Pelikan argues that the sources for the title are not polemics or speculation but devotion, evident in an early Greek version of the hymn to Mary called the *"Sub Tuum Praesidium,"* as we saw earlier.[23] It was used in 324 by Alexander of Alexandria in a letter against the Arians and later confirmed by the First Council of Ephesus in 431 and by Chalcedon in 451. The text of the prayer shows how theology and prayer developed together; it affirms the divinity of Jesus and is evidence that Mary was already being called on as an intercessor, a practice deeply rooted in the church's life.

The Immaculate Conception

The belief that Mary was conceived without sin, long held in the East, has been controversial. While the doctrine is not found explicitly in Scripture, two texts have been cited in its support. In Genesis 3:15

---

[22] Joseph Ratzinger, *Introduction to Christianity* (San Francisco: Ignatius Press, 2004), 274–75.

[23] Jaroslav Pelikan, *The Emergence of the Catholic Tradition (100–600)* (Chicago: University of Chicago Press, 1971), 241.

God says to the Serpent: "I will put enmity between you and the woman, between your offspring and hers; He will strike at your head, while you strike at his heel." Also Luke 1:28 has Gabriel greeting the young Jewish girl, Mary, as "hail, full of grace (Vulgate), the Lord is with you."

Though the concept of original sin had not yet been formulated by Augustine, Ephraem of Syria (306–373) and Ambrose (339–397) taught that Mary was free of all stain of sin. Many of the Eastern fathers followed this opinion and a feast commemorating Mary's conception began in the East in the late seventh century and eventually spread throughout the church. Augustine (354–430) taught that Mary was free from personal sin through God's special grace, but he insisted that as one born of conjugal intercourse she inherited original sin. Bernard of Clairvaux (1090–1153), though greatly devoted to Mary, followed Augustine's opinion. He in turn influenced the thirteenth-century scholastic theologians Bonaventure, Albert the Great, and Thomas Aquinas, all of whom rejected her immaculate conception. John Duns Scotus (1266–1308), by introducing the concept of "preservative redemption," reconciled Mary's freedom from original sin with Christ's universal redemptive work.

Pope Pius IX formally defined the dogma in 1854, but only after asking the bishops of the church what their people believed. His Apostolic Constitution *Ineffabilis Deus* declared: "the Most Blessed Virgin Mary from the first moment of her conception was, by the singular grace and privilege of Almighty God, in view of the merits of Christ Jesus the Savior of the human race, preserved immune from all stain of original sin" (DS 3900). Two things should be observed about this definition. First, it does not deny that Mary herself has been redeemed by Christ; indeed it affirms it. Mary cannot be thought equal to the Redeemer. Second, it asserts that in the divine plan of salvation, Mary has been chosen to benefit from Christ's salvation from the moment of her conception. The dogma emphasizes God's special care for the one who would be closest to Jesus.

The Assumption

Though not in Scripture, accounts of Mary's assumption or dormition were celebrated liturgically in the East since the fourth century and in the West from at least the sixth. The roots of the feast can be found in apocryphal works such as the *Liber Requiei Mariae* (Book of Mary's Repose) and the *Six Books Apocryphon of the Virgin Mary's Assumption and Dormition*, whose provenance is liturgical. A Syriac version of the latter from the sixth century transmits the *Protoevangelium of James* and *Infancy Gospel of Thomas*, making it a sort of "proto-*life* of the virgin," while the Greek original most probably dates to the fourth century.[24]

Pope Pius XII, again after consulting the bishops, defined the assumption of Mary as a dogma in 1950, teaching that "the Immaculate Mother of God, the ever Virgin Mary, having completed the course of her earthly life, was assumed body and soul into heavenly glory" (DS 3903). The pope left open the question of whether Mary actually experienced physical death, the position of the Eastern churches (Orthodox and Eastern Catholic), or was taken up into heaven before death, the position of many Roman Catholics. Pope John Paul II stated in 1997 that Mary experienced natural death.[25]

The dogma really is an affirmation that Mary shares fully in the resurrection of her son, and thus foreshadows the resurrection of all the faithful. But how and when that takes place remains mystery. Traditional teaching holds for an "intermediate state" between the death of the individual and the general resurrection of the dead at the end of time but has difficulty explaining how a soul separated from the body remains personal. Some argue that the resurrection takes place at the moment of an individual's death so that those who have been faithful, like Mary, share fully in the resurrection of Jesus. The CDF has rejected this view, reaffirming the traditional teaching on an intermediate state.[26] Joseph Ratzinger agrees, arguing that the belief in an intermediate state, inherited from Judaism, received

---

[24] See Stephen J. Shoemaker, "Apocrypha and Liturgy in the Fourth Century: The Case of the 'Six Books' Dormition Apocryphon," in *Jewish and Christian Scriptures*, ed. James H. Charlesworth and Lee M. McDonald (New York: T & T Clark, 2010), 156.

[25] John Paul II, "General Audience," June 25, 1997.

[26] CDF, "Letter on Certain Questions Concerning Eschatology," May 17, 1979, http://www.vatican.va/roman_curia/congregations/cfaith/documents/rc_con_cfaith_doc_19790517_escatologia_en.html; this view was amplified in the ITC 1992 document, "Some Current Questions in Eschatology," *Irish Theological Quarterly* 58 (1992): 209–39; for an extended discussion of the intermediate state see the US Lutheran-Roman Catholic Dialogue, "The Hope of Eternal Life," (2010), 6–16; http://www.usccb.org/seia/The-Hope-of-Eternal-Life.pdf.

systematic formulation in the High Middle Ages with its teaching on the immortality of the soul.[27] Rahner is less definitive; he points out that teaching on the intermediate state is only doctrine, not dogma, and so remains open to discussion by theologians.[28]

Conclusion

The idea that Christians share in the very life of God is expressed in various ways. Grace (*charis*) in the New Testament refers to God's favor, help, and salvation offered to us in Christ Jesus. Rahner describes it as God's free self-communication, while Roger Haight suggests a near equivalence of a theology of grace with that of the Holy Spirit. In a sense, the doctrine of the Holy Spirit makes grace more personal, pointing to the indwelling divine presence of the Spirit that gives us a share in the trinitarian life. The term *koinōnia* is also used in the New Testament to express our communion or sharing in God's life in Christ, in his body and blood, and from this union with the divine follows our communion with one another in the church.

The *communio sanctorum*, originally a communion in the holy things of the Eucharist, came to refer to the communion of all those in Christ, both living and dead. The third article of the Apostles' Creed, confessing belief in the Holy Spirit, followed by belief in the holy Catholic church and the communion of saints, is both pneumatological and ecclesiological; those united by the Spirit become one communion. For Irenaeus of Lyons, "where the Church is, there is the Spirit of God; and where the Spirit of God is, there is the Church, and every kind of grace."[29] From the beginning, the church was understood as including the prophets and saints of the first covenant.

Thus the doctrine of the communion of saints grounds the practice of invoking the saints and asking their intercession. If we and they share in God's life, then we share a common life with one another

---

[27] Joseph Ratzinger, *Eschatology: Death and Eternal Life*, 2nd ed. (Washington, DC: The Catholic University of America Press, 1988), 119–22.

[28] Karl Rahner, "The Intermediate State," in *Theological Investigations*, vol. 17 (New York: Crossroad, 1981), 114–15.

[29] Irenaeus, *Against the Heresies* 3.24.1.

and can ask their intercession. The early Christians had this sense of being one community, sharing in the divine life. They venerated the martyrs and prayed at their tombs. From at least the third century, they were directing prayers to Mary, the mother of Jesus, also called the Mother of God, and invoking the saints. Thus Catholic devotion to Mary has deep roots in the *sensus fidelium*.

The Reformers rejected the practice as lacking a biblical foundation; still more they objected to Catholic devotion to Mary as detracting from the role of Christ as the one mediator. Those from nonliturgical traditions generally interpret "communion of saints" in terms of the *congregatio fidelium*, the congregation of the faithful. While this is not incorrect theologically, it misses the deeper meaning of *koinōnia* found in Paul and the early church. The term means more than fellowship, with its connotation of good feeling and partnership. It carries the sense of a true communion in grace, life, and the transforming power of the Spirit.

For Further Reading

Saints

Anderson, H. George, J. Francis Stafford, and Joseph A. Burgess, eds. *The One Mediator, the Saints, and Mary.* Lutherans and Catholics in Dialogue 8. Minneapolis, MN: Augsburg Press, 1991.

Brown, Peter. *The Cult of the Saints: Its Rise and Function in Latin Christianity.* Chicago: University of Chicago Press, 1981.

Cunningham, Lawrence. *The Meaning of Saints.* San Francisco: Harper & Row, 1980.

Johnson, Elizabeth A. *Friends of God and Prophets: A Feminist Theological Reading of the Communion of Saints.* New York: Continuum, 1998. 77–78.

Rahner, Karl. "Why and How Can We Venerate the Saints?" *Theological Investigations,* Vol. 8. New York: Crossroad, 1983. 3–23.

Woodward, Kenneth. *Making Saints.* New York: Simon & Schuster, 1997.

Mary

Anglican-Roman Catholic International Commission. *Mary: Grace and Hope in Christ*. New York: Continuum, 2006.

Athans, Mary Christine. *In Quest of the Jewish Mary: The Mother of Jesus in History, Theology, and Spirituality*. Maryknoll, NY: Orbis Books, 2013.

Boss, Sarah Jane. *Mary: The Complete Resource*. Oxford: Oxford University Press, 2007.

Brown, Raymond E., Karl P. Donfried, Joseph A. Fitzmyer, and John Reumann, eds. *Mary in the New Testament*. Philadelphia, PA/New York: Fortress Press/Paulist Press, 1978.

Gebara, Ivone, and Maria Clara Bingemer. *Mary: Mother of God, Mother of the Poor*. Maryknoll, NY: Orbis Books, 1989.

Graef, Hilda. *Mary: A History of Doctrine and Devotion*, 2 vols. Westminster, MD: Christian Classics, 1985 (first published 1963).

John Paul II. *Redemptoris Mater*. Encyclical Letter on the Blessed Virgin Mary in the Life of the Pilgrim Church. 1987.

Johnson, Elizabeth A. *Truly Our Sister: A Theology of Mary in the Communion of Saints*. New York: Continuum, 2003.

Küng, Hans, and Jürgen Moltmann, eds. *Mary in the Churches. Concilium* 168. New York: Seabury Press, 1983.

Maunder, Chris, ed. *The Origins of the Cult of the Virgin Mary*. London: Burns & Oats, 2008.

Paul VI. "*Marialis Cultus.*" *The Pope Speaks* 19 (1974–1975): 49–87.

Perry, Tim S. *Mary for Evangelicals: Toward an Understanding of the Mother of Our Lord*. Downers Grove, IL: InterVarsity Academic, 2006.

Rahner, Karl. *Mother of the Lord*. New York: Herder & Herder, 1963.

Tavard, George H. *The Thousand Faces of the Virgin Mary*. Collegeville, MN: Liturgical Press, 1996.

Chapter 8

Church

The word "church" (*ekklēsia*) means literally "those called out," from the Greek *ek* and *kaleo*, thus "assembly." In a secular context, *ekklēsia* was used for an assembly or "calling out" of the citizens for some civic purpose. In the Septuagint, *ekklēsia* was used to translate the Hebrew *kahal*, meeting or assembly, or significantly taking on a religious connotation when used to translate the expression *kahal Yahweh*, or assembly of Yahweh, the formal or liturgical assembly of the people, most often in the temple for prayer. Paul often uses the expression "*ekklēsia* of God" (2 Cor 1:2; 10:32; Gal 1:13). The English word church derives from the German *kirche*, which in turn comes from the Greek *kuriakē oikia*, "belonging to the house of the Lord."

The church's origins lie in what scholars refer to today as the Jesus movement. We will consider that movement briefly, look at the beginnings of the church in the New Testament and the controversy over whether the church was originally one or many. Later we will look at the church in history, the church of Vatican II, and some unresolved ecclesiological issues.

The Jesus Movement

In the late 20s of first-century Palestinian Judaism, there were two popular movements—one of the Pharisees, the other of Jesus.[1] Jesus

---

[1] John P. Meier, *A Marginal Jew*, vol. 3: *Companions and Competitors* (New York: Doubleday, 2001), 639.

gathered a group of disciples not to learn his doctrine, as was the case with the disciples of the Pharisees, but to share in his ministry. He sent them forth to heal the sick, cast out demons, and proclaim that the reign of God was at hand (Mark 6:7-13; Luke 10:2-12). In the words of Terrence Tilley, for those in the Jesus movement, discipleship meant "living in and living out the reign of God by engaging in reconciling practices."[2]

It has long been characteristic of liberal theology to portray Jesus as a teacher of social ethics, thus driving a wedge between Jesus and the church. Typical was Alfred Loisy's often-repeated phrase, "Jesus preached the Kingdom of God and what came was the church."[3] But such a view is far too simple. Central to Jesus' ministry was a "gathering" of the scattered people of God, "as a hen gathers her young" (Matt 23:37; Luke 11:23). The theme appears in the Lord's Prayer, where the petition "hallowed be thy name" (Matt 6:9) echoes Ezekiel 26:19-28, where God makes holy his name in gathering Israel from among the nations.[4] Jesus used the metaphor of a new family not based on kinship, clan, or patriarchy but on those who do the will of God (Mark 3:33-35). His movement represented a reconstituted Israel, an eschatological Israel with "the Twelve" symbolizing the twelve tribes at its center. In all the accounts (Q may be an exception), Peter was the spokesman. Thus there was a fundamentally communal dimension to his movement; it was a people, a community.

This eschatological Israel was marked by certain characteristic ritual actions. One entered it through baptism, a washing with water practiced by the disciples and perhaps by Jesus himself in the early days of his ministry (John 3:22) and inherited from Jesus' time with John the Baptist. There was also the tradition of the meal, the continuation of Jesus' practice of table fellowship during his ministry but transformed by his words at the Last Supper and its continuation among the earliest Christians (cf. Luke 24:13-35). The further progress of this movement after Jesus' death and resurrection represents the

---

[2] Terrence W. Tilley, *The Disciples' Jesus: Christology as Reconciling Practice* (Maryknoll, NY: Orbis Books, 2008), 252.

[3] Alfred Loisy, *L'Evangile et l'Eglise* (Paris: Picard, 1902), 111.

[4] Gerhard Lohfink, *Jesus of Nazareth: What He Wanted, Who He Was* (Collegeville, MN: Liturgical Press, 2012), 59–71.

beginning of the church. As Daniel Harrington says, one can trace "continuities of belief, personnel, and practice between the group gathered around Jesus in his earthly ministry (the disciples) and the group gathered around the risen Lord (the church)."[5] In founding the eschatological "people of God," Jesus established what in the post-Easter community would be the church.

Churches in the New Testament

How can we envision the church of the New Testament? Certainly it was not a single community, monolithic in structure. Institutionalization was to come later, beginning toward the end of the New Testament period as the apostles and first disciples faded from the scene. But was it one church in different forms? Was it many churches? Or was it simply diverse?

One or Many?

Ernst Käsemann posed this question at an ecumenical symposium at Göttingen in Germany in 1951: Does the New Testament canon ground the unity of the church or the diversity of the churches? He argued that the extraordinary variety of theological positions evident in the canon, some of them mutually incompatible, does not constitute the foundation for the unity of the church but "provides the basis for the multiplicity of the confessions."[6]

Käsemann repeated his argument in an address to the WCC Fourth World Conference on Faith and Order at Montreal in July, 1963, arguing that the New Testament gave not a uniform ecclesiology but a series of ecclesiologies, Jewish-Christian, Hellenistic, Pauline,

---

[5] Daniel J. Harrington, *God's People in Christ* (Philadelphia, PA: Fortress Press, 1980), 29.

[6] Ernst Käsemann, "The Canon of the New Testament and the Unity of the Church," in Käsemann, *Essays on New Testament Themes* (London: SCM Press, 1964), 103; some like Bart D. Ehrman go beyond the canon to include other communities, usually considered heterodox; see his *Lost Christianities: The Battles for Scripture and the Faiths We Never Knew* (Oxford/New York: Oxford University Press, 2003).

"enthusiastic," Johannine, and "early Catholic."[7] His address was followed by another by Raymond Brown. Brown acknowledged the differences that could be found among the various New Testament writers, but he argued that there was a *"unity in belief* that is present in all stages of NT thought about the Church."[8] He pointed to three common elements: a consciousness of continuity with Israel; apostolicity, in the sense that the church from the beginning possessed some kind of organization based on the Twelve and the apostles in general; and that from its inception, the Christian community practiced baptism and shared in the Eucharist.

In a later book, Brown outlines a number of different New Testament ecclesial traditions: a Pauline heritage visible in the Pastoral Epistles, another Pauline heritage in Colossians and Ephesians, a different Pauline heritage in Luke/Acts, a Petrine heritage in 1 Peter, the heritage of the beloved disciple in the Fourth Gospel, a continuation of this in the Johannine epistles, and the heritage of Jewish/Gentile Christianity in Matthew.[9] Roger Haight, in his study of historical ecclesiology, argues that there was neither a single organization nor a plurality of isolated churches. "The early church is a pluralistic organization. On the one hand, the value of unity suffused the community wherever it existed and according to all of its historical witnesses. The metaphors for the unity of the church abound. On the other hand, it is hard to exaggerate the differences among the Christian communities that made up the early church."[10]

Writing toward the end of the first century, the author of the Acts of the Apostles offers a summary of ecclesial life at the end of his recounting of Peter's Pentecost sermon: "Those who accepted his message were baptized. . . . They devoted themselves to the teaching of the apostles and to the communal life (*koinōnia*), to the breaking of the bread (Luke's term for Eucharist) and to the prayers" (Acts

---

[7] Ernst Käsemann, "Unity and Diversity in New Testament Ecclesiology," *Novum Testamentum* 6 (1963): 295.

[8] Raymond E. Brown, "Unity and Diversity in New Testament Ecclesiology," *Novum Testamentum* 6 (1963): 302, emphasis in original.

[9] Raymond E. Brown, *The Churches the Apostles Left Behind* (New York: Paulist Press, 1984).

[10] Roger Haight, *Christian Community in History*, vol. 1: *Historical Ecclesiology* (New York: Continuum, 2004), 132–33.

2:41-42). What constitutes ecclesial life? At its heart one finds baptism, the apostolic teaching or tradition, communal life, Eucharist, and prayer.

While the New Testament uses various images to describe the church, among them the bride of Christ, the vine and the branches, the family of God, and the flock, three images predominate.

People of God

Though predicated explicitly of Christians only once (1 Pet 2:10), the awareness of the church as the People of God, the renewed or eschatological Israel, is implicit throughout the New Testament. The church begins as a movement within Judaism, and some of the early Christians remained within the Jewish community until a break came toward the end of the century, driven by the increasing number of Gentile converts and the Pharisees' efforts to redefine Judaism after the destruction of the temple (70 BCE). Resentment over eventual efforts to exclude Christian Jews from the synagogue is reflected in the anti-Jewish polemic in John (cf. 9:22) and Matthew. Paul presupposes the continuity of his converts with Israel, referring to them as baptized into Moses in the cloud and the sea and partaking of the same spiritual food and drink (1 Cor 10:1-5). His letter to the Galatians explains how traditional divisions between Jews and Gentiles have been broken down through faith in Christ and baptism (Gal 3:7-29).

The first letter of Peter adopts the language of Exodus, telling the largely Gentile Christians of Asia Minor that they are "a chosen race, a royal priesthood, a holy nation, a people of his own" (1 Pet 2:9; cf. Exod 19:6). The letter to the Hebrews parallels Israel as the people of God, with the church as the new people of God, with the priesthood and sacrifice of Christ superseding the levitical priesthood, temple sacrifice, and cult, though Hebrews should not be read as suggesting a supercessionist approach to Judaism.

Body of Christ

Paul's most powerful metaphor is the Body of Christ. Used to refer to a political or social body, Paul gives "body" a theological meaning in his first letter to the Corinthians, linking it to the ecclesial and eucharistic bodies. Written to bring together a community fractured into parties or divisions, he reminds the Corinthians that they have been united into the one body of Christ by baptism (1 Cor 12:12-13) and their sharing in the Eucharist (1 Cor 10:16-17). He develops the metaphor of the church in its diversity by comparing it to the human body with all its different members, concluding that "you are Christ's body, and individually parts of it" (1 Cor 12:27; cf. Rom 12:4-5). Colossians and Ephesians further develop the metaphor in terms of Christ as the head of his body the church (Col 1:18; 2:19; Eph 5:23), now understood in a universal sense. The theology of the body of Christ means, as Pope Benedict says in his encyclical *Deus Caritas Est*, "I cannot possess Christ just for myself; I can belong to him only in union with all those who have become, or who will become, his own" (no. 14).

Temple of the Spirit

A third metaphor is Temple of the Spirit. Paul's vision of the church is fundamentally charismatic; he sees the church as a Spirit-filled community, rich in a diversity of members, gifts, and ministries. The letter to the Ephesians, most probably Deutero-Pauline, describes the church as "The household of God, built upon the foundation of the apostles and prophets, with Christ Jesus himself as the capstone. Through him the whole structure is held together and grows into a temple sacred in the Lord; in him you also are being built together into a dwelling place of God in the Spirit" (Eph 2:19-22).

In the Acts of the Apostles, it is the Spirit that dominates. Bestowed on those baptized (Acts 2:38; 8:16-18; 9:17), the Spirit is manifested in tongues and prophecy (10:46; 19:6) and enables the leaders of the church of Jerusalem, the "apostles and presbyters," to reach a decision about Gentile converts and the Mosaic Law (Acts 15:28). John's Gospel presents the church as a community of disciples guided by the Spirit; one does not find here the emphasis on developing structures of authority evident in other, even earlier New Testament documents. This later led to problems; according to Ray Brown, the "Paraclete-centered ecclesiology" led to a schism in the later Johannine communities, with the larger part of the community moving in the direction of Gnosticism.[11]

---

[11] Raymond E. Brown, *The Community of the Beloved Disciple* (New York: Paulist Press, 1979), 146–49.

Koinōnia/*Communion*

Most important for contemporary ecclesiology is the recovery of the concept of *koinōnia*, Latin *communio*, English communion or fellowship. As we have seen in chapter 7, *koinōnia* can be used in a soteriological, ecclesial, and sacramental sense, providing the foundation for understanding the church as a communion of the faithful in the life of the triune God and with one another. As Ludwig Hertling shows in his classic study, communion was expressed in the post–New Testament church through visible signs such as eucharistic hospitality, letters of communion, communion among the bishops themselves, and as early as the third century, communion with the bishop of Rome.[12]

Other signs of communion included the participating of several bishops in the ordination of a new bishop to indicate that he and his church were in communion with the other bishops and churches and the sending of the *fermentum* or particle of bread from the bishop's Eucharist to the priests or bishops of neighboring churches to be consumed at their liturgies as a sign of communion.[13] This practice, mentioned by Irenaeus (c. 202), may well have originated in Rome. This ecclesial meaning of the Eucharist is still strong in Aquinas, who taught that the reality (*res*) of the sacrament was the unity of the mystical body.[14] Since the 1961 WCC New Delhi Assembly, *koinōnia* has been used ecumenically to express how the life and unity of the church is to be understood, most recently in the 2013 WCC statement, *The Church: Towards a Common Vision*, no. 13.[15]

The Church in History

Toward the end of the New Testament period, the various churches began to formalize their structures. With the apostles and original witnesses gone from the scene, the churches began going through a

[12] Ludwig Hertling, *Communio: Church and Papacy in Early Christianity* (Chicago: Loyola University Press, 1972), 23–36.

[13] Archdale A. King, *Eucharistic Reservation in the Western Church* (London: A. R. Mowbray, 1965), 8–9.

[14] Aquinas, *Summa Theologica*, III, q. 73, a. 3.

[15] World Council of Churches, *The Church: Towards a Common Vision*, Faith and Order Paper no. 214 (Geneva: WCC, 2013).

process of institutionalization that was to give the church the organization that would keep it united through the centuries that followed.

Early Catholicism

Lutheran New Testament scholar Ernst Käsemann has called the process of church institutionalization "early Catholicism," which he defines as "that transition from earliest Christianity to the so-called ancient Church, which is completed with the disappearance of the imminent expectation."[16] He points to a number of developments, evident in the "early Catholic" writings such as Colossians and Ephesians, 1 and 2 Timothy, Acts, Jude, 2 Peter, the Johannine letters, as well as noncanonical works from the same period such as 1 Clement (c. 96) and the letters of Ignatius of Antioch (110), reflective of a more Catholic understanding of the church. They include an emphasis on "Catholic" structures—the threefold ministry, ordination, and the teaching responsibility of pastors in apostolic succession. Käsemann, who favors a more charismatic structuring of the church, rejects these developments as an effort to limit grace, binding the Spirit to an institutionalized office.[17]

This period also shows the office of the presbyter/bishops in the process of developing into the traditional threefold office of bishop, presbyters (from which the English word "priest" and its cognates are derived), and deacons; it is in place at Antioch by the end of the first century, and by the end of the second it had become almost universal in the church, described by Bishop Ignatius of Antioch as early as 110 as "catholic" (*katholikē*), meaning whole or universal (*Smyrneans* 8:2). Catholics, Orthodox, and Anglicans see these developments as the work of the Spirit.

The Great Church

As Christianity grew, the different ecclesial traditions visible in the New Testament began to take on the common features of one great

---

[16] Ernst Käsemann, "Paul and Early Catholicism," in *New Testament Questions of Today* (London: SCM Press, 1969), 237.

[17] Ibid., 245–48.

church constituted by a communion of local churches. By the second century, the church had the beginning of a liturgical calendar, with Sunday, the Lord's Day, and the Pasch, the annual celebration of Christ's death and resurrection. Hegesippus (c. 180), Irenaeus (d. c. 200), and Tertullian (c. 200) pointed to lists of bishops from churches that claimed apostolic foundation to show that these churches were in visible continuity with the apostolic church. By the end of the second century, bishops were recognized as successors to the apostles and authoritative teachers.[18] Each church had a bishop, assisted by presbyters and deacons, the rituals of baptism and Eucharist, and a collection of sacred writings. An interrogatory baptismal confession from the church of Rome, dating from the last decades of the second century, developed into the Apostles' Creed. The church was composed of local communities around the Mediterranean, with diverse theological and liturgical traditions and a strong sense of unity among themselves. The patriarchates of Jerusalem, Antioch, Alexandria, Constantinople, and Rome emerged as local centers of authority, while by the late fourth century, Rome's primacy of honor was widely recognized.

By the year 300, there were as many as six million Christians in the empire, perhaps 10 percent of the overall population. After the conversion of Constantine, the church began to play an important role in society. In 325, anxious to unify his empire, he invited the bishops to assembly at Nicaea to deal with the heterodox teaching of Arius; more than two hundred showed up, mostly from the Greek-speaking East, but also some from Southern Italy, Gaul, Armenia, Persia, and representatives of the bishop of Rome. Nicaea's creed or confession of faith, slightly revised by the Council of Constantinople (381), became the most widely used Christian creed. As early as the middle of the third century, the bishop of Rome was being recognized as having an unparalleled authority, at least in the West. By the late fourth century, Roman bishops began to see themselves as successors of Peter, the chief of the apostles, and appealed to his authority. At the same time, as Rome diminished in political power, the popes had to take on political responsibilities, ruling over lands that came to be

---

[18] See Francis A. Sullivan, *From Apostles to Bishops: The Development of the Episcopacy in the Early Church* (New York: Paulist Press, 2001), 229.

known as the Papal States. Pope Gregory the Great (590–604), who some consider the first medieval pope, saw the expansion of Christianity over the Alps, into Europe.[19]

The Gregorian Reform, begun by Pope Gregory VII (1073–1085) did much to renew church life by addressing abuses such as simony (the selling of church offices and benefices), lay investiture (the appointment of bishops, abbots, and other officials by feudal lords or kings), and strengthening clerical celibacy, but it also led to a centralization of power in an increasingly powerful papacy. Ghislain Lafont describes what he calls the Gregorian form of the church, based on three axes, a concern for the primacy of truth as it relates to salvation, the primacy of the pope to defend the truth, and a holy and continent priesthood charged with the pastoral care of the faithful. He sees this form as lasting until the Second Vatican Council.[20]

Divisions in the Church

The communion so important to the life of the church and the churches has often been lost in the course of church history. The first divisions came as early as the fifth century, when some of the ancient churches found themselves unable to accept the developing christological doctrine of the early councils: the Nestorian Church of the East after the Council of Ephesus (431) and the Copts in Egypt and the Armenians after Chalcedon (451). In 1054, developing tensions between Rome and Constantinople resulted in a break between the Eastern churches and the Latin West that has never been healed.

The Reformation in the sixteenth century led to the emergence of several new traditions, the Lutheran in Germany and Scandinavia, the Reformed or Calvinist in Switzerland, France, the Netherlands, and later Scotland, and the Anglican in England. The Reformation's left wing saw the emergence of the more radical Anabaptist communities, among them the Swiss Brethren, the Hutterites in Moravia, and the Dutch Mennonites. These Anabaptist communities, often

---

[19] Robert Louis Wilken, *The First Thousand Years: A Global History of Christianity* (New Haven, CT: Yale University Press, 2012), 171.

[20] Ghislain Lafont, *Imagining the Catholic Church: Structured Communion in the Spirit* (Collegeville, MN: Liturgical Press, 2000), 37–64.

peace churches, sought not so much to renew the church but to restore Christian life on the model of the church of the New Testament. From the Reformation came different ecclesiologies and polities, episcopal, presbyteral, congregational, and free church as well as countless denominations.

The Church of Vatican I

The First Vatican Council (1869–1870), called by Pope Pius IX, was in large part a reaction to the Enlightenment attack on church author-ity as well as to the French Revolution. Because of the outbreak of the Franco-Prussian War, the council was adjourned prematurely on October 20, 1870, and thus remained incomplete. Its intended Dog-matic Constitution on the Church, *Pastor Aeternus*, succeeded only in defining papal primacy and papal infallibility, though the first draft of the constitution would have enshrined the notion of the church as a perfect society, with its constitution conferred by the Lord himself.[21] It is important to note that the constitution speaks of infal-libility as a gift of the church, not a personal possession of the pope, though it could be exercised by the pope under limited circumstances in defining a doctrine to be held by the universal church.

Avery Dulles has described the view of the church that found its clearest expression at Vatican I as an institutional ecclesiology. Divid-ing the church into three powers and functions, teaching, sanctifying, and governing, all in the hands of the bishops, it led to further dis-tinctions between the church teaching (*ecclesia docens*) and the church taught (*ecclesia discens*), the church sanctifying and church sanctified, the church governing and the church governed.[22] For example, in his encyclical addressed to the people of France, *Vehementer Nos* (1906), Pope Pius X, using language from Gratian's decretals (1140), defined the church as a fundamentally unequal society:

> It follows that the Church is essentially an *unequal* society, that is, a society comprising two categories of persons, the Pastors and

[21] See Avery Dulles, *Models of the Church* (New York: Doubleday, 1974), 33; see also "The First Draft of the Constitution on the Church," chap. 3 in *The Teaching of the Catholic Church*, Josef Neuner and Heinrich Roos (Staten Island, NY: Alba House, 1967), 213–14.

[22] Ibid., 34.

the flock, those who occupy a rank in the different degrees of the hierarchy and the multitude of the faithful. So distinct are these categories that with the pastoral body only rests the necessary right and authority for promoting the end of the society and directing all its members toward that end; the one duty of the multitude is to allow themselves to be led, and, like a docile flock, to follow the Pastors. (no. 8)

The Church of Vatican II

The Second Vatican Council (1962–1965) ranks among three great reforming movements in the church's history, along with the Gregorian Reform in the eleventh century and the Reformation in the sixteenth.[23] It also marked the transformation of a church largely of Europe and North America into a world church.[24] Others speak today of a globalization of the church, with the center of gravity shifting from the North to the global South. It is estimated that by 2050, 75 percent of the world's Catholics will live south of the equator. Ecclesiology today must attend to the tensions that will result from these global shifts and what the experience of the new churches of Africa and Asia, many of them neopentecostal, might mean for ecclesiology.

From the beginning of the discussion at the council's first session, it was evident that the ecclesiology found in the schema on the church prepared by the Theological Commission, entitled *De Ecclesia*, was not going to be acceptable to the council fathers. In their interventions, the bishops objected to the schema's use of Cardinal Bellarmine's (1542–1621) description of the church as a "perfect society" and its exclusive identification of the mystical body of Christ with the Roman Catholic Church, as Pope Pius XII had done in his 1943 encyclical *Mystici Corporis* (nos. 13, 22). In his intervention, Cardinal Liénart stressed that the church was a mystery. Bishop Emile de Smedt of Bruges criticized the schema for its triumphalism, clericalism, and juridical approach. Cardinal Suenens suggested that the schema be

---

[23] John W. O'Malley, *Tradition and Transition: Historical Perspectives on Vatican II* (Wilmington, DE: Michael Glazier, 1988), 17.

[24] Karl Rahner, "Towards a Fundamental Theological Interpretation of Vatican Council II," *Theological Studies* 40 (1979): 718.

redrafted, reminding the fathers that the church should reflect Christ as the "light of the nations." Cardinal Montini seconded his proposal. Finally, Cardinal Lecaro, speaking on behalf of many of the Latin Americans, urged the council to speak of the church as the "church of the poor," a theme Pope John XXIII had mentioned in his radio address to the assembling bishops on September 11 as the council opened. After Lecaro's address, the pope called for a revision of the schema.[25]

On June 3, 1963, Pope John XXIII died. He was succeeded by Giovanni Montini, Cardinal Archbishop of Milan, who took the name Paul VI. Montini had already shown himself to be on the side of re-form and immediately began to play an active role in moving the council forward. At the beginning of the second session, the fathers received a second draft of the schema, very different from the first. Though the fathers remained divided, a vote on October 30 showed a strong majority in favor of recognizing the episcopacy as the highest level of the sacrament of orders, the inclusion of a bishop into the episcopal college by consecration, the succession of the college to that of the apostles, and their exercise of full and supreme power in the church with the pope by divine right.

When the fathers returned for the third session, the new draft of the schema on the church, now known by the title Dogmatic Constitution on the Church, or as Cardinal Suenens had suggested, *Lumen Gentium*, was a very different document. When the minority contin-ued to protest, Pope Paul was forced to intervene. The pope reminded them that Vatican I had addressed primacy and infallibility but had been unable to complete its work by developing a theology of the episcopal office. *Lumen Gentium* sought to do just that. We need to consider some of the key themes of the constitution.

Image of the Church

Instead of the perfect society model of church which dominated at Vatican I, describing the church in terms of its structures and hi-erarchy, *Lumen Gentium* describes the church as a sacrament, mystery,

[25] See Xavier Rynne, *Vatican Council II* (New York: Farrar, Straus and Giroux, 1968), 109–34.

body of Christ, people of God, and pilgrim church. It could be argued that its dominant model was people of God, developed in chapter 2 of the constitution. The model introduces an element of historicity; the church is real people journeying together toward an eschatological future (LG 9). Church as sacrament (LG 1) sees the church as a sign and instrument of the union of all humanity with God and one another, relating it to the kingdom of God. Mystery points to the church as a sharing in the divine life (chap. 1); it can never be reduced to its structure. Body of Christ underlines the church's eucharistic nature (LG 3, 7). People of God stresses the unity and equality of all the baptized, constituted as a holy priesthood (LG 10), sharing in Christ's threefold office as prophet, priest, and king (LG 31), and by their anointing by the Holy One, partaking implicitly in the church's infallibility (LG 12; 25). The image of a pilgrim church (chap. 7) suggests a church still on the way that "will attain its full perfection" only in heaven (LG 48).

Teaching on the Episcopate

Most significant was the council's teaching on the episcopal office. Bishops together with the pope govern the house of the living God (LG 18); they do this not by delegation but by divine institution (LG 20), reversing the idea that the pope is the source of all power. Episcopal consecration confers the fullness of the sacrament of orders, and with it the office of sanctifying, teaching, and governing, though these offices can only be exercised in hierarchical communion with the head and members of the college (LG 21). As the apostles constituted one apostolic college, so the bishops as their successors constitute a college or body in communion with the Roman Pontiff (LG 22). "The individual bishops . . . are the visible principle and foundation of unity in their particular churches, fashioned after the model of the universal church, in and from which churches comes into being the one and only Catholic Church" (LG 23). Thus they are not vicars of the pope but "vicars and ambassadors of Christ" who govern the particular churches entrusted to them (LG 27).

Lumen Gentium went a long way toward retrieving the way bishops were understood in the first millennium. In formally teaching that the bishops shared with the pope in the governance of the church, the council underlined that the church was not a single, monolithic institution. Nor was it a papal monarchy but a communion of churches, each governed by a bishop, providing a foundation for the theology of communion (*koinōnia*) that would prove so fruitful in the postconciliar church. Pope John Paul II once referred to ecumenical councils, synods of bishops, and national or regional episcopal conferences, as "instruments of collegiality," [26] though their exercise was carefully controlled. In including the bishops in the exercise of the church's charism of infallibility, implicit in Vatican I, the council reinterpreted that council's one-sided emphasis on the role of the pope, and the laity were implicitly included in the references to the inability of the whole body of the faithful to err in matters of belief when they are united in matters of faith and morals (LG 12; cf. LG 25).

Particularly important in this regard is a 2014 statement of the International Theological Commission, titled *The Sensus Fidei in the Life of the Church*. The statement argues that the faithful "are not merely passive recipients of what the hierarchy teaches and theologians explain; rather, they are living and active subjects within the Church" (no. 67). They play a role in the development of doctrine, sometimes when bishops and theologians have been divided on an issue (no. 72) and in the development of the church's moral teaching (no. 73). This means that the old distinction between the church teaching (*ecclesia docens*) and the church taught (*ecclesia discens*), where the church teaching was identified exclusively with the hierarchy, is no longer theologically appropriate. The statement points to the need for ways that the magisterium can consult the faithful (no. 74) and for principles to distinguish the true *sensus fidelium* from mere majority opinion and affirms that separated Christians also participate in some manner in the *sensus fidei*, suggesting the Catholic Church might have something to learn from other churches.

Relation to Other Churches

According to the schema *De Ecclesia*, "The Roman Catholic Church is the Mystical Body of Christ . . . and only the one that is Roman

---

[26] *L'Osservatore Romano*, September 17–18, 1979; cited by Charles M. Murphy, "Collegiality: An Essay Toward Better Understanding," *Theological Studies* 46 (1985): 41.

Catholic has the right to be called church."[27] This exclusive language was not something new; it appeared also in two encyclicals of Pope Pius XII, *Mystici Corporis* and *Humani Generis* (1950). But it was criticized by the council fathers. The 1963 text modified it somewhat, asserting that "many elements of sanctification can be found outside its total structure," things that properly belong to the church of Christ. But the 1964 text that became *Lumen Gentium* revised it even more; it changed the phrase "[this] one Church of Christ . . . constituted and organized in the world as a society, *is* the Catholic Church" to this one church of Christ *subsists* in the Catholic Church (LG 8). In other words, the council was no longer claiming a exclusive equation between the church of Christ and the Catholic Church. This also suggested that while the church of Christ was fully present in the Catholic Church, some ecclesial reality was present in those referred to as ecclesial communities; in the words of the official commission responsible for the Decree on Ecumenism, "In these communities the one sole Church of Christ is present, albeit imperfectly . . . and by means of their ecclesiastical elements the Church of Christ is in some way operative in them."[28]

This language was tightened in the 2000 declaration *Dominus Iesus*; while recognizing those churches that had preserved the apostolic succession as true particular churches in which the church of Christ is present, it argued that "the ecclesial communities which have not preserved the valid Episcopate and the genuine and integral substance of the Eucharistic mystery, are not Churches in the proper sense," though according to Sullivan, the mind of the commission responsible for the Decree on Ecumenism was that those Western communities that lack the full reality of the Eucharist still have an ecclesial character and are analogous to particular churches of the Catholic Church.[29] Echoing *Unitatis Redintegratio* no. 3, *Dominus Iesus* went on to say that "those who are baptized in these communities are, by Baptism, incorporated in Christ and thus are in a certain communion, albeit imperfect, with the Church" (no. 17).

---

[27] *Acta Synodalia Concilii Vaticani II* (Vatican City: 1970), 1/4, 15; cited by Francis A. Sullivan in *The Church We Believe In* (New York: Paulist Press, 1988), 23.

[28] Ibid., AS 3/2, 335; cited by Sullivan, *The Church We Believe In*, 32.

[29] Sullivan, *The Church We Believe In*, 32.

Teaching on the Laity

Lumen Gentium also took a number of significant steps toward developing a theology of the laity. It placed chapter 2, which describes the church as the people of God, before chapter 3, on the hierarchy, underlining the fundamental equality and dignity of all the baptized. It also emphasized that the whole church was called to holiness (chap. 5). Both the baptized and the ordained share in the one priesthood of Christ, though in different ways (LG 10). Most important, it retrieved the *charismata* or spiritual gifts, "both hierarchic and charismatic" (LG 4; cf. 12; 30), thus stressing the laity's share in the charismatic structure of the church. Finally, it began using, though somewhat tentatively, ministry language in regard to the laity. It did so some nineteen times.[30]

Chapter 4 teaches that laymen and laywomen also share in their own way in Christ's priestly, prophetic, and kingly functions; their vocation is to "seek the kingdom of God by engaging in temporal affairs" and to carry out for their own part the mission of the whole Christian people in the church and in the world (LG 31). While an older language described the laity as cooperators in the apostolic tasks proper to the hierarchy, the apostolate of the laity is "a participation in the salvific mission of the Church itself. Through their baptism and confirmation, all are commissioned to that apostolate by the Lord Himself" (LG 33). They can also be called to more direct cooperation in the apostolate of the hierarchy, exercising certain church functions (LG 33), and "if some of them have to fulfill their religious duties on their own, when there are no sacred ministers or in times of persecution; and even if many of them devote all their energies to apostolic work; still it remains for each one of them to cooperate in the external spread and the dynamic growth of the Kingdom of Christ in the world" (LG 35). This somewhat hesitant language was to lead to the explosion of lay ministry in the postconciliar church.

---

[30] See Elissa Rinere, "Conciliar and Canonical Applications of 'Ministry' to the Laity," *The Jurist* 47 (1987): 205.

The Mission of the Church

The postconciliar years saw a clarification of how the church understood its mission. Pre–Vatican II ecclesiology tended to distinguish between the natural and supernatural mission of the church; the natural was to contribute toward building up a just society by practicing the works of mercy, while the supernatural end was to save souls. This kind of dualism can still be seen in *Gaudium et Spes* (no. 42), but the church's understanding of its mission was already changing by the council's reclaiming the importance of evangelization, a term previously associated with Protestants rather than Catholics. As Avery Dulles has pointed out, Vatican I used the word "gospel" only once, while Vatican II mentioned it 157 times, *evangelizations* thirty-one times, and *evangelize* eighteen times.[31] Furthermore, according to the council's Decree on the Mission Activity of the Church, "The pilgrim Church is missionary by her very nature" (AG 2).

But evangelization means more than proclaiming the Gospel to nonbelievers; for Catholics, it now has a richer sense of witnessing to the reign of God through respectful dialogue with representatives of other religious traditions and working for social justice. The 1971 Synod of Bishops on Justice in the World taught that "action on behalf of justice and participation in the transformation of the world fully appear to us as a constitutive dimension of the preaching of the Gospel, or, in other words, of the Church's mission for the redemption of the human race and its liberation from every oppressive situation" (no. 6). In his 1975 apostolic letter, *Evangelii Nutiandi*, Pope Paul VI emphasized that not just individuals but also cultures need to be evangelized, and he stressed that evangelization and liberation are linked because the person "who is to be evangelized is not an abstract being but is subject to social and economic questions" (no. 31). Liberation theology sees the church as the sacrament of historical liberation, as sign and servant of the reign of God, and as people of God,

---

[31] Avery Dulles, "John Paul II and the New Evangelization—What Does It Mean?" in *John Paul and the New Evangelization*, ed. Ralph Martin and Peter Williamson (San Francisco: Ignatius Press, 1995), 26; see also Stephen B. Bevans, "Revisiting Mission at Vatican II: Theology and Practice for Today's Missionary Church," *Theological Studies* 74, no. 2 (2013): 261–83.

submitting its structures, norms, institutional realities, and ministries to the reign of God.[32]

With Pope John Paul II and Pope Benedict XVI, evangelization moved to the center of the church's understanding of its mission, particularly what John Paul called the "new evangelization," calling home to the church those who have lost a living sense of their faith. Pope Francis, for his part, seems to be moving beyond this traditional understanding of the new evangelization; in his 2013 encyclical *Evangelii Gaudium*, he likes to speak of the church as a "community of missionary disciples" (no. 24) and has sought to reposition the church's missionary outreach to the peripheries (no. 20), though he continues to insist like his predecessors that "evangelization is first and foremost about preaching the Gospel to *those who do not know Jesus Christ or who have always rejected him*," not by proselytizing but by attraction (no. 15). Evangelization is Christ centered, not church centered.

Contemporary Ecclesiologies

Models of the Church

In his groundbreaking book *Models of the Church*, Avery Dulles proposed five models to characterize different ecclesiologies.[33] The institution model, dominant in Catholic theology from the Reformation to Vatican II, saw the church as a "perfect society," defined in terms of its visible, hierarchical structures. Given classic expression by Robert Bellarmine (1542–1621), the bonds of union for the church were external, based on union in doctrine, authority, and sacraments. While it gave Catholics a clear sense of identity, its approach was rigid, authoritarian, clerical, and not open to ecumenism.

The mystical communion model, with roots in the church fathers, the Tübingen school's Johann Adam Möhler, and the theology of Yves

---

[32] Alvaro Quiroz Magaña, "Ecclesiology in Liberation Theology," in *Systematic Theology: Perspectives from Liberation Theology*, ed. Jon Sobrino and Ignacio Ellacuría (Maryknoll, NY: Orbis Books, 1996), 185–90.

[33] Avery Dulles, *Models of the Church*, Expanded ed. (Garden City, NY: Doubleday, 1987).

Congar, Jerome Hamer, and Vatican II saw the church as the people of God, with interior bonds of *communio* that were more important than external, juridical structures. While its emphasis on community was very contemporary, it can slight organizational elements, does not support a clear sense of mission, and risks romanticizing the church as an ideal community.

The church as sacrament sees the church as the sacrament of Christ and the union of all humankind, thus defining the church in terms of its visible, symbolic elements. It successfully integrates the inner and outer aspects of the church—its institutional and symbolic dimensions—and mediates between the institutional and mystical communion models. But it runs the risk of a narrow sacramentalism, a loss of a vital sense of mission, and it finds little response in Protestant thought.

The model of the church as herald is a kerygmatic model, based on its mission of proclaiming the Gospel. Typical of much Protestant ecclesiology, it is strongly congregational; it sees each local community as fully church, gathered in response to the preaching of the Word of God. Representative theologians include Martin Luther, Karl Barth, Rudolph Bultmann, and Hans Küng. The basic bond of unity is faith, while the church's mission is proclamation; sacraments are "visible words." Its congregational approach risks making the local congregation completely self-sufficient; it tends to reduce soteriology to an individual message of salvation and, in more conservative congregations, denies saving grace to those who do not come to faith in Christ.

The church as servant reflects a liberation theology model of church. The role of the church is service, its bond of union is the sense of communion and solidarity of those working for justice, often cutting across denominational boundaries. Ministry is seen as working for change and liberation. While it relates the church to the world, it lacks direct biblical foundation and risks secularizing ecclesiology, while its regnocentric approach reduces the church's mission to the transformation of society.

In the expanded edition of his book, Dulles proposed a sixth model, that of the church as a community of disciples. Rooted in the earthly ministry of Jesus and his establishing an alternative society or eschatological Israel, founded on his disciples with "the Twelve" at the center, the model can mediate between the institutional and community models, remaining bound to the church's worship and sacramental life. None of the models Dulles offers is fully adequate for describing the church, while each brings out important dimensions.

Ecclesiology from Below

Recently, some theologians have proposed doing ecclesiology "from below," ruling out in advance the idea that there is one exclusive, God-given form of the church. Building on the work of Friedrich Schleiermacher, Roger Haight seeks to develop a transdenominational ecclesiology, one that begins with history, building on the aspects of ecclesial existence that all Christians share in common.[34] With reference to the work of Bernard Lonergan, Paul Lakeland argues for an "inductive" ecclesiology, one that begins not from some ideal, Platonic definition of church but rather with all those places that claim the name church. Lonergan would call such an ecclesiology empirical. "Ecclesiology from above always excludes; from below, it seeks to include."[35] Gerard Mannion provides an example of such an ecclesiology in his *Ecclesiology and Postmodernity*.[36]

But such a broadly inclusive approach is not quite as open as it might seem; it does not disregard the tradition. Both Haight and Lakeland stress the centrality of the Eucharist. Lakeland says unequivocally, "Without the Eucharist we have no Church," while Haight points approvingly to the 1982 World Council of Church's *Baptism, Eucharist and Ministry* (*BEM*) statement's common apostolic understanding of the Eucharist "as the central act of the church's worship."[37] According to *BEM*, it is "appropriate" that the Eucharist should take place at least every Sunday (Eucharist, no. 31). This will be a challenge in the Global South, where 70 percent of the world's

---

[34] Roger Haight, *Christian Community in History*, vol. 3: *Ecclesial Existence* (New York: Continuum, 2008), 10–27, 28–30.

[35] Paul Lakeland, *Church: Engaging Theology: Catholic Perspectives* (Collegeville, MN: Liturgical Press, 2009), 120–26, at 121.

[36] Gerard Mannion, *Ecclesiology and Postmodernity* (Collegeville, MN: Liturgical Press, 2007).

[37] Lakeland, *Church*, 179; Haight, *Ecclesial Existence*, 3:210; see also World Council of Churches, *Baptism, Eucharist and Ministry* (Geneva: WCC, 1982), Eucharist, no. 1.

Christians live today. Many of their churches are evangelical, Pentecostal, and neopentecostal; they are seldom eucharistic communities.

WCC on the Church

On June 21, 2012, the World Council of Churches' Faith and Order Standing Commission unanimously approved as a convergence (not consensus) statement *The Church: Towards a Common Vision*.[38] This and the 1982 WCC *Baptism, Eucharist and Ministry* text may be the two most significant ecumenical documents since the Second Vatican Council's Decree on Ecumenism. Structured in terms of four ecclesiological issues, the relatively brief text treats successively the church's essentially missionary origin, its nature as a communion, its growth toward the kingdom, and its relation to the world.

Chapter 1 sees the church's origin in the saving activity of the Trinity. Visible unity is important for the nature and mission of the church, a point that is emphasized repeatedly. Visible unity may require in some instances changes in doctrine, practice, and ministry so that the churches may recognize in each other the "one, holy, catholic, apostolic Church" (no. 9). Chapter 2 stresses the nature of the church as a communion. While diversity is a gift of the Lord (no. 28), the unity and catholicity of the church means that each local church should be in communion with all the other local churches (no. 31).

Chapter 3 focuses on the church growing in communion toward visible unity: this requires "communion in the fullness of the apostolic faith; in sacramental life; in a truly one and mutually recognized ministry; in structures of conciliar relations and decision-making; and in common witness and service to the world" (no. 37), though many differences remain about the number of the sacraments or ordinances, who presides at the Eucharist, how ordained ministry is structured and whether it is restricted to males, the authority of councils, and the role of the bishop of Rome.

Chapter 4 underlines the missional nature of the church. Participating in the Divine Mystery, the church serves God's plan for the transformation of the world. It proclaims the Gospel, celebrates the

---

[38] World Council of Churches, *The Church: Towards a Common Vision.*

sacraments, and in manifesting the newness of life given by Christ, anticipates the kingdom already present in him (no. 58), though it acknowledges a need of the churches to be accountable to each other because of new conflicts over moral principles and ethical questions (no. 63).

The WCC text on a common vision of the church is significant for a number of reasons. First, it presents a transdenominational ecclesiology that should find resonances in the different churches. Second, sharing a trinitarian faith, each church is called to living in visible unity with other Christian communities, and each has a structure, consisting of apostolic faith, sacramental life, and a recognized ministry. The centrality of the Eucharist in the text is remarkable; it clearly sees the church as a eucharistic community. At the same time, it has been criticized as being too traditional and excessively Western in its approach. If Christianity is diminishing in the West, it is flourishing in Asia, Africa, and Latin America (usually referred to as the Global South) where two-thirds of the world's Christians are living today.[39] The WCC text does not deal adequately with the different ecclesial experiences of the new churches of Asia and Africa, many of them neopentecostal and nonliturgical.[40]

Some Unresolved Issues

While divisions among the bishops at Vatican II surfaced in the debates on the floor of the council, the majority of the documents passed with virtual unanimity. A few issues remained unresolved or called for further development, while others surfaced by the council's hope for reform continued to be debated in the postconciliar church. Here we can mention only a few.

---

[39] Philip Jenkins, *The Next Christendom: The Coming of Global Christianity* (Oxford: Oxford University Press, 2002), 6–7.

[40] See Thomas P. Rausch, "Towards a Common Vision of the Church: Will It Fly?" *Journal of Ecumenical Studies* 50, no. 2 (Spring 2015): 265–85; Veli-Matti Kärkkäinen's *An Introduction to Ecclesiology: Ecumenical, Historical and Global Perspectives* (Downers Grove, IL: InterVarsity, 2002) is one study that takes the churches of Asia, Africa, and Latin America seriously.

Eucharistic Hospitality

Massimo Faggioli has argued convincingly that Vatican II's *Sacrosanctum Concilium*, the Constitution on the Liturgy, was the real ecclesiological heart of the council, with its vision of a eucharistic ecclesiology. It was the council's beginning, both chronologically and theologically, centered in Scripture and on the Eucharist.[41] But the theology of *Lumen Gentium* was in many ways a compromise between a theology of communion and a more juridical ecclesiology.[42]

A juridical ecclesiological has tended to dominate on the difficult ecumenical question of eucharistic hospitality. According to *Unitatis Redintegratio*, the Decree on Ecumenism:

> worship in common (*communicatio in sacris*) is not to be considered as a means to be used indiscriminately (*indiscretim*) for the restoration of Christian unity. There are two main principles governing the practice of such common worship: first, the bearing witness to the unity of the Church, and second, the sharing in the means of grace. Witness to the unity of the Church very generally forbids common worship to Christians, but the grace to be had from it sometimes commends this practice. The course to be adopted, with due regard to all the circumstances of time, place, and persons, is to be decided by local episcopal authority, unless otherwise provided for by the Bishops' Conference according to its statutes, or by the Holy See. (UR 8)

According to George Tavard, "*Indiscretim* does not mean that *communicatio in sacris* may be practiced, not indiscriminately but discriminately or with discretion; it means that the two aspects of communion (means of grace, and expression of unity) cannot be separated."[43] While the council left concrete cases up to the local episcopal authority, canon law sets out very limited conditions when

---

[41] Massimo Faggioli, "Sacrosanctum Concilium and the Meaning of Vatican II," *Theological Studies* 71 (2010): 437–52; see also Faggioli, *Vatican II and the Battle for Meaning* (New York: Paulist Press, 2012).

[42] See Walter Kasper, *Theology and Church* (New York: Crossroad, 1989), 158.

[43] George Tavard, "Praying Together: *Communicatio in sacris* in the Decree on Ecumenism," in *Vatican II: By Those Who Were There*, ed. Alberic Stacpoole (London: Chapman, 1986), 214.

eucharistic sharing is permitted for those in Protestant churches (844). The Orthodox who were seen as having "true sacraments, above all, by apostolic succession—the priesthood and the Eucharist" (UR 15; *Orientalium Ecclesiarum* nos. 26–29) should be welcomed to receive Catholic sacraments when they have need, with due respect for the discipline of their churches.

While this has remained a painful impasse to ecumenical progress, in the years since the council there has been progress in the post-conciliar Ecumenical Directories and Codes of Cannon Law which have attempted to formulate rules, not for intercommunion between churches, but occasionally for individuals on the basis of an existing *communio*, including the occasion of an interchurch marriage. The legislation, however, has not yet taken account of the council's dialectic between the Eucharist as a sign of unity and as a means of grace but only as a means of grace for the individuals belonging to other ecclesial communities, and that by way of exception.[44] A less juridical ecclesiology, more focused on Scripture and the nature of the church as a eucharistic community, might find ways to welcome occasional eucharistic hospitality for those who share a common eucharistic faith and want to live in communion with another church, but this remains an unresolved issue.[45]

Ordination of Women

Another unresolved issue concerns the ordination of women. At the end of the second session of the council, Belgian cardinal Leon Suenens asked why the council fathers were discussing the reality of the church when half of the church was not represented. This led Pope Paul VI to invite some twenty-three women (of whom only one was married) to attend as auditors.[46] This might be seen as the beginning of the women's movement in the church. It was not long before some were raising the question of admitting women to the church's

[44] Myriam Wijlens, *Sharing the Eucharist: A Theological Evaluation of the Post Conciliar Legislation* (Lanham, MD: University Press of America, 2000), 364–65.

[45] See Thomas P. Rausch, "Occasional Eucharistic Hospitality: Revisiting the Question," *Theological Studies* 74 (2013): 399–419.

[46] Carmel McEnroy, *Guests in Their Own House: The Women of Vatican II* (New York: Crossroad, 1996).

ordained ministry, something that by the second half of the twentieth century was common in most mainstream Reformation churches, but there has been little official discussion of the question of ordaining women in the Catholic Church.

A leaked report of an ultimately unfinished document of the Pontifical Biblical Commission, a subcommittee of the Congregation for the Doctrine of the Faith (CDF), reached the unanimous conclusion that: "It does not seem that the New Testament by itself alone will permit us to settle in a clear way and once and for all the problem of the possible accession of women to the presbyterate." [47] But other Roman documents have stressed the impossibility of ordaining women.

With the Anglican Church moving toward the ordination of women in 1976, that same year the Congregation for the Doctrine of the Faith published *Inter Insigniores*, the Declaration on the Admission of Women to the Ministerial Priesthood. It argued that the Catholic Church does not consider itself authorized to admit women to priestly ordination for a number of reasons. First, the constant tradition of the church is against it. Second, Christ, in spite of his freedom in dealing with women, did not call any women to the group of the Twelve. Third, the apostles did not call women to the ministry of publicly proclaiming the Gospel. Fourth, the CDF finds that the attitude of Jesus and the apostles to be of permanent value for the church. And finally, the priest's role of acting *in persona Christi* demands a "natural resemblance" between Christ and the priest who represents him.

In his 1994 apostolic letter *Ordinatio Sacerdotalis*, without repeating the argument based on "natural resemblance," Pope John Paul II stated, "I declare that the Church has no authority whatsoever to confer priestly ordination on women and that this judgment is to be definitively held by all the Church's faithful" (no. 4). A year later, the CDF under Cardinal Joseph Ratzinger published a *Responsum ad Propositum Dubium*, affirming in the face of any doubt that Pope John Paul's judgment was "definitive," arguing that the teaching of

---

[47] Leonard Swidler and Arlene Swidler, eds., *Women Priests: A Catholic Commentary on the Vatican Declaration*, Appendix 2, "Biblical Commission Report: Can Women be Priests?" (New York: Paulist Press, 1977), 346; see also John R. Donahue, "A Tale of Two Documents," in *Women Priests*, 25–34.

Ordinatio Sacerdotalis has been set forth infallibly by the ordinary and universal magisterium and is to be understood as belonging to the deposit of faith. Nevertheless, the question has not been discussed in a wider forum, drawing on all the bishops, theologians, and representatives of the faithful, leading some to question its infallibility.[48]

The Church Local and Universal

Catholic ecclesiology speaks of both the "particular church" and the "local church"; the particular church is the diocese, while "local churches" refers to regional groupings of particular churches. Vatican II moved Catholic ecclesiology forward by highlighting the concept of the particular church, each of which was governed by the bishop with "proper, ordinary, and immediate" power, exercised in Christ's name. Thus bishops shepherd their churches as vicars of Christ; they are not to be regarded as vicars of the pope (LG 27). The universal church is fully realized in each particular church, gathered around the Eucharist and united in visible communion with the universal church or communion of churches. As Joseph Komonchak says, "A first dimension of the local churches is liturgical."[49] The universal church is not to be regarded as some superstructure; according to *Lumen Gentium* 23, the individual bishops "are the visible principle and foundation of unity in their particular churches, fashioned after the model of the universal Church, in and from which churches comes into being the one and only Catholic Church" (LG 23).[50]

Still, the council did not fully spell out the relation between the local church and the universal church, with the result (as Christopher Ruddy notes) that the conciliar documents remain universalistic, and so "a juridical ecclesiology triumphs over an ecclesiology of com-

---

[48] See Francis A. Sullivan, *Creative Fidelity: Weighing and Interpreting Documents of the Magisterium* (New York: Paulist Press, 1996), 181–84.

[49] Joseph A. Komonchak, "The Significance of Vatican Council II for Ecclesiology," in *The Gift of the Church*, ed. Peter Phan (Collegeville, MN: Liturgical Press, 2000), 80.

[50] See Komonchak, "The Local Church," *Chicago Studies* 28 (1989): 320–34; see also Komonchak, "The Local Church and the Church Catholic: The Contemporary Theological Problematic," *The Jurist* 52 (1992): 416–47.

munion."[51] Walter Kasper also sees two ecclesiologies in the conciliar texts of Vatican II, a juxtaposition of the sacramental *communio*-ecclesiology and the juridical unity-ecclesiology.[52] In the postconciliar period, this was reflected in a debate between Kasper and Joseph Ratzinger, who had long maintained the ontological and temporal priority of the universal church over local churches, a debate Kasper maintained was not over any point of Catholic doctrine but represented rather a "conflict between theological opinions and underlying philosophical assumptions," Platonic in Ratzinger's case, starting from the primacy of the idea, while his own position was more Aristotelian, seeing the universal as existing in the concrete reality of local churches.[53]

Failure to maintain the proper tension between the local and universal churches can violate the principle of subsidiarity, resulting in a universalist ecclesiology. In the early centuries, the idea was that all the faithful, clergy and laity, participate in the election of the bishop, a right that by the tenth century had been taken over by monarchs, powerful feudal families, or cathedral chapters. It was only in recent times that bishops throughout the church were appointed by the pope, made a matter of law for the first time by the 1917 Code of Canon Law (c. 329, no. 2). While this has helped preserve the unity of the church, too often it means that the laity and clergy are disenfranchised in the governance of their particular churches and bishops too often look to Rome rather than to the needs of their faithful.[54]

Recognizing the existential priority of the local church has significant ecclesiological implications. Joseph Komonchak stresses the event character of the local church, each of which is the historical subject of its own self-realization. Practically, this means that local churches should be able to acknowledge and sacramentally confirm

---

[51] Christopher Ruddy, *The Local Church* (New York: Herder & Herder, 2006), 51–52, at 52;

[52] Walter Kasper, "Church as '*Communio*,'" *Communio* 13 (1986): 111.

[53] Walter Kasper, "On the Church: A Friendly Reply to Cardinal Ratzinger," *America* 184, no. 4 (2001): 13; see also Kilian McDonnell, "The Ratzinger/Kasper Debate: The Universal Church and Local Churches," *Theological Studies* 63, no. 2 (2002): 227–50.

[54] See John M. Huels and Richard R. Gaillardetz, "The Selection of Bishops: Recovering the Traditions," *The Jurist* 59 (1999): 348–76.

genuine charisms for leadership. This was better expressed historically in local churches when men received "relative" ordination for
ministry in their own communities, with the consent of the people,
and sometimes even against the will of the man ordained. Today a
universal, "descending" ecclesiology ordains absolutely. Vocations
are considered individualistically, so that a man is ordained and is
then assigned to some community without a prior relationship or
made a "titular" bishop without a community over which to preside.
Komonchak concludes that if indeed the one and universal church
is fully realized in local churches, then much more needs to be done
to allow all members to exercise their common responsibility. Authority is not the monopoly of the clergy.[55] This has obvious implications
for a theology of ministry.

Conclusion

Komonchak notes that ecclesiology is among the youngest of the
theological disciplines, though it has become increasingly important
in the last two centuries,[56] especially given the importance of the
ecumenical movement. We have traced the roots of the church in the
movement of those gathered by Jesus to share in his ministry and in
the communities that assembled in his memory after his resurrection.
These communities, formed in the image of the eschatological Israel,
were united by a common mission inherited from Jesus and by the
rituals of baptism and Eucharist under the leadership of the Twelve.

The New Testament describes the church with the metaphors of
people of God, Body of Christ, and Temple of the Spirit. Never a
monolithic institution, the various churches lived under their bishops
in communion with one another and with the bishop of Rome, though
some lost communion with the whole church as early as the fourth
and fifth centuries. Communion was lost between the Greek East and
the Latin West in 1054, with still greater divisions in the West coming

---

[55] Joseph A. Komonchak, "Ministry and the Local Church," *Proceedings of the Catholic
Theological Society of America* 36 (1981): 56–82, esp. 76–82.

[56] Ibid., 61.

in the sixteenth century. The one, holy, catholic and apostolic church has remained divided down to the present day.

If the First Vatican Council sought to finalize an institutional understanding of church, centered in Rome, Vatican II opened Catholic ecclesiology to a more inclusive understanding of church and committed the Catholic Church to the ecumenical movement. It also initiated a movement that would put evangelization at the heart of the church's understanding of its mission. Still, its very progress raised new questions which remain unresolved. Contemporary ecclesiologies are multiple and diverse.

The new churches of Asia and Africa continue to grow. China may soon be the largest Christian country in the world. Meanwhile, Christianity in Europe and North America is in a state of serious decline. One third of those born Catholic in the United States no longer practice their faith; 10 percent of all Americans are ex-Catholics,[57] making them the second largest religious group in the country. Many of those who remain, while they remain committed to core doctrines such as the bodily resurrection of Christ, Mary as Mother of God, the centrality of the sacraments, and helping the poor, are far more comfortable making up their own minds on questions such as regular Mass attendance, marriage rules, and sexuality.[58] The Catholic Church has become a voluntary society. Mainstream Protestant churches have lost members at an even greater rate.

The challenge today is for a "new" evangelization that does not simply seek to call those who have strayed back to the practice of their faith but can enter into a genuine dialogue with the secular culture of modernity and can reach out to so many in need. Pope Francis, in particular, wants a church focused not on itself but on those living on the peripheries, a church that is centrifugal in its movements. This means a church able to recognize that God's presence is not confined to its own community and structures but is already present in the world. Thus it cannot successfully proclaim the Gospel if it is not also willing to listen and to learn. Hosting such a

---

[57] "America's Former Catholics," Pew Forum; http://www.pewresearch.org/daily -number/americas-former-catholics/.

[58] See William V. D'Antonio, Michelle Dillon, and Mary L. Gauthier, *American Catholics in Transition* (Lanham, MD: Rowman and Littlefield, 2013).

mission demands an ecclesiology that not only looks back to the church's apostolic foundations—to its visible unity, trinitarian faith, and sacramental life—but also is genuinely open to the different, the new, and to those surprises that the Spirit often brings.

For Further Reading

Cahill, Lisa Sowle. "Feminist Theology and a Participatory Church." In *Common Calling: The Laity and Governance in the Catholic Church*, edited by Stephen J. Pope. Washington, DC: Georgetown University Press, 2004.

Clément, Olivier. *You Are Peter: An Orthodox Theologian's Reflection on the Exercise of Papal Primacy.* New York: New City Press, 2003.

Doyle, Dennis M. *Communion Ecclesiology: Vision and Versions.* Maryknoll, NY: Orbis Books, 2000.

Dulles, Avery. *Models of the Church*, Expanded Edition. Garden City, NY: Doubleday, 1987.

Gaillardetz, Richard R. *By What Authority? A Primer on Scripture, the Magisterium, and the Sense of the Faithful.* Collegeville, MN: Liturgical Press, 2003.

———. *Ecclesiology for a Global Church: A People Called and Sent.* Maryknoll, NY: Orbis Books, 2008.

Gaillardetz, Richard R., and Edward P. Hahnenberg. *A Church with Open Doors: Catholic Ecclesiology for the Third Millennium.* Collegeville, MN: Liturgical Press, 2015.

Haight, Roger. *Ecclesial Existence.* Volume 3, *Christian Community in History.* New York: Continuum, 2008.

Kärkkäinen, Veli-Matti. *An Introduction to Ecclesiology: Ecumenical, Historical, & Global Perspectives.* Downers Grove, IL: InterVarsity Press, 2002.

Küng, Hans. *The Church.* New York: Sheed and Ward, 1967.

Lakeland, Paul. *Church: Engaging Theology: Catholic Perspectives.* Collegeville, MN: Liturgical Press, 2009.

Mannion, Gerard. *Ecclesiology and Postmodernity: Questions for the Church in Our Time.* Collegeville, MN: Liturgical Press, 2007.

Rausch, Thomas P. *Towards a Truly Catholic Church: An Ecclesiology for the Third Millennium*. Collegeville, MN: Liturgical Press, 2005.

Ruddy, Christopher. *The Local Church: Tillard and the Future of Catholic Ecclesiology*. New York: Crossroad, 2006.

Schatz, Klaus. *Papal Primacy: From Its Origins to the Present*. Collegeville, MN: Liturgical Press, 1996.

Schillebeeckx, Edward. *Church: The Human Story of God*. New York: Crossroad, 1990.

Sobrino, Jon. *The True Church and the Poor*. Maryknoll, NY: Orbis Books, 1985.

Sullivan, Francis A. *The Church We Believe In: One, Holy, Catholic, and Apostolic*. New York: Paulist Press, 1988.

———. *Magisterium: Teaching Authority in the Catholic Church*. New York: Paulist Press, 1983.

Tillard, J. M. R. *The Bishop of Rome*. Wilmington, DE: Michael Glazier, 1983.

World Council of Churches. *The Church: Towards a Common Vision*. Faith and Order Paper Number 214. Geneva: WCC, 2013.

Chapter 9

Sacramentality and Christian Initiation

According to Andrew Greeley, Catholics live in an enchanted world, a world of statues and holy water, stained glass, votive candles, saints, religious medals, rosary beads, and holy pictures—all hints of a deeper religious sensibility he calls the Catholic sacramental imagination. This imagination enables Catholics to see created reality itself as a "sacrament" that reveals the presence of God.[1] He traces his vision to the influence of David Tracy, particularly his *Analogical Imagination*, which in Greeley's words argues that "the classic works of Catholic theologians and artists tend to emphasize the presence of God in the world, while the classic works of Protestant theologians tend to emphasize the absence of God from the world."[2] Catholics stress the immanence of God, Protestants God's transcendence. Scholars like Robert Neelly Bellah have made similar observations.[3]

In this chapter, we will consider the principle of sacramentality, the disclosure of grace through symbols that has so formed the Catholic imagination. We will look at sacramentality in its biblical roots, its important place in the church's tradition, and in contemporary theology. Then we will consider the traditional rite of Christian

---

[1] Andrew Greeley, *The Catholic Imagination* (Los Angeles: University of California Press, 2000), 1.

[2] Ibid., 5; see also David Tracy, *The Analogical Imagination* (New York: Crossroad, 1982).

[3] Robert N. Bellah, "Religion and the Shape of National Culture," *America* 181, no. 3 (1999): 9–14.

initiation based on what are now recognized as the sacraments of baptism, confirmation, and Eucharist.

Sacramentality

Langdon Gilkey notes that for Catholics, the divine mystery is communicated "not merely through rational consciousness nor through ecstasy alone, but through a wide range of symbols related to all the facets of ordinary life."[4] Such symbols are powerful; they speak not only to our heads but also to our hearts, our feelings, intuitions, and affective natures. Some are natural symbols, a beautiful sunset or a sky filled with stars, a meadow with its grass flowing gently in a breeze, or a silent forest. Others are specifically religious, an icon or statue, vigil lights burning in a dark church, the crucifix. Some are prophetic figures from Scripture or in our daily lives. Catholic churches or chapels are sacramental in their ornamentation. All of these symbols raise our hearts and minds to God. They are portals to the holy.

Consider the difference between a typical Catholic church building, say an Italian or Mexican church, and a Baptist or evangelical church. One is rich in art, statuary, holy water, candles, and stained glass, with an altar and tabernacle in its "sanctuary" or holy place. The other is spare, unadorned, light filled, and dominated by a Bible on a table or free-standing pulpit. One appeals unabashedly to the senses and the imagination; the other tends to restrict knowledge of the divine to the biblical word.

At the root of the Catholic sacramental imagination is the doctrine of the incarnation, the divine Word becoming flesh and so God's presence to creation. The word "sacrament," *sacramentum* in Latin, does not appear in the Bible. But the early Christian communities, like the Jewish communities from which Christianity developed, were able to recognize God's self-disclosure in symbol and story and in prophetic speech and ritual action. Judaism stressed the transcendence of God; its Decalogue forbade any attempt to represent the

---

[4] Langdon Gilkey, *Catholicism Confronts Modernity* (New York: Seabury Press, 1975), 47.

divine "in the shape of anything in the sky above or on the earth below or in the waters beneath the earth" (Exod 20:3; cf. Deut 5:8). Israel's God dwells in an impenetrable "cloud" (Exod 20:21; 24:15). Nothing built by human hands could contain the divine (1 Kgs 8:27). But this apophatic approach to the mystery of the divine was balanced by a kataphatic sense that God was present and active in Israel's history (Gen 26:3; 31:3; Isa 43:2). Israel had a rich sense of God's presence mediated by its rituals of sacrifice and purification, prophets, priests, and kings, and especially the temple, the "house of the Lord" (Ps 122) with its sanctuary or "holy of holies" housing the ark and the sacred vessels.

The early Christians shared this sacramental tradition. God's presence was mediated and disclosed in the ritual washing of Christian initiation, in gestures of healing or appointment to ministry, often accompanied by prayer, the anointing with oil, or the laying on of hands to communicate the Spirit. Most of all, they recognized the risen Jesus present in the ritual remembering (*anamnēsis*) of his sacrificial death and communion in his body and blood in the church's sacramental meal.

Paul speaks of God's ministers as "stewards of the mysteries of God" (1 Cor 4:1). In secular Greek, mystery (*mystērion*) meant "secret" or "hidden." The word was used in the Greek mystery religions for a hidden reality made present symbolically through ritual. Earlier in 1 Corinthians, Paul referred to the mysterious Wisdom of God now revealed through the Spirit (1 Cor 2:7-10). The concept of mystery is further developed in Ephesians and Colossians. Colossians speaks of the mystery hidden from ages past but now revealed to the Gentiles (1:26-27), Ephesians describes the union of husband and wife in marriage as a "mystery" which points to the union of Christ and his church (5:32); thus human love becomes a sign of divine presence. In the post–New Testament period, *mystērion* was used of the Christian rites, while around the year 210, Tertullian used the Latin *sacramentum* as a correlative term, comparing the *sacramentum* or oath which initiated a soldier into the Roman army to the initiation of Christian baptism. The terms *mystērion* and *sacramentum* both represent sign language; they suggest the disclosure of grace through symbol or ritual. The church fathers, including Augustine, used both *mystērion* and *sacramentum* broadly to refer to a great number of ceremonies, rites, symbols, blessings, liturgical objects, and feasts.

Augustine

In his controversy with the Donatists, rigorists who held for the invalidity of sacraments celebrated by those who in times of persecution had repudiated their faith, Augustine distinguished between the sacrament itself (*sacramentum*) and its grace (*res sacramenti*). He held that sacraments celebrated by schismatics were true sacraments but not fruitful until the recipient entered into the communion of the church. For example, baptism, even by schismatics, conferred a character or mark, but the character remained a mere sign until the person receiving the baptism moved into the true church, at which point it became not just a sign but true communion in the grace of Christ and the Spirit.[5]

Scholasticism

As theology moved from the monasteries and ecclesiastical schools to the new universities, the *magistri* and *doctores* sought to present it as a science (*scientia*) alongside other sciences such as philosophy, law, and medicine. In his famous *Book of the Sentences*, a standard medieval theological text, Peter Lombard (d. 1160) defined a sacrament as both a sign and a cause of invisible grace:

> We therefore properly call "sacrament" that which is a sign of the grace of God and the form of invisible grace, in such a way as to carry its image and to be its cause. Therefore, the sacraments were instituted not only for the sake of signifying, but of sanctifying as well.[6]

Concerned to make the term "sacrament" more precise, Lombard distinguished between sacraments as a *cause* of grace and other signs *pointing to* grace such as statues, crucifixes, holy water, oils, and other church ceremonies, thus engaging the question of sacramental efficacy and the relation between the sign, its effect, and the minister.

---

[5] See Augustine, *On Baptism against the Donatists*, Nicene and Post-Nicene Fathers, ed. Philip Schaff (New York: Christian Literature Company, 1886–1890), 1/4, 407–514.

[6] Cited by Philipp W. Rosemann, *Peter Lombard* (New York: Oxford University Press, 2004), 145; Peter Lombard, *Liber sententiarum* 4.1.4.

Aquinas used an analogy with Aristotle's idea of efficient causality to argue that sacraments effect the grace they signify. God was the principal agent in the sacrament, though in a secondary sense, it could be said to be the work of the minister who acts in the name of the whole church. But the sacramental effect came not from the minister but from the merits of Christ who works in the sacraments, making good any defects in the faith of the minister.[7] Some have found Aquinas's sacramental doctrine insufficiently attentive to the role of the Holy Spirit. Bonaventure stressed that what the sacraments signified was divine love, present in creation, drawing human beings into communion with God. Therefore for him sacraments were less instruments than vessels of grace.[8]

The Reformation

The Reformers, using a narrower criterion of christological foundation, recognized only baptism and the Lord's Supper as sacraments in the proper sense, though today both Catholics and Protestants would agree that these two are the primary sacraments. Looking back to Augustine's emphasis on the importance of the Word in sacramental action, Luther spoke of a sacrament as a visible word, deriving its power from the Word which must be received in faith. He objected to the traditional emphasis on sacramental efficacy *ex opera operato* for failing to stress the role of faith and overemphasizing priestly mediation. What mattered was faith, not performance of the rite. Calvin's concern was similar. Following Augustine, he emphasized the role of the Spirit, without which there was no communication of grace. But the Reformation emphasis on the Word led not infrequently to a lack of appreciation for the power of symbol and ritual.

The Council of Trent, in placing its treatment on sacraments after its decree on justification, acknowledged the gratuitous nature of sacramental grace and its reception as dependent on faith. But fearing that the Reformers' doctrine of justification by faith alone had challenged the efficacy of the sacraments, they used the traditional language of *ex opera operato* to reaffirm sacramental efficacy. Since the

---

[7] Aquinas, *Summa Theologica* III, q. 64.

[8] See David N. Power, *Sacrament: The Language of God's Giving* (New York: Crossroad, 1999), 53.

main concern of the council fathers was to respond to what they saw as the errors of the Reformers, they did not develop a comprehensive theology of the sacraments, nor did they seek to resolve those questions still disputed by Catholic theologians. They reaffirmed the traditional number seven for the sacraments and the conferral of a permanent sacramental character in baptism, confirmation, and orders.

The notion of sacramental character was originally associated with the unrepeatability of baptism, confirmation, and ordination, mentioned by Augustine in his controversies with the Donatists. The term itself dates from the twelfth century. Aquinas taught that the sacramental character empowers one to share in the one priesthood of Christ and take part in divine worship, an active power for the ordained and a passive power for all the baptized. The Council of Florence (1439) spoke of the sacramental character as a spiritual sign imprinted indelibly on the soul (*Decree for the Arminians*). Contemporary theologians emphasize sacramental character as incorporating one into the Body of Christ (baptism), sealing and strengthening one in the Spirit for sharing in the church's mission (confirmation), and bestowing a share in the church's ministerial office (ordination).

Contemporary Sacramental Theology

In the post-Tridentine church, the emphasis on sacramental causality too often hardened into the mechanical notion that sacraments conferred grace simply by the correct and valid performance of the rite (*ex opere operato*). Even though the tradition had stressed the subjective disposition of the recipient (*ex opere operantis*), this aspect did not stand out in Augustine's theology. As a result, the tradition that followed too often stressed correct ritual rather than personal disposition. This often led to sterile discussions of the requirements for sacramental validity.

Symbolic Causality

A new focus on the symbolic and personal character of the sacramental action begins to emerge in the work of the Tübingen School, especially that of Johann Adam Möhler, with his description of the church, not as an institution or hierarchical structure but as an organic community, rich in charisms and ministries. He saw the Spirit's presence both realized and expressed in the sacraments. Relating the sacraments to human experience, together with new studies on the function of symbol, myth, and ritual, was to lead to a shift from an emphasis on instrumental causality to a new appreciation of symbolic causality. Sacraments mediate grace by symbolizing; signs and symbols manifest God's self-communication, particularly in the humanity of Christ, the Word become flesh.[9] We saw this earlier in talking about the symbolic character of revelation.

An example of symbolic causality can be found in the way that the human spirit is disclosed through bodily gestures even more profoundly than through words. A glance, handshake, hug, or caress—each is a symbolic action disclosing the inner spirit of a person. This gift of person to person finds its most powerful expression in the union of a couple in marital intercourse; for the act of intercourse, while it can be an expression of violence and exploitation, can also disclose in the love of the couple the tender and life-giving love of God. In showing how the invisible grace of God becomes visible, both Karl Rahner and Edward Schillebeeckx emphasized the symbolic and personal character of sacramental causality. Both develop the idea of Christ as the fundamental sacrament (*Ursakrament*) and the church as the sacrament of Christ.[10]

Church as Sacrament

Starting from his theological anthropology, Rahner's sacramental theology recognizes God's self-disclosure in nature and in the self-transcending character of the human being as spirit in the world. Like Aquinas, for whom sacramental grace was not limited to the sacraments, he argues that the particular grace (*res sacramenti*) of baptism, penance, and the Eucharist can also be realized apart from

[9] See David N. Power, *Unsearchable Riches: The Symbolic Nature of Liturgy* (New York: Pueblo, 1984), 196–206.

[10] Karl Rahner, *The Church and the Sacraments* (New York: Herder and Herder, 1963); Edward Schillebeeckx, *Christ the Sacrament of the Encounter with God* (New York: Sheed and Ward, 1963); see also David N. Power, *The Eucharistic Mystery: Revitalizing the Tradition* (New York: Crossroad, 1994), 269–77.

these sacraments.[11] Given the transcendental character of the human person manifest in knowledge, freedom, and love, grace is present wherever humans open themselves to the divine mystery, respond in love and compassion to another, or commit themselves to transcendent values such as truth, justice, or mercy. God's dialogue with creation achieves its full realization in the person of Jesus who is himself the visible embodiment of God's saving grace. As such, he is sign and reality, *sacramentum* and *res sacramenti*. With the risen Jesus no longer present in his humanity, the church carries on God's offer of salvation, made visible in space and time. Thus the church becomes the fundamental sacrament of salvation, the sign of God's self-communication in Christ and ultimate victory over sin and death.[12]

Schillebeeckx views religion as a saving dialogue between God and human beings, a perspective that moves sacramentality away from a mechanical approach, based on physicalist categories, to one modeled on human, personal encounter. From this perspective, Jesus becomes the personal, visible realization of the divine grace of redemption, "the primordial sacrament."[13] Those who encountered the historical Jesus encountered the living God visibly present in him. But the glorified Christ, no longer visible, remains visible through his body the church, the sacrament of the risen Christ. "What Christ is doing invisibly in this world through his Spirit, he is at the same time doing visibly through the mission of his apostles and of the members of the Church community."[14]

Schillebeeckx brings the signifying and causal nature of sacramentality together; the sacramental sign, like the offer of love in gestures of friendship or compassion, is an invitation that, when accepted or entered into, symbolizes God's love and mediates God's transforming presence. In his later work, influenced by liberation theology, Schillebeeckx's sacramental theology took on a more explicitly political dimension. Using the phrase, "No salvation outside the world,"

---

[11] Karl Rahner, "Theological Reflections on the Priestly Image of Today and Tomorrow," *Theological Investigations* vol. 12 (New York: Seabury Press, 1974), 48.

[12] Karl Rahner, *Foundations of Christian Faith: An Introduction to the Idea of Christianity* (New York: Seabury Press, 1978), 411–12; Rahner, *The Church and the Sacraments*, 15–23.

[13] Schillebeeckx, *Christ the Sacrament of the Encounter with God*, 3–15, at 15.

[14] Ibid., 50.

he argued that the language of following Jesus does not make sense apart from social/political praxis in the world, while it is precisely the world with its experience of suffering, evil, oppression, and injustice that makes the language of Christian faith and praxis necessary.[15]

Others working in sacramental theology have seen sacramental efficacy moving in different directions. Feminist theologians, concerned for a more inclusive community, have sought to give women greater expression in the church's symbolic and ministerial life and to value gender difference.[16] Hans Urs von Balthasar's theological aesthetics stresses a contemplative entry into the mystery of God's glory revealed to the world in the eternal self-emptying of the Son and his return to the Father in the Spirit.[17] Louis-Marie Chauvet and Jean-Luc Marion prefer the language of the gift-exchange between lovers to that of being and causality.[18]

As the basic sacrament, for Schillebeeckx the church, the sacrament of Christ, is the wellspring of the seven sacraments; the church realizes its own essence in privileged moments of encounter with grace at defining moments of a person's life. The traditional number of seven sacraments comes from Lombard's *Book of the Sentences*.[19] The Reformers recognized only two sacraments, baptism and the Lord's Supper or Eucharist on the basis of a strict principle of Dominical institution, as we have seen.

Christian Initiation

The ancient practice of Christian initiation involved a washing with water (a real bath), anointing with oil, invoking the Spirit, and

[15] Edward Schillebeeckx, *Church: The Human Story of God* (New York: Crossroad, 1990), 5–15.

[16] Susan A. Ross, *Extravagant Affections: A Feminist Sacramental Theology* (New York: Continuum, 1998).

[17] Hans Urs von Balthasar, *The Glory of the Lord: A Theological Aesthetics*, vol. 1, *Seeing the Form* (San Francisco: Ignatius Press, 2009).

[18] Louis-Marie Chauvet, *Symbol and Sacrament: Sacramental Reinterpretation of Christian Existence* (Collegeville, MN: Liturgical Press, 1995); Jean-Luc Marion, *God without Being* (Chicago: University of Chicago Press, 1991).

[19] The Council of Florence (1439) made Lombard's enumeration official church teaching.

admission to the Eucharist, incorporating a person into Christ and his body the church. As the anointing was eventually separated from baptism and reserved to the bishop, Christian initiation came to be seen as comprised of three sacraments: baptism, confirmation, and Eucharist.

Baptism

The Greek *baptismos* means a "dipping in water," a ritual practiced by John the Baptist as a sign of repentance and apparently by Jesus in the early days of his ministry (John 3:22). The early Christian communities adopted the ritual as a sign of initiation into Christ and his body, the church. The New Testament writers stress different aspects of baptism.

Paul's theology of baptism is complex. He sees baptism as incorporating a person into the mystery of Christ's dying and rising to new life (Rom 6:3-4). This participation in Christ's union with the father in life, death, and resurrection is at the heart of the Paschal Mystery. This is celebrated in the Catholic funeral ritual when the white pall is placed over the casket, with words that recall the deceased incorporation into the mystery of Christ's dying and rising. But Paul also sees baptism as a sacrament that unifies the diverse members of the community as Christ's body, overcoming differences of origin, race, social status, and gender (1 Cor 12:12-13; Gal 3:28). Those baptized have been "clothed with Christ" and made heirs to the promise given to Abraham and his descendants (Gal 3:27). There is no longer either Jew or Greek, slave or free, male or female; all are one in Christ.

John's theology of baptism emerges in Jesus' dialogue with Nicodemus, when he says that no one can enter the kingdom of God without being born from above, clarifying Nicodemus's misunderstanding about the impossibility of reentering his mother's womb by referring to being born again of water and the Spirit (John 3:3-5). Evangelicals have understood this to mean being "born again," though the text says literally "born from above." Still the metaphor is a good one; baptism demands a conversion of life which is analogous to a new birth. Luke also sees baptism as contingent on faith (Acts 2:41).

From the second century, those "catechumens" preparing for baptism went through a long period of catechesis, prayer, exorcisms, and investigation called "scrutinies" before they were led down into the pool and baptized at the Easter Vigil. While the place of baptismal anointing and prayers for the Spirit differed between the East and the West, the different rites expressed cleansing from sin and the gift of the Spirit. Thus Basil of Caesarea speaks of baptism as our being buried with Christ, a dying to sin, and coming to life again in the Spirit as adopted sons and daughters, sharing in the grace of Christ.[20] The ancient catechumenate was restored in the Rite of Christian Initiation of Adults after the Second Vatican Council (1972).

Unfortunately, in the Middle Ages, under the influence of Augustine, with infant baptism now the norm, the initiatory aspect of the sacrament with the importance of faith was replaced by an emphasis on cleansing from original sin. While the mainstream Reformers continued the practice of infant baptism, the so-called "left wing" or radical Reformation rejected infant baptism in favor of "believers' baptism," hence the name "Anabaptists." Karl Barth was strongly against infant baptism. The World Council of Churches' consensus statement *Baptism, Eucharist and Ministry* argued that both practices had deep roots in the tradition, and each should be respected, though it cautioned against indiscriminate baptism.[21]

Since baptism is incorporation into Christ through incorporation into the church, which for the infant means the home, there should be some realization of the "domestic church" in the family. Today the Catholic Church's canon law states that where there is no hope that the infant will be brought up in the faith, the baptism is to be put off until there is some hope of practice (canon 868, 2). Ministers, however, should be sensitive to cultural differences; sometimes baptism is delayed because couples can't afford the stipend required by the priest; in other cultures the extended family can serve to provide an experience of church. The old fear of limbo is no longer a reason for baptism; a 2007 document of the International Theological Commission said that the meaning of baptism was to be found in incorpora-

---

[20] Basil of Caesarea, *On the Holy Spirit* 15, 35–36.
[21] World Council of Churches, *Baptism, Eucharist and Ministry* (Geneva: WCC, 1982).

tion into Christ and the church, not in freeing children from eternal punishment.[22]

How does baptism mediate grace? Because grace builds on the human, context is key. We are shaped by the network of relationships, familial, social, and cultural, which form us for better or for worse. We know the tragic consequences for those who come from dysfunctional families or violent environments or who have been rejected or suffered emotional or physical abuse. We know how easy it is to assume the values of our materialistic, secular culture. Similarly, we know how we ourselves are changed when we experience that we are loved or how we have been moved by the goodness of others; we feel a new energy, and new possibilities open up for us.

Baptism mediates new life in Christ by moving the person baptized from a world still under the rule of sin to one shaped and informed by the Spirit of Jesus. Becoming a Christian is not a question of some kind of *gnosis*. It is not primarily a doctrinal matter, though doctrine is important; nor is it a matter of proof. As Chauvet says in commenting on the Emmaus story (Luke 24:13-35), "You cannot arrive at the recognition of the risen Jesus unless you renounce seeking/touching/finding him by undeniable proofs. Faith begins precisely with such a *renunciation of the immediacy* of the see/know and with the assent to the mediation of the church."[23] Faith is fundamentally performative. To be a Christian means to live in Christ's body, a community of men and women who gather in Jesus' name, proclaim his Gospel, experience him in word and sacrament, strive to imitate his example, and live in his Spirit. Such relationships are transformative. To live in a graced community gives one the power to avoid sin, open oneself to God, and live a new life. The church points to Christ and mediates his grace in its preaching (*kerygma*) and teaching (*didachē*), its fellowship (*koinōnia*), worship (*liturgia*), and ministry (*diakonia*).

[22] ITC, "The Hope of Salvation for Infants Who Die without Being Baptized," *Origins* 36 (April 26, 2007): 725–46.

[23] Louis-Marie Chauvet, *The Sacraments: The Word at the Mercy of the Body* (Collegeville, MN: Liturgical Press, 2001), 25, emphasis in the original.

Confirmation

Originally part of the baptismal ritual, the postbaptismal anointing with chrism, sometimes accompanied by the laying on of hands, gradually emerged in the West as a separate sacrament called confirmation. The Eastern churches have preserved the original form of Christian initiation—washing with water, postbaptismal anointing with oil or "chrismation," and reception of the Eucharist. Even infants baptized in Orthodox churches receive the Eucharist by means of a spoon dipped in the consecrated wine. As the church grew in the West, however, spreading into rural areas distant from the episcopal see and increasing in the number of candidates for baptism, many of them infants, the bishop could not always be present. As the postbaptismal anointing was increasingly reserved to the bishop, probably to show the link between the bishop and the local church and the church universal, confirmation became a separate sacrament.

However ultimately explained, the separation of confirmation from its proper place in Christian initiation has led to confusion over its meaning. It should not be understood as bestowing the Spirit, since the Spirit is given in baptism and is often active even before. Aquinas saw confirmation as a sacrament conferring spiritual strength to confess the faith, making the one confirmed "a front-line fighter for the faith of Christ."[24] But it should not be seen as a sacrament of Christian adulthood. Rather, confirmation is a celebration and intensification of the Spirit's presence in a person's life. While liturgists argue for a return to the proper order of Christian initiation, a challenge further complicated by Pope Pius X granting children access to the Eucharist at the "age of reason," others argue that given the universality of infant baptism, confirmation makes more sense as the moment when a young person personally appropriates the commitment made by parents and godparents for them at their baptism.

Eucharist

The Eucharist or Lord's Supper has its origins in the memorial character of Jewish blessings, specifically the grace after meals or *birkat-ha-mazon* prayed by the host in thanksgiving. Just as Jewish

---

[24] Aquinas, *Summa Contra Gentiles* 4.60.

prayer continued to look back to the saving event of the Exodus, so the Eucharist memorializes or remembers Christ's saving death and resurrection. Its roots lie in the Isaian image of the eschatological banquet in the heavenly Jerusalem (Isa 25:6-8) used also by Jesus (Luke 13:26-30; Matt 22:1-14) and in the table-fellowship tradition so important in his ministry. But this is transformed in view of the Last Supper, when Jesus identified the bread and wine of the table with his body and blood, soon to be broken and poured out on the cross.

NEW TESTAMENT FOUNDATIONS

The New Testament gives us two different accounts of the "institution narrative." Common elements include the notions of memorial (*anamnesis*), sacrifice, covenant, communion in the body and blood of Christ, and eschatological hope. One form (Mark 14:22-24; Matt 26:26-28) speaks of the bread as his body and his blood as the blood of the covenant to be shed for many, with Matthew adding for the forgiveness of sins. The second and perhaps earlier form in Paul and Luke (1 Cor 11:24-25; Luke 22:19-20) speaks of the bread as Christ's body and the wine as a new covenant in his blood and contains the command to repeat. Paul also recognizes the ecclesial character of the Eucharist, uniting its participants into the one body of Christ: "The cup of blessings that we bless, is it not a participation (*koinōnia*) in the blood of Christ? The bread that we break, is it not a participation (*koinōnia*) in the body of Christ? Because the loaf of bread is one, we, though many, are one body, for we all partake of the one loaf" (1 Cor 11:16-17).

John's Gospel does not mention the institution of the Eucharist, but the long sixth chapter on the bread of life, which moves from Jesus as the true bread come down from heaven to a more literal invitation to partake of his body and blood most likely represents the eucharistic theology of the Johannine community: "unless you eat of the flesh of the Son of Man and drink his blood, you do not have life within you. Whoever eats my flesh and drinks my blood has eternal life, and I will raise him on the last day" (John 6:53-54). Luke's story of the two disciples on the road to Emmaus who recognize the risen Jesus in the breaking of the bread (Luke 24:30) most likely comes out of the experience of the early Christians who continued to break the bread and share the cup in his memory and so came to recognize his presence among them, as the church has done ever since.

EUCHARIST IN THE TRADITION

The *Didache*, dating from the mid-to-late first century, offers a prayer of thanksgiving thought to have been used at the Eucharist (*Didache* 9). Justin Martyr (d. c. 165) has left us a description of an early Eucharist, noting that "the president offers prayers of thanksgiving according to his ability," suggesting that he prayed in his own words (*Apology* 67). The *Apostolic Tradition* attributed to Hippolytus contains a eucharistic prayer or anaphora that is generally considered to date from the late second or early third century.[25]

From the second century on, the church fathers stressed Christ's real presence in the Eucharist, though they did not always use the language of substantial change. Thus Ignatius of Antioch (d. 110), in arguing against the Docetists' denial of the true humanity of Jesus, observed that they abstain from the Eucharist because they do not believe that it "is the flesh of our Savior Jesus Christ" (*Smy* 6.7). Justin Martyr compared the union of the bread and wine with Christ's body and blood to the joining of the divine and human in the incarnation (*First Apology*, 66). Ambrose (d. 397) speaks of a change of the elements, arguing that the power of grace was superior to that of nature: "But if the word of Elijah had such power as to bring down fire from heaven, shall not the word of Christ have power to change the nature of the elements?" (*On the Mysteries*, 52).

A controversy in the eleventh century over Christ's eucharistic presence led to the language of substantial change, transubstantiation. Berengar (d. 1088), a theologian and head of the school of St. Martin at Tours, took what seemed to many to be an overly symbolic approach to the sacrament. He seems to have taught that Christ was present in the Eucharist *only* as sign, rather than that the bread was identical with his body. In response, the Fourth Lateran Council (1215) used the term "transubstantiation" to affirm that while the

---

[25] See Paul F. Bradshaw, Maxwell E. Johnson, and L. Edward Phillips, *The Apostolic Tradition: A Commentary*, Hermeneia: A Critical and Historical Commentary on the Bible (Minneapolis, MN: Fortress Press, 2002), 37.

appearances of the bread and wine remained the same, the substance of both really changed.

The controversy with Berengar contributed to an unfortunate shift in meaning that contributed to a loss of the relationship between eucharistic participation and church, uniting the members into the one Body of Christ, so evident in Paul (1 Cor 1:16-17). The phrase "mystical body" (*corpus mysticum*) originally referred to the sacramental body of the Lord or "the mystery of the body," while "body of Christ" or "true body of Christ" (*verum corpus*) referred to the church. As "mystical body" shifted from eucharistic to ecclesial usage, an overly individualistic eucharistic piety developed.[26] Joseph Ratzinger acknowledges that this development led to a diminishment of the corporate character (the sense of the "we") of eucharistic faith, though he does not judge this to be entirely an unhappy development, as deeper theological reflection on Christ's presence led to a spiritual deepening and adoration which he argues is in no way opposed to communion.[27]

THE REFORMATION

The Reformers had difficulty with the notion of the Eucharist as sacrifice and with the mediating role of the priest, but they did not intend to deny Christ's eucharistic presence. Their problem was with the term transubstantiation, thus with a particular theological language. Luther's formula was that Christ was present "in, with, and under" the elements of bread and wine, which has often been interpreted as "consubstantiation." He saw the sacraments in relation to the Lordship of Jesus, giving him power over all things, thus allowing him to be present wherever the sacraments are celebrated ("ubiquity").

Calvin's concern was to avoid overly physicalist language. He wrote that Christ is present through "that marvelous communion of his body and blood—provided we understand that it takes place by

---

[26] Henri de Lubac, *Corpus Mysticum* (Notre Dame, IN: University of Notre Dame Press, 2006), 79–80; 256–59.

[27] Joseph Ratzinger, *The Spirit of the Liturgy* (San Francisco: Ignatius Press, 2000), 87–90.

the power of the Holy Spirit, not by that feigned inclusion of the body itself under the element."[28] But it was not just a spiritual communion. "I am not satisfied with those persons who, recognizing that we have some communion with Christ, when they would show what it is, make us partakers of the Spirit only, omitting mention of flesh and blood. As though all these things were said in vain: that his flesh is truly food, that his blood is truly drink [John 6:55]."[29] As Kilian McDonnell points out, Calvin wants to move from the philosophical concept of substance to that of person, even though he uses "substance" frequently. But his concept is soteriological; there is a real encounter with Christ the Mediator and Redeemer in the Lord's Supper.[30] Other Reformers were more radical. For Zwingli the Eucharist was a sign, an aid to memory to remember Jesus in his passion; it was a remembering of a past event: "Therefore our eucharist is a visible assembling of the church, in which together we eat and drink bread and wine as (*veluti*) symbols, that we may be reminded of those things which Christ has done for us."[31]

COUNCIL OF TRENT

Trent (1545–1563) was concerned with what it understood as the Reformers' errors, but, unfortunately, it addressed the doctrine of the real presence and that of the Mass as sacrifice in different sessions and decrees.[32] In speaking of the change of the bread and wine into the body and blood of Christ, it said that the Catholic Church "properly and appropriately (*aptissime*)" calls this change transubstantiation (DS 1642). Its language did not commit the church to the scholastic analysis of change or to scholastic categories, nor was it giving a philosophical explanation of how this takes place; the council fathers' concern was to safeguard Christ's eucharistic presence. Canon 1 on the sacrament of the Eucharist affirms that in the Eucharist, the whole

[28] Calvin, *Institutes* 4.17.26.

[29] Ibid., 4.17.7.

[30] Kilian McDonnell, *John Calvin, the Church, and the Eucharist* (Princeton, NJ: Princeton University Press, 1967), 246–47.

[31] Cited by W. P. Stevens, *The Theology of Huldrych Zwingli* (Oxford: Clarendon Press, 1986), 239–40.

[32] See Power, *The Eucharistic Mystery*, 253–62.

Christ, body and blood, soul and divinity are contained truly, really, and substantially (DS 1651). This language recognizes that the presence of the risen Jesus is not physical; it is sacramental. Through the action of the Holy Spirit in the liturgy, Christ is present in the bread and wine; in sharing in the gifts we enter into a profound communion with the Lord and with one another. Against the Reformers, who rejected the idea of the Eucharist as sacrifice, the Decree on the Sacrifice of the Mass (DS 1738–59) reaffirmed its propitiatory sacrificial character, though the council did not define precisely what it understood by sacrifice.[33] And it did little to address the clericalization of the liturgy that had developed in the Middle Ages.[34]

EUCHARIST AND LITURGY

The renewal of the liturgy had to wait for the liturgical movement beginning in the late nineteenth century, the ecumenical movement, and especially the Second Vatican Council. The council's constitution on the liturgy, *Sacrosanctum Concilium*, spoke of the multiple presences of Christ in the church's liturgical celebrations, in the minister, the sacraments, the Word, and especially in the eucharistic species (SC 7). It called for full, conscious, and active participation of the faithful, the simplification of the rites, and somewhat cautiously for liturgical inculturation. Reformation churches have also benefited from the renewal of the liturgy occasioned by Vatican II, while the long years of ecumenical dialogue have moved the churches beyond many of the Reformation controversies, putting them in a new light.

According to the council's *Unitatis Redintegratio*, the Decree on Ecumenism, the ecclesial communities stemming from the Reformation "have not retained the proper reality of the eucharistic mystery in its fullness" because of the lack (*defectus*) of the sacrament of orders (UR 22). What then is missing from Protestant celebrations of the Eucharist? Few would want to argue today that it means a lack of eucharistic presence. In a famous 1993 letter to Lutheran bishop

---

[33] See Robert J. Daly, *Sacrifice Unveiled: The True Meaning of Christian Sacrifice* (New York: T & T Clark International, 2009), 149.

[34] See David N. Power, *The Sacrifice We Offer: The Tridentine Dogma and Its Reinterpretation* (New York: Crossroad, 1987).

Johannes Hanselmann, Joseph Ratzinger wrote, "Even a theology oriented to the concept of succession such as that which holds in the Catholic and in the Orthodox church, need not in any way deny the salvation-granting presence of the Lord [*Heilschaffende Gegenwart des Herrn*] in a Lutheran [*evangelische*] Lord's Supper." [35]

The 1982 WCC statement, *Baptism, Eucharist and Ministry*, described the Eucharist as a thanksgiving to the Father, *anamnesis* or memorial of Christ, invocation of the Spirit (*epiclesis*), communion of the faithful in the body and blood of Christ, and meal of the kingdom. It maintained that "As the eucharist celebrates the resurrection of Christ, it is appropriate that it should take place at least every Sunday" (Eucharist no. 31). This stands as a challenge to many Protestant churches, for whom Sunday celebration is no longer the norm. For example, David Fergusson observes that Sunday celebration of the Lord's Supper "is still largely foreign to the worship of most Reformed communities in the world today, and, if ecumenical progress is to be achieved, a commitment to the more frequent celebration of the Lord's Supper is probably required alongside a reassessment of its theological significance." [36] The same could be said for many evangelical communities.

The inability of Christians from different traditions to join in the celebration of the Eucharist highlights the divisions that still remain between them. Roman Catholic and Orthodox Christians understand sharing in the Eucharist as a sign of the communion of the church. Protestants generally argue that it is the Lord who invites baptized believers to his Supper, and no church has the right to exclude them. For Catholics, there has been some progress on this difficult question. Some developments in canon law focus not on relations between churches but on the needs of individuals, suggesting certain occasions when eucharistic hospitality is permissible. [37]

---

[35] "Briefwechsel von Landesbischof Johannes Hanselmann und Joseph Kardinal Joseph Ratzinger über das Communion-Schreiben der Römanischen Glaubenkongregation," *Una Sancta* 48 (1993): 348; see also Ratzinger, *Pilgrim Fellowship of Faith: The Church as Communion*, ed. Stephan Otto Horn and Vinzenz Pfnür (San Francisco: Ignatius Press, 2005), 248.

[36] David Fergusson, "The Reformed Churches," in *The Christian Church: An Introduction to the Major Traditions*, ed. Paul Avis (London: SPCK, 2002), 41.

[37] See Thomas P. Rausch, "Occasional Eucharistic Hospitality: Revisiting the Question," *Theological Studies* 74 (2013): 399–419.

Conclusion

If Charles Taylor is correct that the Reformation, with its emphasis on personal faith and its discomfort with sacraments, priesthood, and the sacred,[38] began the process of abolishing the enchanted medieval cosmos, the Catholic imagination still finds traces of the divine in nature, art, symbols, stories, and persons. Implicit here is the concept of sacramentality, the idea that the symbolic in its many forms can raise the imagination, the heart, and the mind to God.

If it took centuries to develop an explicit theology of the sacraments and to fix their number at seven, rituals, images, symbols, even art was valued from the earliest days of the church. The battle over icons that took place in the Eastern church in the eighth and ninth centuries found no echo in the West. In his battle against the iconoclasts, John of Damascus (c. 675–749), after distinguishing between worship and veneration, pointed to the material as the medium through which salvation came. At root of this conviction is the doctrine of the incarnation, in which God takes on the material and becomes flesh in the person of Jesus of Nazareth. Thus the human embodies the divine; the material manifests the sacred.

If an emphasis on sacraments can and at times has hardened into a mere ritualism, a new appreciation of the power of the symbolic has helped restore the balance between an overly intellectual approach to faith and ritualism or even superstition. More recent theology such as that of Edward Schillebeeckx has seen in the man Jesus the fundamental sacrament of the hidden God and the church as the sacrament of the risen Christ, with the seven sacraments as the actualization of the church. And for those who have eyes to see, nature itself is sacramental, revealing in the beauty of creation and the incredible diversity of species the goodness and inexhaustible love of God.[39]

The early church initiated neophytes into the community with the waters of baptism and prayers for the gift of the Spirit, often with the laying on of hands. The catechumenate, already in place by the third

---

[38] Charles Taylor, *A Secular Age* (Cambridge, MA: Belknap Press of Harvard University, 2007), 70–77.

[39] See Elizabeth A. Johnson, *Ask the Beasts: Darwin and the God of Love* (London: Bloomsbury, 2014), 255.

century, was a lengthy period of preparation that culminated with the baptizing of the candidates, anointing them with oil, and leading them dressed in white into the church for the celebration of the Eucharist at the great Easter liturgy. In the West, confirmation emerged later as a separate sacrament. Vatican II restored the catechumenate in the Rite of Christian Initiation of Adults (RCIA).

From the beginning, the church has gathered on the Lord's Day to break the bread and share the cup in memory of Jesus. In the words of Joseph Ratzinger, "The Church is the celebration of the Eucharist; the Eucharist is the Church; they do not simply stand side by side; they are one and the same."[40] The language of transubstantiation, introduced to safeguard Christ's eucharistic presence against the tendency to reduce it to simple sign, was rejected by the Reformers, though most recognized that Christ was truly present, even if they expressed it differently. But in subsequent history, the Eucharist in many Reformation traditions was marginalized or reduced to a private devotion. The modern liturgical movement and the years of ecumenical dialogue that followed Vatican II have challenged all the churches to the renewal of their eucharistic practice.

The sacraments of initiation that we have been considering incorporate one into the church, the Body of Christ, and thus into Christ. Formed by the Word of God and nourished by the bread of life in the Eucharist, Christians are united in the Spirit of Jesus. They come to a new experience of reconciliation and communion and are missioned to witness to God's reign or kingdom in the world. Christianity is thus not a recondite personal philosophy; still less can it be reduced to a system of ethics. To be a Christian is to be part of Jesus' movement, to be incorporated into his body which continues to mediate his presence to the world.

---

[40] Joseph Ratzinger, *Principles of Catholic Theology* (San Francisco: Ignatius Press, 1987), 53.

For Further Reading

Sacramentality

Chauvet, Louis-Marie. *The Sacraments: The Word of God at the Mercy of the Body*. Collegeville, MN: Liturgical Press, 2001.

———. *Symbol and Sacrament: A Sacramental Reinterpretation of Christian Existence*. Collegeville, MN: Liturgical Press, 1995.

Cooke, Bernard. *Sacraments & Sacramentality*. Mystic, CT: Twenty-Third Publications, 1983.

Downey, Michael. *Clothed in Christ: The Sacraments and Christian Living*. New York: Crossroad, 1987.

Duffy, Regis. *Real Presence: Worship, Sacraments, and Commitment*. San Francisco: Harper & Row, 1982.

Greeley, Andrew. *The Catholic Imagination*. Los Angeles: University of California Press, 2000.

Mitchell, Nathan. *Meeting Mystery*. Maryknoll, NY: Orbis Books, 2006.

Power, David N. *Sacrament: The Language of God's Giving*. New York: Crossroad, 1999.

Rahner, Karl. *The Church and the Sacraments*. New York: Herder & Herder, 1963.

Ross, Susan A. *Extravagant Affections: A Feminist Sacramental Theology*. New York: Continuum, 2001.

Schillebeeckx, Edward. *Christ the Sacrament of the Encounter with God*. New York: Sheed & Ward, 1963.

Baptism

Duffy, Regis. *On Becoming Catholic: The Challenge of Christian Initiation*. San Francisco: Harper & Row, 1984.

Ferguson, Everett. *Baptism in the Early Church: History, Theology, and Liturgy in the First Five Centuries*. Grand Rapids, MI, and Cambridge, UK: Eerdmans, 2009.

Johnson, Maxwell E. *The Rites of Christian Initiation: Their Evolution and Interpretation*. Collegeville, MN: Liturgical Press, 1999.

Kavanagh, Aidan. *The Shape of Baptism*. New York: Pueblo, 1978.

Osborne, Kenan. *The Christian Sacraments of Initiation*. New York: Paulist Press, 1987.

Confirmation

Austin, Gerard. *The Rite of Confirmation: Anointing with the Spirit*. New York: Pueblo, 1985.

Kavanagh, Aidan. *Confirmation: Origins and Reform*. New York: Pueblo, 1988.

Turner, Paul. *Confirmation: The Baby in Solomon's Court*. New York: Paulist Press, 1993.

Eucharist

Irwin, Kevin. *Models of the Eucharist*. New York: Paulist Press, 2005.

Kilmartin, Edward J. *The Eucharist in the West: History and Theology*. Edited by Robert J. Daly. Collegeville, MN: Liturgical Press, 1998.

LaVerdiere, Eugene. *The Eucharist in the New Testament and the Early Church*. Collegeville, MN: Liturgical Press, 1996.

Léon-Dufour, Xavier. *Sharing the Eucharistic Bread: The Witness of the New Testament*. New York: Paulist Press, 1987.

Pierce, Joanne M., and Michael Downey, eds. *Source and Summit: Commemorating Josef A. Jungmann, SJ*. Collegeville, MN: Liturgical Press, 1999.

Power, David N. *The Eucharistic Mystery: Revitalizing the Tradition*. New York: Crossroad, 1994.

———. *The Sacrifice We Offer: The Tridentine Dogma and Its Reinterpretation*. New York: Crossroad, 1987.

Schillebeeckx, Edward. *The Eucharist*. London: Burns & Oats, 2005.

Chapter 10

Sacraments of Healing and Vocation

Familiarity with the history of the sacraments reveals how much they have changed over the centuries. In this chapter we will consider the sacraments of healing—penance and the anointing of the sick—and what we might call sacraments of vocation—marriage and order.

Penance and Reconciliation

The history of the sacrament of penance, now called reconciliation, is complicated.[1] The New Testament recognizes the Christian community's power of proclaiming the forgiveness of sin and sees church leaders as playing a role in the process. Paul excludes from the community a man living in an incestuous relationship with his stepmother (1 Cor 5:1-13) and later bids the community to welcome back someone who has been similarly disciplined (2 Cor 5:5-11). Matthew's Gospel gives church leaders the authority of "binding and loosing," excluding sinners and readmitting those who had repented, as in the synagogue tradition (Matt 18:15-18). The Fourth Gospel sees the risen Jesus as bestowing on the disciples the same power to forgive or retain sins (John 20:23). Post–New Testament texts (1 Clement, the *Didache*) speak of postbaptismal forgiveness and reconciliation, though the *Shepherd of Hermas* seemed to limit it to one occasion,

---

[1] The classic study is Bernhard Poschmann, *Penance and the Anointing of the Sick* (New York: Herder & Herder, 1964).

referring to it as a "second chance." Less serious sins were confessed to one another (Jas 5:16) or collectively acknowledged at the Eucharist.

Canonical Penance

As imminent eschatological expectation began to fade, the churches in the second and third centuries began to develop a process for penance and reconciliation known as canonical penance. Analogous to the catechumenate, those guilty of serious sin—apostasy, murder, and adultery—were required to enter the order of penitents. Like the catechumens, they were led out of the Sunday assembly after the Liturgy of the Word and could return only after a period of prayer and penance, sometimes lasting years. Penances often included fasting, abstinence from sexual relations or the use of arms, so seriously was the baptismal commitment taken. Some churches anointed those entering the order of penitents with ashes, from which was to develop the Ash Wednesday tradition.[2] After completing their penance, penitents were welcomed back by the bishop. Underlying the bishop's role in reconciliation is the sense that serious sin damages the community, and that the one who represents the community extends the grace of reconciliation.

Canonical penance was thus public and not to be repeated. The process was rigorous, sometimes called a "second baptism" or "second plank" (Tertullian). Many chose to wait for sacramental reconciliation until close to death. Rigorists like the Novatians and Montanists objected to the process, seeing no pardon for idolatry, murder, and adultery. Others, like Tertullian, had longer lists of serious sins. But by the sixth century, the practice had been largely abandoned.

In the East, perhaps as early as the fifth century, the theology of repentance in the context of what would be called today spiritual direction had come to include reconciliation.[3] In the West, sixth-century penitents, under the influence of the Irish monks, began

---

[2] See James Dallen, *The Reconciling Community: The Rite of Penance* (Collegeville, MN: Liturgical Press, 1992).

[3] Alexis Torrance, *Repentance in Late Antiquity: Eastern Asceticism and the Framing of Christian Life* (Oxford: Oxford University Press, 2013).

confessing their sins to a monk or spiritual guide, not always a priest. The confessor would assign a penance, and after the penance was performed, the penitent would receive reconciliation. The Irish monks developed penitential books that provided lists of penances appropriate to the various sins. Gradually this affected a change in the ritual of reconciliation, from public penance to private "confession," with the option of repeating the sacrament. Various synods and councils tried to proscribe the new practice, but because it met a pastoral need, the Fourth Lateran Council decreed in 1215 that everyone who had committed a serious sin should confess it within the year. By this time, a ritual for confession had developed; a penitent would confess to a priest, receive a penance, and then receive absolution. Scholastic theology attributed forgiveness to the sacramental power of the keys, exercised by the priest, though Aquinas recognized confession to a layperson in an emergency as an imperfect sacrament.[4]

Penance Post-Reformation

Luther kept the practice of confessing one's sins, though he did not consider it a sacrament because it was not clearly instituted by Christ. Article 11 of the Augsburg Confession says, "Private Absolution ought to be retained in the churches, although in confession an enumeration of all sins is not necessary. For it is impossible according to the Psalm: Who can understand his errors?"[5] The Council of Trent defined penance in terms of contrition, confession, absolution, and satisfaction, countering the Reformers that it had been instituted by Christ. The 1614 *Rituale Romanum* required listing sins by species and number. For many Catholics, frequent or weekly confession, even of venial sins, became the norm; most American Catholics grew up with what were called "confessions of devotion," part of what Jay Dolan described as a "culture of sin."[6]

---

[4] Aquinas, *Summa Theologica*, supplementum q. 8, a. 2.

[5] *The Book of Concord: The Confessions of the Lutheran Church*, http: //bookofconcord .org/augsburgconfession.php.

[6] Jay P. Dolan, *The American Catholic Experience* (Garden City, NY: Doubleday, 1985), 221.

A post–Vatican II Rite of Penance was promulgated in 1973 providing three forms: individual confession with absolution, a communal penance service with opportunity for individual confession, and general absolution, though permission for the third form has rarely been given. Communal celebration adds thanksgiving, the reading of Scripture, and a sense of solidarity in both sin and grace to the celebration of reconciliation.[7] Few Catholics "go to confession" today, but those who do often see it as an opportunity for spiritual counseling and direction. When one approaches the sacrament with a deep sense of contrition, it can be a genuine experience of grace. In parishes, communal penance services are popular especially during Advent and Lent.

Sacrament of the Sick

The author of James writes, "Is anyone among you sick? He should summon the presbyters of the church, and they should pray over him and anoint [him] with oil in the name of the Lord, and the prayer of faith will save the sick person, and the Lord will raise him up. If he has committed any sins, he will be forgiven" (Jas 5:14-15). This prayer in James is not only for physical healing but also for God's saving grace. In the early centuries, oil blessed by the bishop was used in various healing rituals. The *Apostolic Tradition* includes a prayer for the bishop's blessing of oil that it might "give strength to all that taste of it and health to all that use it" (*Apostolic Tradition* 5). Family members might use it to anoint the sick, or the sick persons might anoint themselves or even drink it.

More formal rites appear in the Gelasian and Gregorian Sacramentaries stemming from the Carolingian Reform (740–840); they included prayers for anointing the sick and dying, and Viaticum, "food for the journey." From this period forward, the rite was restricted to the ministry of priests and included pardon for sins.[8] Thus it became

---

[7] James Dallen, *The Reconciling Community: The Rite of Penance* (Collegeville, MN: Liturgical Press, 1992).

[8] John J. Ziegler, *Let Them Anoint the Sick* (Collegeville, MN: Liturgical Press, 1987), 68–70.

associated with a sacrament for the dying; Peter Lombard included this "extreme unction" or last anointing in his list of the seven sacraments. Comparing it to baptism and penance, Aquinas called it "a spiritual healing or cure."[9] Though Trent left open the possibility of the sacrament giving physical healing (DS 1696), it continued to be seen as a sacrament for the dying, as the name unfortunately suggested.

Following Vatican II, the revised rite reinstituted the last anointing in the broader context of the pastoral care of the sick.[10] Now known as the sacrament of the anointing of the sick (SC 73), it is seen as an act of the church and so should be celebrated communally. It includes the proclamation of the Word, the prayer of faith, the laying on of hands, and the anointing of the forehead and hands with oil. Particularly important is the human touch. The new rite sees the sacrament as a help toward salvation that may restore health or prepare one for death. Not just the seriously ill, but the elderly, those expecting surgery, or the infirm in body or mind can receive the sacrament.

Marriage

It is obvious to many that marriage as an institution is changing. As of 2012, it was estimated that probably 40 to 50 percent of marriages would end in divorce. The number of petitions for annulments in the United States has dropped from a high of 72,308 in 1990 to 18,558 in 2014, while between 1970 and 2014 the number of Catholic marriages dropped from 420,000 to 154,000, suggesting that fewer Catholics are marrying in the church or seeking to take advantage of the annulment process.[11] Thus from a sacramental perspective, an increasing number of Catholics forego both the sacrament and the institution. Stephen Schloesser sees a shift brought on by the "biopolitics" of the twentieth century from marriage and family as an

---

[9] Aquinas, *Summa Theologica*, supplementum, q. 30, a. 1.

[10] The revised rite was originally called the *Rite of Anointing and Pastoral Care of the Sick*; it was revised and translated as *Pastoral Care of the Sick: Rite of Anointing and Viaticum* (Washington, DC: ICEL, 1982).

[11] Statistics for the Center for Applied Research in the Apostolate (CARA); http://cara.georgetown.edu/CARAServices/requestedchurchstats.html.

economic unit to what he calls "companionate" marriage, an emotional union.[12] Civil recognition of gay marriage challenges the procreative meaning of the institution and thus its heterosexual meaning.

Marriage in Scripture

The first creation story (Gen 1:1-2:4a) teaches that humankind (Hb *ʾāḏām*) is created male and female in the image and likeness of God and told by the Creator to be fertile and multiply. The second story (Gen 2:4b-25) suggests that man and woman are created for each other: "That is why a man leaves his father and mother and clings to his wife, and the two of them become one body" (Gen 2:25). Marital love is celebrated frequently, for example, in the book of Tobit and in the Song of Songs, a frankly erotic poem. The law contained in Deuteronomy allowed a man to divorce his wife for "something indecent" but did not extend the same right to the wife (Deut 24:1). At the same time, the Old Testament, a period in which polygamy was widespread, does not offer a developed theology of marriage.

The New Testament goes further. Jesus forbade divorce for either partner (Mark 10:11-12; Matt 5:31-32; Luke 16:18). Paul's view of marriage could be described as quasi sacramental, a sign of grace and union. Paul sees marriage as a charism (1 Cor 7:7), a gift of the Spirit for the building up of the church, and he recognizes the transforming power of a marriage lived in faith to make holy both the spouses and their children, even in the case where one partner is a nonbeliever (1 Cor 7:14). What is interesting about this passage is that though Paul knows of Jesus' prohibition of divorce, he makes an exception based on pastoral need for the believer in the case where the nonbeliever will not live in peace. Ephesians sees the union of husband and wife as a great *mysterion* or symbol of the intimate union of Christ and the church (Eph 5:32). Jerome would translate *mysterion* as *sacramentum*, though there are other reasons for seeing marriage as a sacrament.

---

[12] Stephen R. Schloesser, " 'Dancing on the Edge of the Volcano': Biopolitics and What Happened after Vatican II," in *From Vatican II to Pope Francis: Charting a Catholic Future*, ed. Paul Crowley (Maryknoll, NY: Orbis Books, 2014), 6.

Marriage in the Tradition

Marriage was the last sacrament to be officially named as such, and its theology was slow in being developed.[13] In the early centuries, Christian marriage was a secular affair, though not without Christian and ecclesial significance. Augustine used the Ephesians text to speak of its sacramental nature; in his *On the Good of Marriage* (no. 32), he listed fidelity, offspring, and the sacrament as its primary values. Fidelity meant a commitment of love and faithfulness to each other, excluding the reducing of either partner to a mere sexual object. Children were to be accepted lovingly from God and brought up in the faith. Sacrament meant the marital union was indissolvable, a visible sign of the union of the blessed in heaven. Thus marriage had both individual and social meaning. From the fourth to the eleventh centuries, increasing emphasis was placed on its ecclesial dimension, including liturgical ceremonies, while its sacramental nature was developed in the following centuries.

By the twelfth century, a ritual wedding ceremony at which the priest officiated was in place. Lombard included marriage among the seven sacraments in his *Sentences* (c. 1150). It was declared a sacrament by the Council of Verona in 1184. Trent, against Luther, affirmed the sacramentality of marriage and imposed the requirement of canonical form, that is, marriage in the presence of an ordained minister. Augustine's influence may have shaped the tendency to make the primary end of marriage procreation and treat it in contractual terms.

More personalist themes began to enter Catholic teaching on marriage prior to Vatican II, while the council itself acknowledged the importance of conjugal love by moving beyond the old language of the primary and secondary ends of marriage and replacing the older contract language with that of covenant. *Gaudium et Spes* sees marriage as ordained for the begetting and education of children, though that is not the sole reason for which it was instituted. The constitution describes marriage in the language of conjugal love and intimacy, self-gift, vocation, covenant, indissolubility, and the equal dignity of

---

[13] Edward Schillebeeckx provides a history of the sacrament in *Marriage: Human Reality and Saving Mystery* (New York: Sheed and Ward, 1965); see also *Marriage, Readings in Moral Theology 15*, ed. Charles E. Curran and Julie Hanlon Rubio (New York: Paulist Press, 2009).

the spouses (GS 48–50). It is the love of the spouses and their faithfulness to each other that can sustain and nourish the new life which marital love, in cooperating with divine love, brings forth. In his theology of the body, Pope John Paul II sought to integrate the personal and sexual nature of the person into an ecclesial understanding of sex and marriage,[14] though some have criticized his understanding of women as based primarily on motherhood.

Contemporary Theology of Marriage

Contemporary Roman Catholic approaches to marriage suggest moving from an individualistic emphasis on interpersonal fulfillment to a social view of marriage, relating it to community and church.[15] For Karl Rahner, marriage is a sign of a love that opens a person to include rather than exclude, becoming in this way a sign of God's love that is open to all. "Christian marriage has at all times the force of a real representation of the unifying love of God in Christ for mankind. In marriage the Church is made present."[16] Similarly, Edward Schillebeeckx treats marriage as a secular reality transformed by the grace of salvation, becoming an eschatological sign of God's love revealed in the death and resurrection of Jesus. Thus for Schillebeeckx it becomes a sacrament—a culminating point of an event set in motion by God: "In these two who love each other, God himself arouses a new and greater love—a love like that which he himself has for his people, the church."[17] For Francis Schüssler Fiorenza, marriage as a sign of Christian discipleship is a sign and symbol of the church brought about by God in the Spirit.[18]

Walter Kasper sees the love of husband and wife for each other in Christian marriage as an effective sign of Christ and the love of God. In other words, in sacramental marriage husband and wife help each

[14] John Paul II, *Familiaris Consortio* (1981); see also John Paul II, *Man and Woman He Created Them: A Theology of the Body* (Boston: Pauline Books, 2006).

[15] See Lisa Sowle Cahill, "Marriage: Developments in Catholic Theology and Ethics," *Theological Studies* 64 (2003): 78–105.

[16] Karl Rahner, "Marriage as a Sacrament," in *Theological Investigations* vol. 10 (New York: Crossroad, 1973), 221.

[17] Schillebeeckx, *Marriage*, xxix.

[18] Francis Schüssler Fiorenza, "Marriage," in *Systematic Theology: Roman Catholic Perspectives*, 2nd ed. (Minneapolis, MN: Fortress Press, 2011), 606–11.

other and their children experience the love of God. For Kasper, it is also a sacrament of the church, the church in miniature or "domestic church" and an eschatological sign of the gathering of all people at the end of time, not unlike the approach of Rahner and Schillebeeckx.[19]

Beyond the theological understanding of marriage, the church today faces a number of pastoral issues that touch on marriage, among them, divorce and remarriage, birth control, and same-sex marriage. We need to consider them briefly.

Divorce and Remarriage

From the beginning, it has been obvious that some marriages fail to achieve the ideal of what marriage in Christ should be and so could be said to die. The pastoral problem is how to honor the clear teachings of Jesus against divorce and still respond with compassion to those who want to enter a second marriage and continue to take an active part in the sacramental life of the church. Various pastoral accommodations have been made in Christian history.

Some churches, without necessarily approving of divorce, allow remarriage without penalty. The Orthodox churches, using their principle of economy, generally allow for a second marriage and even a third without excluding sacramental participation. The rite for the second or subsequent marriage has a complicated history; the present rite includes several penitential prayers. Catholic practice recognizes several pastoral accommodations for those whose marriages fail and are in a second marriage.[20] One is the annulment process, a judgment of a matrimonial tribunal that a canonically valid marriage never existed because at the time the marriage was entered into, one of the "goods" of marriage—freedom, intention of permanence, and openness to offspring—was missing, or some "impediment" such as a prior marriage bond stood in the way. Since Vatican II, the grounds for granting an annulment have been enlarged, adding "lack of due discretion," recognizing that entering into a marriage covenant demands discernment and a certain degree of maturity.

---

[19] Walter Kasper, *Theology of Christian Marriage* (New York: Crossroad, 1981), 34–44.
[20] For an overview see Lisa Sowle Cahill, "Marriage and Divorce in Canon Law," in *Theological Studies* 47, no. 1 (1986): 112–17.

A second pastoral approach common in the United States is called the "internal forum" solution. When a person living in a technically invalid second marriage sincerely believes that a first marriage lacked something for indissolubility but is unable to receive a declaration of nullity through the annulment process, he or she, after seeking counsel from a priest confessor or counselor, may decide to approach the Eucharist on the basis of conscience.[21] Though Pope John Paul II in *Familiaris Consortio* (no. 84) disapproved of those not validly married receiving the Eucharist, many priests today make use of this approach. Today many Catholics simply make the decision for themselves.

Cardinal Walter Kasper, with the support of the German Episcopal Conference, has argued that though Jesus' teaching on marriage is clear, to help those Catholics in civil marriages who want to participate more fully in the church's sacramental life, the church could tolerate but not accept a second union, perhaps on an analogy with canonical penance.[22] Pope Francis has called repeatedly for streamlining the annulment process. The issue was presented again at the 2015 Synod of Bishops on the Family, which recommended the internal forum solution.

Contraception and Birth Control

Catholic teaching against contraception goes back to at least to the fourth century, but it did not become a critical question until the end of the nineteenth century when the practice of birth control became more common in Europe. After the 1930 Anglican Lambeth Conference gave qualified approval to the practice, Pope Pius XI condemned any form of contraception in his 1930 encyclical on marriage *Casti Connubii*. His successor, Pius XII, moved Catholic teaching a step forward in approving periodic abstinence during a woman's fertile period, the so-called rhythm method, in an address to the Italian Society of Catholic Midwives in 1951.

---

[21] See Cahill, "Marriage and Divorce in Canon Law," 114; see also Oskar Saier, Karl Lehmann, and Walter Kasper, "Pastoral Ministry: The Divorced and Remarried," in Curran and Rubio, *Marriage*, 391–92.

[22] Cindy Wooden, "Cardinal Outlines Possible Paths to Communion for Divorced, Remarried," *Catholic News Service*, February 28, 2014; see also Kasper, *Theology of Christian Marriage*, 62–71.

The question of contraception was raised with a new intensity with the appearance of the birth control pill in the 1950s. After Pope John XXIII set up an international commission to discuss both it and population, many Catholics hoped that the Second Vatican Council would address the question, but Pope Paul VI kept it off the council's agenda. Instead, he expanded the commission to sixty-nine members, including representatives of the laity. In 1967, the commission voted sixty-four to four (Archbishop Karol Wojtyla, later Pope John Paul II, was absent) in favor of a change in the traditional teaching that all use of contraceptives was immoral. After considering the question carefully, Paul VI reaffirmed the traditional teaching in his 1968 encyclical *Humanae Vitae*, arguing that "each and every marriage act must remain open of the transmission of life" (no. 11) because of the inseparable link between its unitive and procreative meaning.

Few issues have been as divisive for Catholics, introducing the idea of "dissent" into Catholic life as theologians and academics disagreed with the papal teaching. As many as thirteen episcopal conferences tried to soften the encyclical's teaching in their responses.[23] According to Leslie Tentler, many confessors, required by the encyclical to uphold a teaching they did not fully agree with, encouraged their penitents to follow their own conscience, leading to a diminishing of the effective authority of the magisterium on matters of sexuality. Tentler says that a 1969 survey found 43 percent of priests stressing the primacy of conscience, with another 7 percent encouraging the "responsible" use of contraceptives. Only 13 percent of priests over age fifty-five claimed that they would deny absolution to those who refused to follow *Humanae Vitae*.[24] While some claim that 98 percent of Catholic women use contraceptives at some point in their lives, more realistic statistics suggest a number between 68 and 76 percent.[25] In any case, one could argue that the teaching has not been received by the church.

---

[23] See Vincent J. Genovesi, *In Pursuit of Love: Catholic Morality and Human Sexuality* (Wilmington, DE: Michael Glazier, 1987), 237–38.

[24] See Leslie Woodcock Tentler, *Catholics and Contraception* (Ithaca, NY: Cornell University Press, 2004), 273.

[25] Retired archbishop John R. Quinn cited a study at the 1980 Synod of Bishops that gave the 76.5 percent number; see his "New Context of Contraceptive Teaching," *Origins* 10 (1980): 263–67; see also Tentler, *Catholics and Contraception*, 266–68.

Pope Francis has tried to reframe the issue by situating it within the context of "responsible parenthood." While defending Paul VI's teaching, he cautioned against families having too many children, saying that the church has "many licit ways" to limit reproduction. At the same time, he rejected as "ideological colonialization" efforts of governments to force birth control programs on developing countries by tying them to aid.[26]

Same-Sex Marriage

Marriage between persons of the same sex implicitly redefines marriage in terms of partnership rather than procreation. Advocacy for civil recognition of same-sex marriage began in the United States in the 1970s but became a strong movement after the supreme court of Hawaii in 1993 declared in Baehr v. Lewin the state's prohibition of same-sex marriage to be unconstitutional. By 2015, same-sex marriages were recognized in thirty-six states and the District of Columbia as well as in at least eighteen countries, including Ireland, which approved it by popular vote. It was made a constitutional right throughout the United States by the Supreme Court on June 26, 2015.

The Catholic Church, understanding the meaning of marriage as both procreative and unitive and unable to approve of homosexual activity, is not able to recognize same-sex marriages as sacramental.[27] At the same time, many Catholics think that the church needs to do more to include gay people and make them welcome. Some are asking today if marriage must be limited to the possibility of biological reproduction. Pope Francis defends the idea of marriage as a union between a man and a woman but appears to be open to domestic unions as a compromise.[28] The question of how to make same-sex couples more welcome surfaced at the Extraordinary Synod on the Family in 2014.

[26] Francis X. Rocca, "Pope says Catholics Must Practice 'Responsible Parenthood'," Catholic News Service, January 19, 2015; http://cara.georgetown.edu/CARAServices /requestedchurchstats.html.

[27] For another view see Stephen J. Pope, "The Magisterium's Arguments against 'Same-Sex Marriage': An Ethical Analysis," in Curran and Rubio, *Marriage*, 300–329.

[28] John L. Allen, "Caution on Pope Francis and Recognition of Gay Unions," *National Catholic Reporter*, March 20, 2013, http://ncronline.org/blogs/ncr-today/cautions -pope-francis-and-recognition-gay-unions.

Holy Orders

The sacrament of order (or "Holy Orders," as it is officially called) developed out of the need in the church of the postapostolic age to institutionalize appointment to the church's emerging pastoral office. In the primitive church, the apostles exercised oversight over local church leaders and were consulted when problems arose.[29] For Paul, an apostle was someone who had seen the risen Jesus and been sent to preach the Gospel; they were early Christian missionaries. Among the apostles, "the Twelve" held pride of place (cf. Gal 2:9), but identifying them as apostles was probably a later Lukan reflection. The bishops eventually succeeded the apostles, though they were not considered apostles themselves.[30]

New Testament Foundations

In the early communities, leadership beyond that of the apostles was rather fluid; those exercising leadership roles were differently named. Paul refers to them as prophets and teachers (1 Cor 12:28), leaders or presiders (*proistamenoi*; 1 Thess 5:12; Rom 12:8), overseers and ministers (*episkopoi kai diakonoi*; Phil 1:1; Rom 16:1), and heads of house churches (1 Cor 16:19; Rom 16:5; Phlm 2; Col 4:15). Leaders (*hēgoumenoi*) are mentioned in Hebrews (13:7, 17, 24) and Luke (22:26). Prophets and teachers are still visible in some later books (Acts 13:1-3; *Didache* 15.1). Underlying all these roles was the concept of *diakonia*, service, used even prior to Paul, a term adopted from Jesus' reference to himself as a servant. In addition to these leading roles or ministries, Paul recognized a rich variety of charisms or gifts of the Spirit (1 Cor 12:4-11), and while some community members had leading roles, it would be too early to speak of a church office.

Threefold Ministry

As the apostles and original witnesses began to fade from the scene and the churches faced the threat of false teachers and schism, they

---

[29] Edward Schillebeeckx, *Ministry: Leadership in the Community of Jesus Christ* (New York: Crossroad, 1981), 9.

[30] Francis A. Sullivan, *From Apostles to Bishops: The Development of the Episcopacy in the Early Church* (New York: Paulist Press, 2001).

went through a process of institutionalization in which those identified as presbyters or bishops assumed the roles once exercised by the prophets, teachers, and leaders in the local communities, as well as the leaders of the house churches. In the process, community leadership was becoming an office, emerging as early as the early second century as the traditional threefold ministry.

The office of the deacon is already in evidence in the Pastoral Epistles. The office of presbyter, literally "elder," was originally a Jewish institution borrowed from the synagogue (1 Pet 5:1; Jas 5:14), while the overseer (*episkopos*) also seems to have been Jewish in origin—Qumran had overseers with responsibilities similar to those of the presbyters in the Pastoral Letters. The two terms were not at first clearly distinguished; some presbyters seem to have combined the functions of community leadership and teaching (Acts 20:17-35), as did earlier the "pastors and teachers" in Ephesians 4:11. In 1 Timothy (5:17), such presbyters are awarded a double compensation. According to John Meier, these presbyters represented a group emerging within the presbyteral college, exercising not just supervision but also the liturgical roles implied by preaching and teaching. It was these specialized presbyters who may have received the title *episkopos* at Ephesus (cf. 1 Tim 3:1-7).[31] According to Raymond Brown, "In churches associated with the three great apostolic figures of the NT, Paul, James, and Peter, presbyters were known and established in the last third of the century."[32]

Thus the later New Testament represents a transitional period in which, in a number of churches, the offices of presbyter/bishops and deacons were evolving into the traditional threefold ministry or pastoral office of a bishop, assisted by presbyters and deacons. Already in place at Antioch and some other churches in the early second century, by the end of the century it could be found virtually throughout the church. The laying on of hands as a sign of appointment to community leadership is in place by the early third century. The *Apostolic Tradition* (2.3) refers to it in the context of the ordination of

---

[31] John P. Meier, "*Presbyteros* in the Pastoral Epistles," *Catholic Biblical Quarterly* 35 (1973): 344–45.

[32] Raymond E. Brown, "*Episkopê* and *Episkopos*: The New Testament Evidence," *Theological Studies* 41 (1980): 336.

a bishop, and Eusebius attests to the practice in quoting a letter by Cornelius, bishop of Rome to Fabius, bishop of Antioch (6.43.9). Some see the laying on of hands as appointment to office in earlier texts (1 Tim 4:14; 5:22; 2 Tim 1:6; Acts 13:1-3), but the meaning of these texts is disputed.[33] The word "ordination" comes from the Latin (*ordinare*) "to order" or incorporate into an order, for example, the *ordo episcoporum* or *ordo presbyterorum*.

The bishop's authority was strengthened by the struggle against Montanism and Gnosticism in the second century. To counter the Montanist claim of continuing revelations, the principle developed that revelation had "closed" with the death of the last apostle. Against the Gnostics, who appealed to secret, unwritten traditions, writers such as Hegesippus, Irenaeus, and Tertullian used lists of the bishops from churches with an apostolic foundation to demonstrate visible continuity with the apostolic tradition, leading to the recognition of the bishops as authoritative teachers and bearers of the apostolic faith, thus as successors to the apostles.[34]

Presiding at the Eucharist

The New Testament provides little evidence about who presided at the Eucharist. Some think that those who led house churches included eucharistic presidency among their roles. Luke seems to link the apostles with the Eucharist, situating a tradition on ministry in the context of the Last Supper (Luke 22:24-27) and showing the prophets and teachers at Antioch engaged in the liturgy (*leitourgountōn*) of the Lord (Acts 13:2). The *Didache* recognizes the prophets and teachers as eucharistic leaders (10.7), urging the community to elect bishops and deacons with the encouragement that "they too conduct (*leitourgousi*) the liturgy of the prophets and teachers" (15.1). Ignatius of Antioch (d. 110) clearly links eucharistic presidency with church leadership: "You should regard that Eucharist as valid which is celebrated either by the bishop or by someone he authorizes"

---

[33] See Brian P. Irwin, "The Laying on of Hands in 1 Timothy 5:22: A New Proposal," *Bulletin for Biblical Research* 18, no. 1 (2008): 123–29.

[34] Sullivan, *From Apostles to Bishops*, 229–30.

(*Smyrneans* 8.1). The origins of ordained ministry in community leadership should be taken seriously in calling people to orders today.

Though the New Testament does not refer to Christian ministers as priests, the *Didache* (c. 100) calls the wandering prophets who served as eucharistic leaders (10.7) "high priests" (13.3). In the early third century, the word "priest" (*hiereus, sacerdos*) began to be used for bishops. The prayer of consecration attributed to Hippolytus of Rome (c. 215) refers to the bishop as "high priest," while Tertullian (d. 225) and Cyprian (d. 258) also speak of the bishop as *sacerdos*. Cyprian extended the term to presbyters (from which the English word "priest" is derived), but only when referred to jointly with the bishop, a usage that has been traditional in the church. It is also in Cyprian that we find the first reference to presbyters presiding at the Eucharist without the bishop (Letter, 5).

Emergence of the Sacral Model

In the second and third centuries, presbyters and bishops were not distinguished from others by dress or special privileges, but after Constantine's Edict of Milan in 313, when the church received legal status, bishops began to receive certain honors and privileges and to wear the insignia of high officials such as the pallium and the stole. Before long, as the liturgy became more ornate, other clergy began wearing distinctive clothing. Recent studies have described the "sacerdotalizing"[35] and "clericalization"[36] of the church's pastoral office in the period between the fourth and the tenth centuries, turning it into a sacral office. From the 1100s on, theologians defined holy orders not in terms of the bishop but in terms of the priest, who differed from others in the church by his "sacred power" (*sacra potestas*) to "confect" the Eucharist. The Council of Florence (1439) defined the sign of ordination as the handing over of a chalice with wine and a paten with bread, though today the sign is seen as the laying on of hands.

---

[35] Edward Schillebeeckx, *The Church with a Human Face* (New York: Crossroad, 1985), 144–47.

[36] Kenan B. Osborne, *Priesthood: A History of Ordained Ministry in the Roman Catholic Church* (New York: Paulist Press, 1988), 145–48.

The Council of Trent, in reacting to the Reformers' emphasis on the ordained ministry as a preaching office (*Predigamt*) or simply ministry (*Dienst*), reaffirmed its cultic dimension; it emphasized a visible priesthood with "the power of consecrating, offering, and administering" the body and blood of Christ and forgiving sins (DS 1764). The priestly spirituality of the so-called French School founded by Cardinal Pierre de Bérulle furthered the cultic understanding of the priest's office by centering it on the priest's role in celebrating the Eucharist. It was this model of priesthood that informed Catholic thinking down to Vatican II.

The Second Vatican Council

The Second Vatican Council provided a new rationale for the bishop in its collegial teaching on the episcopal office, and it elaborated a theology of the laity, but it said relatively little about the priest. They were prudent cooperators with the episcopal order, consecrated to preach the Gospel, shepherd the faithful, and celebrate divine worship. They constitute one priesthood with the bishop and are bound together with other priests in intimate brotherhood, symbolized by their joining the bishop in laying on of hands on the one being ordained (LG 28). *Presbyterorum Ordinis*, the Decree on the Ministry and Life of Priests, speaks of priesthood in terms of ministry and service rather than sacramental power, with the word "ministry" appearing more than forty-five times in the document. It chose the concept of the priest acting in the person of Christ the head (*in persona Christi capitis*) (PO 2) as foundational to its theology of the presbyteral office.

The council also restored the ancient office of the deacon, on whom hands were imposed "not unto the priesthood, but unto a ministry of service" (LG 29). This once important office had been reduced to a step on the way to presbyteral ordination. As of 2014, there were 17,464 permanent deacons in the United States alone. Women also were once ordained as deaconesses in the Greek Byzantine and Syriac traditions. An important part of their ministry was to care for sick women and assist for reasons of decency at the baptism of women; their liturgical tasks were much restricted compared to those of the deacons and they did not preach publicly or baptize. Cipriano

Vagaggini and Roger Gryson argue that their ordination was equal to that of the male deacons.[37] There were no deaconesses in the West before the fifth century, when "deaconess" began to be used as an honorary title for professed widows, associated with a particular liturgical blessing.[38] Some argue on the basis of precedent that women could be ordained deacons today.[39]

The council's failure to develop more fully the theology of the presbyteral office has led to different interpretations of the office in the postconciliar church and to a crisis of identity for many priests. Karl Rahner stressed the kerygmatic aspect of the priest's role; Otto Semmelroth and John Paul II emphasized the cultic or sacramental aspect; Thomas O'Meara, Robert Schwartz, and Hans Küng emphasized community leadership. Many priests who lived through the council adopted the model of priest as spiritual leader of the community, especially after Schwartz's book, defining the priest as a servant leader.[40] In the 1980s, many younger priests, often called "John Paul II priests," began reclaiming the cultic model, stressing the priest as a "man set apart," with an ontological difference from the faithful.

The Vatican also moved toward claiming a more cultic understanding of the priest, stressing an identity distinct from the faithful. A 1997 instruction published jointly by eight Vatican congregations was titled, "On Certain Questions Regarding the Collaboration of the Non-Ordained Faithful in the Sacred Ministry of the Priest," reclaiming the concept of *"potestas sacra"* as the faculty to act in the person of Christ the head and forbidding the nonordained faithful from using titles such as "pastor," "chaplain," "coordinator," "moderator," or other similar titles. In a new translation (2000/2002) of the "Rites of Ordination of a Bishop, of Priests, and of Deacons,"

---

[37] Cipriano Vagaggini, *Ordination of Women in the Diaconate in the Eastern Churches*, ed. Phyllis Zagano (Collegeville, MN: Liturgical Press, 2013), 59; Roger Gryson, *The Ministry of Women in the Early Church* (Collegeville, MN: Liturgical Press, 1976), 120; arguing against this is Aimé Georges Martimort, *Deaconesses: An Historical Study* (San Francisco: Ignatius Press, 1986), 245–46.

[38] Gryson, *The Ministry of Women in the Early Church*, 100–102.

[39] Phyllis Zagano, *Holy Saturday: The Argument for the Restoration of the Female Diaconate in the Catholic Church* (New York: Crossroad, 2000); Vagaggini, *Ordination of Women*, 59.

[40] Robert Schwartz, *Servant Leaders of the People of God* (New York: Paulist Press, 1989).

the terms "presbyter" and "presbyterate," appearing in the earlier 1993 translation were changed to "priest" and "priesthood." The homily for the rite speaks of the ones ordained being advanced "to the Order of Priests," language that is neither traditional nor theologically appropriate, since there is no order of priesthood, only the orders of the bishop, presbyter, or deacon.[41]

Contemporary Catholic Theology

The concept of the priest acting in the person of Christ is an ancient one, based on the bishop's role as leader of the local church. Edward Kilmartin traces it back as far as 1 Clement (96); he sees the concept developing from the author's description of church leaders as successors of the apostles, sent by Christ, who in turn was sent by God.[42] Cyprian (d. 258) described the bishop as acting in the place of Christ (*vice Christi*) as priest and judge (Ep 59.5.1) and in presiding at the Eucharist (Ep 63.14.1). Medieval theology saw the priest acting *in persona Christi* at the Eucharist in virtue of the power of consecration received at ordination, while the bishop did so in virtue of his pastoral office. At the same time, scholastic theologians spoke of the priest as acting *in persona ecclesiae* in virtue of his role as president of the liturgical assembly.

Pope Pius XII adopted this theology of the priest acting *in persona Christi* in his encyclicals *Mystici Corporis* (1943) and *Mediator Dei* (1947), extending it so that the priest is said to represent Christ in offering the sacrifice of the cross, and so represents the whole church.[43] But this makes the priest's acting *in persona ecclesiae* dependent on his acting *in persona Christi*. There remains a difference of opinion as to whether the christological or ecclesial representation has priority.[44]

---

[41] For a further discussion, see Thomas P. Rausch, "Vatican II on the Priesthood: Fifty Years Later," *Seminary Journal* (Winter 2012): 9; see also the *Catechism of the Catholic Church*, 2nd ed. (Vatican City: Libreria Editrice Vaticana, 1997), no. 1538.

[42] Edward J. Kilmartin, "Apostolic Office: Sacrament of Christ," *Theological Studies* 36 (1975): 245; 1 Clement 42.1-4.

[43] Pius XII, *Mystici Corporis*, AAS 35 (1943): 232–33; *Mediator Dei*, AAS 39 (1947): 556.

[44] See Thomas P. Rausch, "Forum: Priestly Identity: Priority of Representation and the Iconic Argument," *Worship* 73 (March 1999): 169–79.

David Coffee has argued that *Presbyterorum Ordinis* and later magisterial texts assume that ordained priesthood is to be understood immediately in christological terms. He criticizes this notion, arguing that the only place where the priest can exercise the headship of Christ is the church, and therefore, his function is directly ecclesiological and only indirectly christological. He also rejects the conclusion, drawn by others but not by the council, that the common priesthood which derives from baptism and is oriented to ecclesial worship is ecclesiological. Unfortunately, the council was unable to reconcile the two priesthoods in the person of Christ, leaving in place "the popular impression of the priest as above the Church rather than as a part of it."[45] Coffee argues that each priesthood possesses properly an ecclesiological nature, and both can have a christological reference. Their essential difference, something the council affirmed but did not describe, should be seen here: "The common priesthood, like that of Christ, is a dynamism of faith, of divine sonship or daughterhood, which the ordained priesthood is not. And the ordained priesthood is a charism, of official witness, which the common priesthood is not."[46]

The key is the question of authorization. In his book *The Priestly Office*, Avery Dulles emphasized the importance of ordination. Though he acknowledges that talk about a priest's "sacred powers" can be misleading,[47] he placed the ecclesial dimension of the priest's representative role before the christological. Ordination incorporates the priest into the order of presbyters, the church's apostolic office. Through ordination in the apostolic succession the priest is enabled "to act in the name of the church and in the name of Christ as head of the church."[48] But as Kilmartin says, "Pastoral office can only represent and act in the name of the Lord when it represents the life of faith of the Church."[49]

---

[45] David Coffee, "The Common and the Ordained Priesthood," *Theological Studies* 58 (1997): 235.

[46] Ibid., 228.

[47] Avery Dulles, *The Priestly Office: A Theological Reflection* (New York: Paulist Press, 1997), 15.

[48] Ibid., 35; see also Richard R. Gaillardetz, "The Ecclesiological Foundations of Ministry within an Ordered Communion," in *Ordering the Baptismal Priesthood*, ed. Susan K. Wood (Collegeville, MN: Liturgical Press, 2003), 36.

[49] Kilmartin, "Apostolic Office," 260.

This theology of authorization is helpful for a number of reasons. It helps clear up Vatican II's inability to reconcile the two priesthoods' relation to Christ. First, laymen and laywomen can indeed represent Christ in their charitable works or in witnessing to their faith, but the priest, authorized by the church to act in its name, represents Christ officially in celebrating the sacraments and particularly in presiding at the Eucharist. Second, while the language of ontological difference is not particularly helpful, it does have some meaning. After ordination, a new relationship exists between the priest and the church; the priest has been incorporated into the church's apostolic office, and consequently a real (ontological) change has come about. This does not suggest some kind of ontological clericalism, placing the priest on a higher level, but acknowledges that there are different orderings in the church's life.[50] Finally, stressing authorization does not mean that the priest is simply a delegate of the community; one must be ordained by legitimate authority. To deny this is to risk dissolving the church into a plurality of self-authorizing groups, thus substituting a congregationalism for Catholicism.

The ministerial priesthood serves the priesthood of the whole church, the Body of Christ, in celebrating the sacraments and particularly the Eucharist. Saying that the priests acts *in persona Christi capitis* (in the person of Christ the head) means that Christ himself truly acts in the church through the one authorized to act in its name, especially in celebrating the Eucharist and the other sacraments. As coworkers with the bishop, the priest expresses the communion between the local community and the universal church.[51]

One final point is important. Given the origins of ordained ministry in community leadership, a charism of pastoral ministry and leadership should be a *sine qua non* for ordination. This also means that a vocation to priesthood should not be considered a private possession of the individual, a felt inner call.[52] It must always be related to a community, as was the case with relative ordination (ordination

---

[50] See Richard R. Gaillardetz, "The Ecclesiological Foundations of Ministry within an Ordered Communion," in Wood, *Ordering the Baptismal Priesthood*, 26–51.

[51] See Roger Mahony and the Priests of the Archdiocese of Los Angeles, *As I Have Done for You: A Pastoral Letter on Ministry* (Chicago: Liturgical Training Publications, 2000), 24–27.

[52] See Edward Hahnenberg, *Awakening Vocation: A Theology of Christian Call* (Collegeville, MN: Liturgical Press, 2010).

for a particular community) in the early church. One is called to orders if and when an aptitude for pastoral leadership, for discerning and empowering the gifts of others, has been recognized.

Ecumenical Consensus

The 1982 WCC text *Baptism, Eucharist and Ministry* was formulated as a consensus of Catholic, Orthodox, and Protestant theologians, though it does not yet represent a consensus of their churches. In the section on ministry, it says that the apostles prefigure the church and those within it entrusted with specific authority, the ordained. Ordained and lay members are interrelated. The responsibility of the ordained is to assemble and build up the Body of Christ by proclaiming and teaching the Word of God, celebrating the sacraments, and guiding the life of the community. The deep communion between Christ and the members of his body is most visible when the ordained minister celebrates the Eucharist (nos. 10–14). The episcopal succession is seen as a profound sign but not a guarantee of the apostolicity of the church (no. 38). Ordination by the laying on of hands is "invocation of the Holy Spirit; sacramental sign; acknowledgement of gifts and commitment" (no. 41). Questions still unresolved include the ordination of women, the necessity of an ordained presider (not required by all churches), and the language of priest and priesthood, though the text recognizes this language as traditional and appropriate, relating the ordained minister to the priestly reality of Christ and the whole community (no. 17).

Conclusion

The history of the sacraments shows considerable change in form and nomenclature. A "second chance" for postbaptismal forgiveness and reconciliation through public penance eventually gave way to a new form of private, "auricular" confession that began emerging in the sixth century; penitents would confess to a monk or priest (or occasionally a layperson), receive a penance, and after the penance was performed, receive reconciliation. By the second millennium, confession was generally to the priest, who would give a penance, sometimes prayers in place of fasting or stipends for prayers by those in monasteries, though confessing to a layperson in an emergency when no priest was available was still recognized. The Second Vatican Council authorized three different forms for what was now called the sacrament of reconciliation.

Prayer and anointing of the sick, mentioned in the letter of James (5:14-15), evolved into using blessed oil for healing and then to a service for the dying called "Extreme Unction." Vatican II reformed the rite to stress communal prayer and anointing by a priest for the sick or dying, called now the sacrament of the sick. Today the sacrament is celebrated for the infirm or those expecting surgery.

If Christian marriage has always been seen as a medium of grace, for Paul a charism, its theology was slow in developing. Opposition to the Albigensian teaching that marriage was evil, as well as the liturgical celebration of marriage with elements from Roman and Germanic traditions, contributed to a sacramental understanding of marriage. Trent established the requirement of sacramental form. Recent Catholic teaching has replaced contractual language with that of covenant and emphasizes the social meaning of the sacrament as an eschatological sign of the union of all people in God's love. Relationality is at the heart of this union.

The sacrament of orders developed out of the institutionalizing of ministry and authority in the late first and early second centuries. By at least the early third century, the laying on of hands had emerged as the sign of appointment to the "order" of bishop or presbyter. In the Middle Ages, the ministry of the priest underwent a clericalization or sacerdotalization, setting the priest apart by dress, language, and privilege and defining the sacrament of orders not in terms of the bishop as head of the local church but in terms of the sacred power received by the priest to "confect" the Eucharist.

Vatican II restored the proper balance by teaching that the bishop received the fullness of the sacrament of orders (LG 21) and by using the language of ministry rather than sacred power to describe the role of the priest. Its concept of the priest acting *"in persona Christi capitis"* (PO 2) suggests a representative understanding of ordained ministry; the bishop, presbyter, or deacon is one officially authorized to act in the name of the church (*in persona ecclesiae*) in kerygmatic and sacramental ministry and thus in the person of Christ, the head of the church. Basic to this ministry is to support the priesthood of all the baptized.

For Further Reading

Reconciliation

Coffey, David M. *The Sacrament of Reconciliation*. Collegeville, MN: Liturgical Press, 2001.

Dallen, James. *The Reconciling Community: The Rite of Penance*. Collegeville, MN: Liturgical Press, 1992.

Poschmann, Bernhard. *Penance and the Anointing of the Sick*. New York: Herder & Herder, 1964.

Anointing of the Sick

Duffy, Regis. *A Roman Catholic Theology of Pastoral Care*. Philadelphia, PA: Fortress Press, 1983.

Empereur, James. *Prophetic Anointing: God's Call to the Sick, the Elderly, and the Dying*. Wilmington, DE: Michael Glazier, 1982.

Larson-Miller, Lizette. *The Sacrament of Anointing of the Sick*. Collegeville, MN: Liturgical Press, 2005.

Meyendorff, Paul. *The Anointing of the Sick*. Crestwood, NY: SVS Press Books, 2009.

Ziegler, John J. *Let Them Anoint the Sick*. Collegeville, MN: Liturgical Press, 1987.

Marriage

Curran, Charles E., and Julie Hanlon Rubio, eds. *Marriage*. Readings in Moral Theology 15. New York: Paulist Press, 2009.

Kasper, Walter. *Theology of Christian Marriage*. New York: Crossroad, 1983.

Lawler, Michael G. *Marriage and Sacrament: A Theology of Christian Marriage*. Collegeville, MN: Liturgical Press, 1993.

Mackin, Theodore. *The Marital Sacrament*. New York: Paulist Press, 1989.

Rubio, Julie Hanlon. *A Christian Theology of Marriage and Family.* New York: Paulist Press, 2003.

Schillebeeckx, Edward. *Marriage: Human Reality and Saving Mystery.* New York: Sheed and Ward, 1965.

Holy Orders

Bradshaw, Paul F. *Ordination Rites of the Ancient Churches of East and West.* New York: Pueblo Publishing, 1990.

Dulles, Avery. *The Priestly Office: A Theological Reflection.* New York: Paulist Press, 1997.

O'Meara, Thomas. *Theology of Ministry.* New York: Paulist Press, 1983.

Osborne, Kenan B. *Orders and Ministry.* Maryknoll, NY: Orbis Books, 2006.

———. *Priesthood: A History of the Ordained Ministry in the Roman Catholic Church.* New York: Paulist Press, 1988.

Power, David N. *Mission, Ministry, Orders: Reading the Tradition in the Present Context.* New York and London: Continuum, 2008.

Rausch, Thomas P. *Priesthood Today: An Appraisal.* New York: Paulist Press, 1992.

Schillebeeckx, Edward. *The Church with a Human Face: A New and Expanded Theology of Ministry.* New York: Crossroad, 1985.

Sullivan, Francis A. *From Apostles to Bishops: The Development of the Episcopacy in the Early Church.* New York: Paulist Press, 2001.

Wood, Susan K. *Sacramental Orders.* Collegeville, MN: Liturgical Press, 2000.

Chapter 11

Creation and Eschatology

Creation is a theological term; it presupposes a Creator. Rooted in Scripture, it envisions God's mysterious work of bringing into existence and sustaining the earth and the cosmos in which our planet shines so brightly. The biblical view differed from that of the ancient philosophers who presupposed the eternity of the world. Modernity saw the rise of a new tension between science and religion; Darwin's great work, *The Origin of Species*, in particular, challenged the biblical view in the minds of many.

Today Catholic theology has moved considerably beyond its initial hesitancy to embrace an evolutionary universe. In this chapter we will consider the biblical roots for a theology of creation, see how the later tradition added to this theology, consider the challenge of Darwinism, and look at some examples of Catholic evolutionary thinking. Then we will look at eschatology, the theology of the "Last Things"—heaven and hell, death and judgment—that is correlative to a theology of creation.

Creation in Scripture

Creation theology is found throughout the Old Testament. The Bible opens with the words, "In the beginning . . . God created the heavens and the earth" (Gen 1:1). Genesis actually has two stories of the creation of the earth, its plants and animals, and the man and woman whose offspring will populate it. The book of Job celebrates God's work founding the earth, clothing it with clouds, setting the seas within their boundaries, placing the stars in their constellations, and watching over the animals (Job 37–39). Psalm 104 describes God's care for creation, raising grass for the cattle and plants for the beasts of burden, bringing forth bread from the earth, wine to cheer people's hearts, providing food for the young lions, and creating monsters or great fish to play in the seas. The Wisdom literature, developing late in the Jewish tradition, celebrates God's creative work and is echoed in the New Testament.

Old Testament

The ancient Near East was rich in creation myths, but none portrayed a creator deity like the God of Israel. *Enuma Elish*, the ancient Babylonian creation story, may go back as far as the eighteenth century BCE. *Atrahasis*, telling the story of the creation of humans and the great flood, dates from roughly the seventeenth century BCE. The *Epic of Gilgamesh*, containing the story of the flood, comes from the tenth to the thirteenth centuries, while an early version can be traced back to the eighteenth century BCE.[1] All were written in either Sumero-Akkadian cuneiform or Mesopotamian cuneiform.

Enuma Elish portrays creation as the result of a cosmic struggle between the storm god Marduk, head of the Babylonian pantheon, and Tiamat, the monster of chaos who represents the formless but relentless waters of the sea, sometimes appearing as a dragon or sea serpent. Marduk overcomes Tiamat by driving an evil wind into her, bloating her monstrous body, then piercing her heart with an arrow. Dividing her in two with his sword, he fashions the sky or firmament above and the earth below. There are obvious parallels between the Babylonian account and the first creation story from the Old Testament's Priestly (P) account (Gen: 1-2:4a). Both refer to a watery chaos at the beginning of creation, personified in the Babylonian account by Tiamat. The names for chaos in both accounts are etymologically

---

[1] See Richard J. Clifford and John J. Collins, eds., "Introduction: The Theology of Creation Traditions," in *Creation in the Biblical Traditions* (Washington, DC: Catholic Biblical Association of America, 1992), 4–5; see also *Myths from Mesopotamia: Creation, the Flood, Gilgamesh, and Others*, trans. with introduction and notes by Stephanie Dalley (Oxford: Oxford University Press, 1989).

related, Tiamat in *Enuma Elish* and *Tehom*, the Deep, in Genesis. Both refer to the alternation of day and night before the creation of the heavenly bodies, fashioned later in the story. In both accounts, the earth appears after a division of the primeval waters. The order of creation is the same; first the sky, then the dry land, the heavenly bodies, and finally the man and the woman.[2]

The second creation story (Gen 2:4b–3:24), from the more ancient Yahwist account, so called for its anachronistic use of the divine name Yahweh, focuses more on the creation of the man and the woman, with the creation of the plants and living creatures mentioned only in passing. This account evidences the influence of the *Atrahasis* epic, including an early version of the story of the flood which was later incorporated into the *Epic of Gilgamesh*. *Atrahasis* shows the god Enki creating the first humans by mixing clay with the blood of a slain god associated with knowledge. Fashioned to serve the gods, but "generated partially from a divine principle, humankind shared a commonality with the gods." Aspiring also to the status of divinity, they revolt against their role.[3] Disturbed, the gods send various plagues, and finally a great flood, with Enki rescuing Atrahasis in a boat.

But if the Babylonian stories influenced those in Genesis, the differences are significant. The biblical authors can be seen as demythologizing the Babylonian accounts. *Enuma Elish* portrays creation as the result of a violent struggle, traces of which can be found in other parts of the Old Testament where the ancient monster, variously known as Leviathan or Lotan, the Sea-River, or sometimes Rahab, appears (Pss 74:13-14; 89:9-11; Isa 27:1; Job 3:8; 26:12-13). But in the P account creation takes place effortlessly by the sovereign power of the divine Word. The sun, moon, and stars are not deities to be worshiped but placed in the heavens to mark the days and seasons, to tell time. The man and woman are created in the divine image and likeness, not to be servants for the gods, as in the Akkadian stories, but to have dominion over the living things of the earth (Gen 1:26,

[2] See *The Ancient New East: An Anthology of Texts and Pictures*, ed. James B. Pritchard (Princeton, NJ: Princeton University Press, 1958), 31–39; see also Alexander Heidel, *The Babylonian Genesis: The Story of Creation* (Chicago: University of Chicago Press, 1951).

[3] Bernard F. Batto, "Creation Theology in Genesis," in Clifford and Collins, *Creation in the Biblical Traditions*, 23.

28). The first account ends with the command of Sabbath rest (Gen 2:3), linking creation with covenant (Exod 20:8-11) and thus with God's saving grace. Its repetitive character, repeating "God saw how good it was," suggests that it was composed for use in the liturgy.

Unlike the first creation account, in which God is portrayed as transcendent, the second is remarkably anthropomorphic. It shows God, like a potter, forming the man from clay, blowing into his nostrils the breath of life, casting a deep sleep on him, to fashion a woman from his rib, finally closing up its place with flesh. Thus it gives an account of sexual difference, showing that man and woman are made for each other as partners and providing a divine foundation for marriage (Gen 2:25). The temptation of the serpent to "be like gods" (Gen 3:5) may reflect the reason given for the revolt of humans in *Atrahasis*.

We might summarize the themes of these two creation stories as follows. First, creation is good, the work of God's hands in overcoming the primeval chaos and fashioning the earth and its creatures. Evil comes not from God but from the man and woman's refusal to honor God's command. Still, the earth remains under threat. The monster of chaos is described as bound or restrained, rather than killed (Pss 89:10; 104:6-8; Job 26:12-13; 38:8-11). The cosmos is sustained only by God's power.[4]

Second, there is an emphasis on the dignity of humankind. They are created innocent, naked yet unashamed, created in the image and likeness of God, destined for intimacy with the God who walks with them "at the breezy time of the day." Respect for life in all its forms is rooted in the dignity of the human person.

Third, original innocence is lost when the first couple succumbs to the temptation to become like gods themselves. Sin ruptures the harmony of creation; the man and woman are alienated from God, from their world, as the woman will bear her children in pain and be subject to her husband, and the man will have to earn his living by the sweat of his brow. What follows in succeeding chapters is fratricide, strife, and the near-destruction of the earth in the story of the flood and later the division of the languages, dividing people

[4] Bernard W. Anderson, ed., *Creation in the Old Testament* (Philadelphia, PA: Fortress Press, 1984), 15.

from each other. As von Rad suggests, the sin of the man and the woman threatens creation itself, as the waters of chaos once confined by the creator return to inundate the earth.[5]

Fourth, God's will is always to save, to deliver humanity from the destruction that follows their refusal to follow God's command. Thus God makes clothes to cover their nakedness, marks Cain to protect him from vengeance at the hands of his brother's tribe, and delivers Noah and humanity from the waters of the flood. Even more, the theology of creation cannot be separated from soteriology, from the doctrine of salvation; creation is the inauguration of God's saving work, a theme that reappears with special emphasis in Second Isaiah. "Creation and redemption belong together, as the obverse and reverse of the same theological coin."[6] The story of the call of Abraham that brings this "prehistory" to a close promises a blessing in which all the nations will share.

Creation theology is echoed in the psalms and the Wisdom literature. The psalms praise God for creation (Pss 8:4-10; 19:1-7; 33:6-8; 96). The old "Combat Myth" or cosmogony between the storm god and Leviathan or Rahab, with the victory now attributed to Yahweh, is echoed in the psalms and elsewhere (Pss 74:13-14; 89:9-11; Isa 27:1; Job 3:8; 26:12-13; cf. Isa 27:1; 59:9; Job 9:13; 26:12; 38:8-11). Yahweh's answer to Job from out of the whirlwind is framed as a long interrogation of Job, asking him how he can possibly understand the mysteries of God's work in nature, the stars, weather, land and sea, the beasts of the field, and birds of the air (Job 38–39). Psalm 104 celebrates God's creative work—especially God's care for living beings, providing them with food and drink as we have seen—and is considered by some as part of the Wisdom tradition.[7]

The emphasis on creation in the Wisdom literature provides an alternative to the saving history model so often emphasized in biblical theology. The book of Proverbs describes "Lady Wisdom" (Roland Murphy's term) or "Woman Wisdom" as a feminine agent of God, the Lord's firstborn, present at creation when he made the sky and

---

[5] Gerhard von Rad, *Old Testament Theology*, vol. 1 (New York: Harper & Row, 1962), 156–57.

[6] Anderson, *Creation in the Old Testament*, 6.

[7] Hans-Jürgen Hermisson, "Observations on the Creation Theology in Wisdom," in Anderson, *Creation in the Old Testament*, 123.

set the limits for the sea, the Lord's handworker, playing in the divine presence (Prov 8:22-31). There remains controversy about how to translate the passage. Approaching the text metaphorically, Gail Yee sees a God that is male, female, and neither, closest to human beings in the experience of birth, making them cocreators.[8]

Creation also plays an important role in the book of Wisdom, though it is complex. The book begins by affirming the wholesome nature of creation and God's undying justice, with death and a "destructive drug" (spiritual death) coming from elsewhere (Wis 1:13-15). Solomon's prayer in chapter 9 sees Wisdom as present when Yahweh created the world and sent forth from heaven with a saving mission (Wis 9:10-18). Creation and salvation are thus emphatically linked; "God uses the cosmos to bring about a re-ordering of creation, particularly the re-establishment of justice. Creation, the Exodus, and Salvation are the continuous spectrum of God's creative activity."[9]

Continuous Creation

It is also important to note that the Old Testament views Yahweh's creative work as continuous, not as something in the past, as deism with its image of the divine watchmaker assumes. Yahweh is portrayed as sustaining creation at every moment, fighting the forces of disintegration, keeping them in check. There is no power equal to that of Israel's God, no dualism as in the pagan mythologies that influenced the Genesis accounts. In Psalm 104, God's creative work continues. It is Yahweh who makes the earth fruitful (Hos 2:10-15; Jer 31:12) and is active in nature (Deut 7:13). Yahweh is identified with the storm and other displays in nature, but this power is always to save; it is not capricious (Pss 18:8-16; 68:8-10; 77:17-21; Ezek 1). "Classical theology speaks of creation in three senses as *creatio originalis, creatio continuo, creatio nova*, that is, original creation in the beginning, continuous creation in the present here and now, and new creation at the redeemed end-time."[10] In the scholastic tradition, the

---

[8] Gale A. Yee, "The Theology of Creation in Proverbs 8:22-31," in Clifford and Collins, *Creation in the Biblical Traditions*, 93–95.

[9] Michael Kolarcik, "Creation and Salvation in the Book of Wisdom," in Clifford and Collins, *Creation in the Biblical Traditions*, 107.

[10] Elizabeth A. Johnson, *Ask the Beasts: Darwin and the God of Love* (London: Bloomsbury, 2014), 123.

philosophical doctrine of the contingency of being means that without God's sustaining presence, the cosmos would cease to exist.[11]

New Testament

The influence of Wisdom theology is particularly evident in Paul and John. Paul sees Jesus as "the Wisdom of God" disclosed in God's plan of salvation (1 Cor 1:24-30) "through whom all things are and through whom we exist" (1 Cor 8:6), the earliest New Testament identification of Christ with the work of creation. This theme is later developed in Colossians: "He is the image of the invisible God, the firstborn of all creation. For in him were created all things in heaven and on earth" (Col 1:15-16). This image of Christ as Wisdom, First-born, active in creation reflects Wisdom theology, perhaps rooted in Wisdom's description of the just one who calls himself the son of God and "boasts that God is his father" (Wis 2:12-20).

The Prologue to the Fourth Gospel reflects Old Testament Wisdom theology to a remarkable degree, though the Greek logos has been substituted for Sophia. The Old Testament describes God's Wisdom as born before creation (Sir 1:4; Prov 8:22-24), coming forth from the mouth of God (Sir 24:3), present and active in forming the earth (Prov 8:28-30; Wis 7:22; 9:9), and coming into the world with a salvific mission (Wis 6:12-16; 9:10-18). God chose the place for Wisdom's tent (Sir 24:8). In John's Prologue, the Word that became flesh in Jesus and made his dwelling among us (literally "pitched his tent") was not just active in creation but was himself God, the one through whom all things came to be, the light shining in the darkness that was coming into the world (John 1:1-14). Like the book of Wisdom, the Prologue links creation and salvation.

Creation in the Tradition

As Christianity moved out of its Palestinian matrix and into the Greco-Roman world, it encountered a different language, more technical and philosophical than the mythopoeic language of the Bible. Yet its task remained the same, to express the Christian mystery in

---

[11] Aquinas, *Summa Theologica*, I, q. 105, a. 5.

language that would be at home in the culture. Two doctrines were to develop from this encounter, the idea of a *creatio ex nihilo* or creation from nothing, and the *imago Dei*, the human person as created in the image of God.

Creatio ex Nihilo

For the ancients, whose view of the world was cyclical rather than sequential, the universe was thought to be eternal. This included Plato, Aristotle, the Stoics, and Plotinus, all of whom had an influence on developing Christian thought. The first to challenge this was the *Shepherd of Hermas* (140–150), the work of an unknown author whose notion of a *creatio ex nihilo* was only implicit. The *Shepherd*'s author wrote, "First of all, believe that God is One, even He who created all things and set them in order, and brought all things from nonexistence into being."[12] This goes beyond the Old Testament, which in Genesis 1:1 spoke of the earth as a formless wasteland covered by the primeval waters.

Irenaeus of Lyons (c. 135–202) further developed the idea of a creation out of nothing in his polemic against the Gnostic teachers Marcion and Valentinus. A philosophical religion that remained a challenge to primitive Christianity, Gnosticism argued the material world was evil, the work of an inferior deity or demiurge. Marcion distinguished between the wrathful God of the Old Testament and the loving Father of Jesus, a misconception still heard today. In his famous *Against the Heresies*, Irenaeus argued that God, the Father of Jesus, was both uncreated and creator of all things out of nothing: "God . . . in the exercise of His own will and power, formed all things (so that those things which now are should have an existence) out of what did not previously exist."[13]

Like Irenaeus, Origen (c. 185–254) defended both the humanity of Christ, so important for the doctrines of redemption, and creation out of nothing, citing the testimony of the *Shepherd*.[14] Tertullian (c. 160–225) used Scripture to argue that if matter were eternal it would be

---

[12] *Shepherd of Hermas*, Mandate 1, 1 [26]: 1.
[13] Irenaeus, *Against the Heresies* 2.10.2.
[14] Origen, *The Writings* (De Principis), nos. 5, 77.

equal to God.[15] Augustine (354–430), moving beyond his Manichean youth, affirmed the goodness and beauty of creation and its origin *ex nihilo*.[16] Thomas Aquinas, influenced by Aristotle, has a variant position. While arguing that God alone is eternal, he could envision an eternal universe. Being eternal, it would not have a beginning, but it could not be the cause of its own existence; it would still have to have a first cause.

The doctrine of *creatio ex nihilo*, defined by the Fourth Lateran Council (1215), affirms several important points: first, that God is distinct from creation as its cause, ruling out pantheism; second, that creation comes from a free act of God rather than from some eternal emanation, which suggests a more personal God who creates out of love. Finally, holding that creation comes from the Father of Jesus rules out the Albigensian view of creation from an evil principle, implying that material creation itself is evil.[17]

Imago Dei

The Priestly creation account teaches that God created humankind as male and female "in the divine image" (Gen 1:26-27). The phrase occurs again, prohibiting murder in the covenant with Noah, "for in the image of God has man been made" (Gen 9:6). Patristic and medieval theologians would further unpack the meaning of this phrase, stressing the spiritual faculties of the human person, intellect and will. The respect in the Catholic tradition for human life in all its forms is rooted in the idea of its creation in the image of God. Unfortunately, the language of the fathers is unhappily androcentric. Clement of Alexandria (c. 150–215) writes that man is "the image and glory of the Lord," but admits that women are able to philosophize equally with men, "though males are preferable at everything."[18]

Augustine's position is similar. In commenting on Genesis 1:26 he says, "This text says that human nature itself, which is complete [only] in both sexes, was made in the image of God; and it does not

[15] Tertullian, *Treatise Against Hermogenes*, chap. 4.
[16] Augustine, *Confessions* 12.7.7.
[17] Anne M. Clifford, "Creation," in Francis Schüssler Fiorenza and John P. Galvin, *Systematic Theology: Roman Catholic Perspectives*, 2nd ed. (Minneapolis, MN: Fortress Press, 2011), 219.
[18] Clement of Alexandria, "The Stromata or Miscellanies," 4.8.

separate the woman from the image of God which it signifies." But Paul's statement that men do not have to cover their heads "because he is the image and glory of God, but woman is the glory of man" (1 Cor 11:7) leads Augustine to say, "The woman together with her own husband is the image of God, so that that whole substance may be one image; but when she is referred separately to her quality of *help-mate*, which regards the woman herself alone, then she is not the image of God; but as regards the man alone, he is the image of God as fully and completely as when the woman too is joined with him in one."[19] More original was Augustine's seeing in the spiritual faculties of memory, understanding, and love an interior image or analogy of the Trinity as Father, Son, and Spirit.[20]

Aquinas treats the *imago Dei* in the context of a theology of creation, using an *exitus-reditus* framework. Human beings are created in the divine image and directed toward God as their ultimate end.[21] The *imago Dei*, rooted in the human person's intellectual nature, is realized by acts of knowing and loving God, though Aquinas reiterates Augustine's position on the secondary status of woman. He acknowledges that both men and women share in the *imago Dei* by their intellectual nature: "in a secondary sense the image of God is found in man, and not in woman: for man is the beginning and end of woman; as God is the beginning and end of every creature."[22]

The notion of the creation of human beings in the image of God calls attention to what is unique in them, specifically their spiritual aspects, their capacity to know, choose, and especially to love. In loving, human beings most resemble the God who is love. Romanus Cessario argues that "Aquinas contends that we should look for the image of God, not primarily in the intellectual capacitates of the soul, but in the very acts of those operative capacities or powers."[23] Karl Rahner referred to this embodied aspect of human beings in his theological anthropology as "Spirit in the World."[24] In his encyclical

---

[19] Augustine, *The Trinity* 12.7.10.

[20] Ibid., 15.22.

[21] J. Augustine de Noia, "Imago Dei–Imago Christi: Theological Foundation of Christian Humanism," 9, http://www.e-aquinas.net/pdf/pl_dinoia.pdf.

[22] Aquinas, *Summa Theologica*, I, q. 93, a. 4.

[23] Romanus Cessario, *Christian Faith and the Theological Life* (Washington, DC: The Catholic University of America Press, 1996), 43.

[24] Karl Rahner, *Spirit in the World* (New York: Herder and Herder, 1968).

Laudato Sì, Pope Francis cites the *Catechism of the Catholic Church* (no. 357) which says creation in God's image and likeness shows the immense dignity of each person who is not something but someone, capable of self-knowledge, self-possession and of freely entering into communion with other persons (no. 65).

Creation and Science

Science's approach to the world is different from that of theology; it studies the observable, speculates, makes hypotheses, and tries to confirm them. "Creation" is not a scientific term. The vastness of our universe is staggering. Our own galaxy, which we call the Milky Way, has approximately 100 billion stars in it, but there are about 10 billion galaxies in the observable universe. Assuming an average of 100 billion stars per galaxy would mean about 1 billion trillion stars just in the observable universe, but there could be billions more because light from stars further than 13.7 light years away has not yet reached us. In her book on Darwin and creation, Elizabeth Johnson describes from a scientific point of view the formation of our solar system which is part of the Milky Way:

> Supernova explosions created a thick interstellar cloud of dust and gas. A great clump was pulled together by gravity and reignited to become the star we call our sun. Much of the rest of this thick cloud got concentrated in smaller chunks not big enough to catch fire, forming the planets and asteroids of our solar system, including the Earth. This planet was beautifully positioned, close enough to the sun to catch a goodly portion of its rays yet not so close to become intolerably hot. Through time and a series of cataclysmic and quiet events, the planet acquired water and an atmosphere. Its basic physical characteristics enabled the development of complex chemistries requisite for life.[25]

The relation between the church and science has not always been easy. While the medieval church had been a patron of science through its monasteries, hospitals, universities, and scholars, modernity

---

[25] Johnson, *Ask the Beasts*, 113.

brought new challenges. When Copernicus, a Polish priest, published his *On the Revolution of the Heavenly Spheres* in 1543, two years before the Council of Trent began, it occasioned only minimal controversy. But in the post-Reformation period, Catholic biblical exegesis became increasingly literal. While Copernicus's work was praised by the Jesuit astronomer Clavius, other Jesuits, none of them mathematicians, criticized it, arguing for the immobility of the earth on the basis both of Scripture and the teaching of Aquinas. One of them, Cornelius à Lapide, wrote that "one must adapt philosophy and physics to Sacred Scripture and the word of God. . . . It is forbidden . . . to subordinate Sacred Scripture to the words of the philosophers or to the light of nature." [26] Today we would call that fundamentalism.

Galileo Galilei

When Galileo (1564–1642) proposed Copernicus's theory in 1616, the reaction was swift. He was ordered by Cardinal Robert Bellarmine, at the command of Pope Paul V, to refrain from teaching or defending Copernicus's doctrine orally or in writing, which he obeyed until 1632 when he proposed heliocentrism as a "hypothesis." Galileo was not without insight into the relation between science and Scripture. In a 1615 *Letter to the Grand Duchess Christina*, he had used Augustine to argue that Scripture and science had different goals and therefore could not conflict. Famously, he argued that the Holy Spirit was not concerned with what we would call today scientific questions but rather with what concerned our salvation: "The intention of the Holy Ghost is to teach us how one goes to heaven, not how heaven goes." [27] Nevertheless, the papal court judged him guilty of violating his agreement with Cardinal Bellarmine and sentenced him to house arrest, under which he lived until his death in 1642. In a 1992 address to the Pontifical Academy of Sciences, Pope John Paul II acknowledged that the church had erred in condemning Galileo.

---

[26] See Irving A. Kelter, "The Refusal to Accommodate: Jesuit Exegesis and the Copernican System," in *The Church and Galileo*, ed. Ernan McMullin (Notre Dame, IN: University of Notre Dame Press, 2005), 42–47, at 46.

[27] Galileo Galilei, "Letter to the Grand Duchess Christina," http://www.fordham.edu/halsall/mod/galileo-tuscany.asp.

Charles Darwin

The name of Darwin is still associated with the rejection of biblical authority by many, but that was far from his purpose. But his keen eye for the variety of species led him to criticize the natural theology of his day which sought to use the new knowledge of the order and design of nature as an argument for the existence of God as intelligent designer, an argument promoted especially by William Paley in his *Natural Theology* which Darwin had studied at Cambridge. When his most famous work, *On the Origin of Species*, was published in 1859, some religious thinkers rejected his work from the start, while others were open to it and worked to incorporate his evolutionary perspective into their own work. At the same time, many naturalists, holding to the view of separate creation for the individual species, found it controversial.

Johnson argues that Darwin did not intend to write as an atheist and denied that he was one before he died. Though he may have been a deist as the HMS Beagle began its journey, his eventual agnosticism was as much due to the trauma of the human condition as to his science.[28] The *Origin* did not address the beginnings of life on earth, nor did it present the development of the species in any kind of order. John Haught maintains that Darwin might well have been concerned about the theological implications of his research, as he hesitated to publish *Origins* until forced to by the anticipated appearance of a similar volume.[29] His main interest was in the incredible variety of life, governed by his principle of natural selection, though in the fifth edition of *Origins* he adopted Herbert Spencer's concept of the "survival of the fittest." This was regrettable as the phrase has often been used as a principle for a social Darwinism, though Darwin's position on this subject remains ambiguous.

Conservative Christians continue to battle against evolution to this day, convinced that the theory of evolution and belief in a creative God are incompatible, and they insist on including in school curricula theories such as "creation science" or "intelligent design." The former seeks to offer scientific evidence for the Genesis creation narrative,

[28] Johnson, *Ask the Beasts*, 36–40.
[29] John F. Haught, *Making Sense of Evolution: Darwin, God, and the Drama of Life* (Louisville, KY: Westminster John Knox, 2010), 16–17.

while "intelligent design" argues that the intricate design of the eye, the brain, and complexity of bodily systems offer *scientific* evidence of an intelligent designer beyond the natural world. Neither represents genuine science.

The majority of Christians see no conflict between evolution and faith in creation. One is a scientific hypothesis to explain the diversity of species; it can say nothing about ultimate causality. The other is a theological statement about the origin of life. Today the evidence supporting the theory of evolution is difficult to deny, nor does the principle of natural selection rule out God's creative, sustaining presence. Pope John Paul II acknowledged that evolution is "more than a hypothesis" in 1996, though he stressed the uniqueness of the human person, created in God's image and likeness.[30]

Evolution and the Drama of Life

How might theology integrate the theory of evolution with Christian faith? One thing is clear; we need new metaphors. As Elizabeth Johnson writes: "Neither overriding monarch nor absent deist god, the Spirit of God moves with extravagant divine generosity to create and sustain the conditions that have enabled the biodiverse community of life to become so interesting and beautiful."[31] John Haught sees evolution essentially as a drama, not with the imposed design of an engineer-God, but one described by Darwin that portrays the incredibly rich story of living beings struggling to be and to flourish. The story is dramatic precisely because it remains a struggle, a risky venture with considerable loss and failure along the way. Tragedy is always possible. Evolutionary materialists cannot see the drama. They reduce the story of life to a mechanism, meaningless moments, a series of accidents leading nowhere, rather than a drama in which contingency, natural laws, and time play key roles.

Haught looks for a "deeper coherence," something more profound than even design that might point beyond adaptive imperfections to

[30] John Paul II, "Message to the Pontifical Academy of Sciences: on Evolution"; http://www.ewtn.com/library/papaldoc/jp961022.htm.
[31] Johnson, *Ask the Beasts*, 179.

a greater future characterized by the promise and liberation so much a part of Judeo-Christian theological reflection on the mystery of God.[32] He turns not to Paley's engineer or designer but to Teilhard de Chardin (1881–1955), the Jesuit paleontologist, evolutionist, and visionary who sought a post-Darwinian understanding of evolution called forward from the future toward the Omega Point by the cosmic Christ. While going beyond a strictly scientific account, Teilhard's synthesis of science and faith, expressed in his main work, *The Phenomenon of Man*, posed a challenge to the materialist.[33] How could they leave subjectivity and the incredible world of thought out of the picture, reducing life and mind to mindless physical components? Does not the increasing complexity of the material world suggest something? There are more atoms in the human eye than there are stars in the known universe.

Teilhard's reading of the story of life sees a movement from the realm of matter (*geosphere*) to life (*biosphere*), and more recently, thought (*noosphere*). For him, life, mind, and "spirit" have been present at least inchoately from the beginning. A strictly materialist narrative leaves no room for God or God's Spirit, but theology can see that some kind of transformation has been going on since the beginning in the complexification of the material and continues to move toward a larger, more dramatic future.[34] But God is immensely patient; like the drama of life, the drama of salvation is played out not just in years but in eons and remains hidden. A theology of evolution sees God as present in this story of an evolving creation. Haught speaks of a God who suffers along with creation, revealing the theme of divine suffering love.[35]

Ilia Delio says that we meet Christ not just in faith but also at the heart of the evolutionary process; we meet him "in the divine, continual act of creation, redemption, and sanctification of the total universe." Christ is the beginning and the end of all unity in the cosmos.[36]

---

[32] Haught, *Making Sense of Evolution*, 61–65.

[33] Pierre Teilhard de Chardin, *The Human Phenomenon*, new ed., trans. Sarah Appleton-Weber (Portland, OR: Sussex Academic Press, 1999).

[34] Haught, *Making Sense of Evolution*, esp. 11–27, 137–48.

[35] John F. Haught, *God and Darwin: A Theology of Evolution* (Boulder, CO: Westview Press, 2008), 54.

[36] Ilia Delio, *Christ in Evolution* (Maryknoll, NY: Orbis Books, 2008), 132.

The same story can be told in biblical terms. But that is to move our focus from creation to eschatology.

Eschatology

From the Greek *eschatos*, the "last" or "end," eschatology, is a theological term for the biblical view of the end times, the ultimate destiny of humanity and indeed of the cosmos, the *eschaton*, when the fullness of God's salvation will be realized. We have seen how the Old Testament links the theology of creation with God's promise of salvation; they are correlative concepts and belong together, two sides of the same coin. As Brian Daley says, eschatology includes "a hope in the final revelation of God's wise and loving activity throughout history, with a longing for final reckonings. It is the logical conclusion of the biblical doctrine of creation, in the attempt to foresee the fulfillment of creation's purpose."[37]

The Hebrew "save" comes from the root Yš, meaning, to possess space, freedom, or security by removing constriction or threat. In the Old Testament, Yahweh's saving activity is manifested in creation, in his presence to Israel in history, and especially in the great story of the Exodus, which remains the archetype of salvation which Jews continue to celebrate to this day. The Exodus was a saving event in their history. But the notion of salvation continued to develop.[38]

The books of Judges and Samuel show God's saving power mediated by heroic figures and prophets raised up in times of crisis, among them Gideon, Deborah, Samson, Jephthah, and Samuel. With the establishment of the monarchy, that same role is filled by the king or "Lord's anointed," Saul, then David—who remained the symbol of the ideal king—and Solomon. But from the ninth to the sixth centuries, under the influence of the prophetic preaching, the religious imagination of Israel began to shift to the future, to the hope for a coming revelation of Yahweh's saving power.

---

[37] Brian E. Daley, *The Hope of the Early Church* (Cambridge, UK: Cambridge University Press, 1991), 2.

[38] See Thomas P. Rausch, *Eschatology, Liturgy, and Christology* (Collegeville, MN: Liturgical Press, 2012).

The prophets rebuked Israel for her infidelity, idolatry, and oppression of the poor, warning of God's judgment, but at the same time they assured the people that Yahweh would not abandon Israel. The imagery varies; the prophets spoke of a future anointed king in the Davidic line or messiah (2 Sam 7:1-16), of a Day of the Lord (Isa 2:11; Joel 4:14) when Yahweh would judge evildoers and vindicate the poor and oppressed (Isa 11:1-9), of a renewed (Ezek 34:25; 37:26) or new covenant (Jer 31:31-34), or of a mysterious figure called the Servant of Yahweh who would bring forth justice on the earth (Isa 49:1-7), freedom to captives (Isa 42:1-9), bringing God's salvation to the ends of the earth (Isa 49:1-7), even giving his life as an offering for sin (Isa 52:13–53:12). The effect of the prophetic preaching was a shift in the Jewish religious imagination, away from what Yahweh had done in the past and toward what would happen in the future, a shift that became explicit in Second Isaiah: "Remember not the events of the past, the things of long ago consider not; See, I am doing something new!" (Isa 43:18-19).

Late in the tradition, when a fierce persecution (168–160) broke out under Antiochus IV Epiphanes as he tried to impose order on his Seleucid kingdom, including Palestine, by mandating the cult of Zeus, many of the Jews found themselves suffering torture and death for their fidelity to their faith and to the traditions of their ancestors (1 Macc 1-2; 2 Macc 6-7). One response was the apocalyptic tradition, which gave expression to the hope that God would intervene definitively in the life of the people, ushering in a new age and raising the dead to life (Dan 12:1-3), a notion that was still controverted in the time of Jesus (cf. Luke 20:27-38).

The preaching of Jesus expanded the notion of salvation; the reign of God proclaimed God's closeness. In the words of Benedict XVI, "Through Jesus' presence and action God has here and now entered actively into history in a wholly new way."[39] At the same time, God's raising of Jesus from the dead gives a new depth to the concept; the kingdom of God in its fullness will mean the victory of justice and a transformation of creation, a "new heaven and a new earth" (Rev 21:1; cf. 2 Pet 3:13) as well as the resurrection of the dead.

---

[39] Benedict XVI, *Jesus of Nazareth: From the Baptism in the Jordan to the Transfiguration* (New York: Doubleday, 2007), 60.

We find such a dual soteriological emphasis in Paul. He wrote that "the kingdom of God is not a matter of food and drink, but of righteousness, peace, and joy in the holy Spirit" (Rom 14:17). He recognized that the Wisdom of God, hidden for the ages and revealed in the crucified Jesus (1 Cor 2:7-8) affected not just individual disciples but creation itself. Jesus was the "firstfruits of those who have fallen asleep," the initial realization of the fullness of God's salvation to be realized at his coming in glory (1 Cor 15:20-24).

The early Christians grasped this implicitly. They prayed for Christ's *parousia* (presence or arrival) or "Second Coming," facing to the East when they celebrated the Eucharist, ready to welcome him like the rising sun, crying out in Aramaic or Greek *Maranatha*, "Come, Lord" (1 Cor 16:22; Rev 22:20; *Didache* 10.6), and praying "Thy kingdom come" in the Lord's Prayer. Geoffrey Wainwright gives numerous examples of how both East and West saw the eucharistic meal as sign, pledge, and anticipation of the meal of the eternal kingdom to come.[40] But as Easter hope was transformed in the following centuries into fear of the coming judgment, the *eschaton*, symbolizing the fullness of salvation, was reduced to a focus on the *eschata*, the last things, death and judgment, heaven and hell. Conservative Christianity, both Catholic and evangelical Protestant, has too often reduced salvation to a narrow vision of the next life, to "getting saved," or sharing in the resurrection. But eschatology, of course, involves both.

The Four Last Things

Death and judgment, heaven and hell, the "four last things," point beyond the life we know and cherish to the mystery that lies ahead. The transcendent dimension of our experience leads us to ask if there is life beyond life, a future that remains veiled, a God who created us and will not let go. Will there be justice for all the victims of history, and will those who have been responsible for so much suffering be in some way held accountable? Does God even care? The New Testament is rich in eschatological hope, but there is considerable disagreement on how to read the New Testament's eschatological texts.

---

[40] Geoffrey Wainwright, *Eucharist and Eschatology* (New York: Oxford University Press, 1981), 51; see also Rausch, *Eschatology*, 1–3.

Fundamentalist Christians have long approached "end-time" texts with a literalist hermeneutic, turning the book of Revelation into a collection of coded prophecies of Christ's Second Coming, seeing "signs" in contemporary events or various millennial visions of a thousand-year kingdom when the elect will reign with Christ. Others, still influenced by the Enlightenment, eliminate from their interpretation the eschatological entirely as well as any idea of judgment. Both approaches are wrong. The Bible does not give us precise information about God's future, but Christian eschatology, rooted in God's self-disclosure in Jesus and his resurrection, expresses Christian hope in the language of metaphor and poetry.

Death

One thing that is certain is death, no matter how much we seek to deny it. Each person will one day face that moment when life slips away, sometimes suddenly and unexpectedly or more slowly as our physical and spiritual energies diminish and old age or disease has the final word. Contemporary culture seeks to deny death. At Forest Lawn "Memorial Park" in Los Angeles—the chain of cemeteries satirized by Evelyn Waugh in his book, *The Loved One*—people repose, rest, or slumber, but death is rarely mentioned.

But if the denial of death is a phenomenon,[41] there is also little recognition of the sacred character of life. Our elderly are hidden away in "managed care" facilities or retirement communities and an increasing number of nations and states have "right to die" laws that allow physicians, with the patient's permission, to administer life-ending drugs. In Belgium this includes children. In the United States there are approximately 1.06 million abortions a year (2011); the number has been declining, but it is still higher than any Western industrialized nation. And many in the United States are reluctant to provide national health care for the poor who do not qualify for medical insurance.

But death, no matter how difficult, is part of life. The Catholic Church celebrates the passing of a Christian in its Mass of Christian Burial, praying for those whose "life is changed, not ended" and who look forward to an eternal dwelling in heaven. Still, dying is never

---

[41] See Ernst Becker, *The Denial of Death* (New York: Free Press, 1973).

easy as a person consciously or unaware enters into that experience of aloneness and abandonment that Jesus experienced on the cross, crying out, "My God, my God, why have you forsaken me" (Mark 15:34). The Paschal Mystery invites each Christian to share in his passage to eternal life by placing themselves, as Jesus did, into the hands of the Father (Luke 23:46).

Last Judgment

Developing out of the prophets' promise of a Day of the Lord when Yahweh would judge Israel and the nations—holding the wicked to account and vindicating the poor—the idea of a Day of Judgment was further developed in the Jewish apocalyptic and intertestamental traditions: "The doctrine of the last judgment is the most characteristic doctrine of Jewish apocalyptic. It is *the* great event towards which the whole universe is moving and which will vindicate once and for all God's righteous purpose for men and all creation."[42] The same theme continues into the New Testament. There are frequent references to the Son of Man being revealed (Luke 17:30) or coming in glory (Matt 16:27), or to Christ's coming or revelation as Lord (1 Cor 1:8; 1 John 2:28; 1 Pet 4:13). The great apocalyptic sermon in Matthew 25 shows the Son of Man coming in glory, judging the nations, separating the sheep from the goats on the basis of whether they recognized him in the poor, the hungry, and the imprisoned and ministered to his needs (Matt 15:31-46).

The New Testament does not say when the Day of the Lord will come, but the idea that everyone will face judgment is everywhere. One of Paul's early letters said it would be announced by an archangel and the blast of a trumpet, after which those disciples still alive will be lifted up "to meet the Lord in the air" (1 Thess 4:16-17), the origin of evangelical "rapture" theology. Fundamentalist evangelicals hold that Catholics will be "left behind."[43] The Day of the Lord will come like a thief, "and then the heavens will pass away with a mighty

---

[42] D. S. Russell, *The Method and Message of Jewish Apocalyptic* (Philadelphia, PA: Westminster Press, 1964), 380.

[43] See Tim La Haye and Jerry B. Jenkins, *Glorious Appearing: The End of Days* (Wheaton, IL: Tyndale House, 2004); see also Carl E. Olson, *Will Catholics be "Left Behind"? A Catholic Critique of the Rapture and Today's Prophecy Preachers* (San Francisco: Ignatius Press, 2003).

roar and the elements will be dissolved by fire" (2 Pet 3:10). Jesus tells us that not even the Son of Man knows the exact time or hour (Mark 13:32). In the Johannine writings, those who refused to believe have already been judged, and those whose deeds were evil will come to the resurrection of condemnation (John 5:29).

The popular religious imagination generally has looked forward to two judgments, one at the moment of death, after which those who have been responsive to God's grace enter into heaven, though they must still await the resurrection of the body, and the last judgment at the end of time. Some theologians reject the idea of an intermediate state between the two judgments, speculating that the resurrection takes place immediately after death. Others, for example, John Thiel and Joseph Ratzinger, reject this view, as does the official church.[44] John Thiel proposed that those he calls the "blessed dead" are still involved in the work of salvation, an idea one finds also in Origen and Gregory of Nyssa.[45] Thiel sees them as engaged in virtuous action, overcoming the effects of sin lingering in themselves and others, filling up so to speak what was revealed as lacking in the particular judgment. In this way, the Last Judgment, rather than being redundant or anti-climactic, completes their participation in the divine plan of salvation.

Heaven

The New Testament has a variety of images for the fullness of our salvation. It speaks of heaven, an Old Testament notion for the place where God dwells above the earth, as the reward for the disciples of Jesus (Matt 5:12; 1 Thess 4:16-17). Paul includes the expression "to inherit the kingdom of God" (1 Cor 6:9; 15:50; Gal 5:21; cf. Eph 5:5); he also uses the expression to see God "face to face" (1 Cor 13:12). John's Gospel refers to "eternal life" (John 3:15, 36; 6:68; 12:50; 20:31;

---

[44] John E. Thiel, *Icons of Hope: The "Last Things" in Catholic Imagination* (Notre Dame, IN: University of Notre Dame Press, 2013), 142–43; Joseph Ratzinger, *Eschatology: Death and Eternal Life*, 2nd ed. (Washington, DC: The Catholic University of America Press, 1988), 119–32; CDF, "Letter on Certain Questions Concerning Eschatology," May 17, 1979, http://www.vatican.va/roman_curia/congregations/cfaith/documents/rc_con_cfaith_doc_19790517_escatologia_en.html.

[45] Daley, *The Hope of the Early Church*, 56, 88.

cf. Rom 2:7; 6:23; 1 Tim 1:16). The historic creeds confess belief in "the life everlasting" (Apostles' Creed) and "the life of the world to come" (Nicene Creed). But the nature of heaven remains mystery. Perhaps Paul captures this most closely when he writes:

> What eye has not seen, and ear has not heard,
> and what has not entered the human heart,
> what God has prepared for those who love him. (1 Cor 2:9)

Of course heaven is not "up there," nor is it a place. We can understand something of what heaven means much better than we can imagine it. To be in heaven means to be fully in God's presence, the fulfillment of our deepest longing. As Augustine said so beautifully: "You have made us for yourself, O Lord, and our hearts are restless until they rest in you" (Confessions 1.1). Classical theology called it the beatific vision. The Orthodox churches of the East speak of *theosis* or divinization, a sharing in the divine nature. Thomas Aquinas says that God alone is capable of fulfilling the desires of the human person:

> It is impossible for any created good to constitute man's happiness. For happiness is the perfect good, which lulls the appetite altogether; else it would not be the last end, if something yet remained to be desired. Now the object of the will, i.e., of man's appetite, is the universal good; just as the object of the intellect is the universal true. Hence it is evident that naught can lull man's will, save the universal good. This is to be found, not in any creature, but in God alone; because every creature has goodness by participation. Wherefore God alone can satisfy the will of man, according to the words of Psalm 102:5: "Who satisfieth thy desire with good things." Therefore God alone constitutes man's happiness.[46]

Joseph Ratzinger's vision of heaven is radically christological: he writes that one is "in heaven" to the degree that he or she is "in Christ," who as God and man makes space for human existence in the very existence of God.[47] But there is also a social, ecclesiological

---

[46] Aquinas, *Summa Theologica*, I–II, q. 2, a. 8.
[47] Ratzinger, *Eschatology*, 214.

dimension to heaven: "If heaven depends on being in Christ, then it must involve a co-being with all those who, together, constitute the body of Christ. Heaven is a stranger to isolation. It is the open society of the communion of saints, and in this way the fulfillment of all human communion."[48]

Hell

Is there the possibility of eternal loss? Origen (c. 184–254) was perhaps the first to propose the doctrine of "*apocatastasis*," the notion that everyone, including the devil, would be saved.[49] The idea has surfaced occasionally in the life of the church. Hans Urs von Balthasar explored it carefully in his little book *Dare We Hope "That All Men Be Saved"?*, supporting the hope of universal salvation but not the doctrine.[50] The common view is that eternal loss remains a possibility. Noting the uncomfortable silence today about hell, eternal damnation, and judgment, Edward Schillebeeckx argues that holding for universal salvation suggests too cheap a view of mercy and trivializes the real drama of the conflict between good and evil in human history. But this does not necessarily mean that we must subscribe to a vision of eternal torment of the wicked such as portrayed by Hieronymus Bosch in his art.

Like Karl Rahner, Schillebeeckx holds that heaven and hell are asymmetrical concepts. Christian hope for eternal life is rooted not in the Greek idea of the immortality of the soul but rather in a bond with the living God that cannot be overcome by death. For the wicked, however, for those whose lives have not included solidarity with others and communion with God, there is no ground for eternal life. Death for them is final, the biblical "second death" (Rev 20:6). He adds that as a Christian he cannot imagine the blessed in heaven next door—so to speak—to those suffering the pains of hell.[51] This position

---

[48] Ibid., 235.

[49] See John R. Sachs, "Apocatastasis in Patristic Theology," *Theological Studies* 54 (1993): 617–40.

[50] Hans Urs von Balthasar, *Dare We Hope "That All Men Be Saved"? With a Short Discourse on Hell* (San Francisco: Ignatius Press, 1988).

[51] Edward Schillebeeckx, *Church: The Human Story of God* (New York: Crossroad, 1990), 136–37; Karl Rahner's position is similar; he says statements about "heaven"

is often called "annihilationism." Others, however, reject it. Dermot Lane says, "There is something incongruous about affirming God as a God of the living alongside a hypothesis about hell as the annihilation of people."[52]

Finally, hell is less God's punishment than separation from the God of life that is the result of the way one chooses to live one's own life. In one of his General Audiences, John Paul II said that eternal damnation or hell "is not a punishment imposed externally by God but a development of premises already set by people in this life. . . . It is the ultimate consequence of sin itself, which turns against the person who committed it. It is the state of those who definitively reject the Father's mercy, even at the last moment of their life."[53] The root of all sin is here, in the refusal to acknowledge the Creator.

Nor can God force a relationship; love is always a gift, freely offered, and freely received. According to Pope Benedict, "Christ inflicts pure perdition on no one. In himself, he is pure salvation. Anyone who is with him has entered the space of deliverance and salvation."[54] In his encyclical *Spe Salvi*, he cites Dostoyevsky to the effect that in the end, evildoers "do not sit at table at the eternal banquet beside their victims without distinction, as though nothing had happened."[55] But if the church believes in the possibility of hell, it has never said that anyone has gone there.

Purgatory

Purgatory, the idea of purgation after death for venial sins or the temporal punishment due to sins already forgiven, is unique to the Catholic tradition. Though not explicitly in Scripture, it is rooted in the ancient practice of praying for the dead found in the late Old

---

and "hell" are not parallel, *Foundations of Christian Faith: An Introduction to the Idea of Christianity* (New York: Seabury, 1978), 435–43.

[52] Dermot A. Lane, *Keeping Hope Alive: Stirrings in Christian Theology* (New York: Paulist Press, 1996), 143.

[53] John Paul II, "General Audience," Wednesday July 28, 1999, no. 1.

[54] Ratzinger, *Eschatology*, 205.

[55] Benedict XVI, *Spe Salvi*, no. 40, http://w2.vatican.va/content/benedict-xvi/en /encyclicals/documents/hf_ben-xvi_enc_20071130_spe-salvi.html.

Testament (2 Macc 12:45) and practiced by the early Christians, especially when they celebrated the Eucharist. Orthodox Christians, though they generally do not believe in purgatory, also pray for the dead. Protestants do not, and they reject the idea of purgatory as unbiblical and contrary to the sufficiency of Christ's sacrifice. The doctrine of purgatory was affirmed by the Second Council of Lyons (1274). Today the emphasis is less on punishment; rather it is on the purification of whatever keeps a person from union with God, a purification of our loves which often remain imperfect and self-centered.

For Ratzinger, purgatory is not "some kind of supra-worldly concentration camp" but an encounter with the transformative power of the Lord through which "a person becomes capable of Christ, capable of God and thus capable of unity with the whole communion of saints."[56] In other words, coming into the presence of the holy is a searing, purifying experience, burning away whatever keeps one from entering into communion with the divine. But this purification has a radically social dimension. Ratzinger argues that our social nature links us inseparably to others; we are present "in others as guilt or as grace." To encounter Christ is to encounter his whole body: "I come face to face with my own guilt vis-à-vis the suffering members of that body as well as with the forgiving love which the body derives from Christ its head."[57]

When this purification takes place, whether after death, in the process of dying, or even in this life remains mystery. It is a sign of ecumenical progress that the Lutheran-Catholic common statement "The Hope of Eternal Life" notes that Catholic and many Lutheran funeral liturgies, celebrated within the context of the Eucharist, contain a prayerful commendation of the dead into the hands of a merciful and gracious God, though in the case of Lutherans this does not extend to a common practice of prayer for the dead beyond funerals.[58]

---

[56] Ratzinger, *Eschatology*, 230.

[57] Ibid., 232.

[58] US Lutheran-Roman Catholic Dialogue, "The Hope of Eternal Life," (2010), 64, http://www.usccb.org/beliefs-and-teachings/ecumenical-and-interreligious /ecumenical/lutheran/upload/The-Hope-of-Eternal-Life1.pdf.

The Fullness of Salvation

Eschatology involves so much more than the four last things and the destiny of the individual. This was clear to Irenaeus, who in Brian Daley's words understood salvation "not so much God's unexpected intervention in history . . . as it is the end-stage of a process of organic growth which has been creation's 'law' since its beginning."[59] This is what modern, Western individualism has so often lost sight of, the idea of the *eschaton*, the fullness of salvation. But that has begun to change. Theologians such as Johann Baptist Metz, Jon Sobrino, Peter Phan, and Terrence Tilley stress how the kingdom of God with its good news for the poor (Luke 4:18) is already breaking into the world through the ministry of Jesus. And thinkers such as Pierre Teilhard de Chardin, Elizabeth Johnson, John Haught, and Ilia Delio argue that eschatology involves the cosmos itself. Thus creation and eschatology are linked.

The Old Testament presents a God who hears the cry of the poor (Pss 34:16, 18; 69:34; Exod 22:26) and promises justice for the oppressed of Israel (Pss 9:8-9; 96:13; 98:9; Jer 17:10). One of the promises of the messianic age was justice for the poor (Isa 11:3-5). Robert Krieg summarizes the eschatological vision of the prophets as looking forward to a new community of love and faithfulness in which Israel will live in communion with God, peace with their neighbor, and harmony with creation.[60] In his preaching of the kingdom of God, Jesus called the poor, the hungry, and those who hunger and thirst for justice blessed (Matt 5:3-10; Luke 6:20-23).

The resurrection of Jesus shows both God's vindication of the just one, God's only Son, and foreshadows God's ultimate embrace of all the innocent victims of history. God's salvation in its fullness means the victory of justice for all those who have suffered unjustly, God's answer to the cries of the poor heard throughout the ages. In the new order, God will wipe away the tears from their eyes and there will be no more death or mourning, wailing, or pain (Rev 21:3-4). Indeed, in his encyclical *Spe Salvi*, Pope Benedict writes "I am convinced that

---

[59] Daley, *The Hope of The Early Church*, 29.
[60] Robert A. Krieg, *Treasure in the Field: Salvation in the Bible and in Our Lives* (Collegeville, MN: Liturgical Press, 2013), 90–100.

the question of justice constitutes the essential argument, in any case the strongest argument, in favor of faith in eternal life" (no. 43).

This "thicker" theology of salvation has led to various forms of liberation theology, for the poor and oppressed, for women and all disadvantaged because of gender discrimination, and for the earth itself. These theologies insist that God's salvation cannot be restricted to the eschatological future; the kingdom of God is already being realized in our history and we are called to witness to it, a theme particularly strong in the theology of Ignacio Ellacuría and Jon Sobrino.[61]

A New Heaven and a New Earth

The New Testament can only suggest how the world itself will share in the fullness of God's salvation, but the linking of creation and salvation that we have seen in the Old Testament is evident also in the New Testament. In Romans, Paul writes of all creation waiting with eager longing for the revelation of the children of God: "for creation was made subject to futility, not of its own accord but because of the one who subjected it, in hope that creation itself would be set free from slavery to corruption and share in the glorious freedom of the children of God. We know that all creation is groaning in labor pains even until now" (Rom 8:20-22). In 1 Corinthians, Paul talks of Christ destroying death and all the powers, gathering all to himself, placing them under his feet: "When everything is subjected to him, the Son himself will [also] be subjected to the one who subjected everything to him, so that God may be all in all" (1 Cor 15:28). Paul thus envisions a return of humanity and creation itself to God. This theme is repeated in Colossians which joins the themes of creation and salvation in Christ, the beginning and the end:

> He is the image of the invisible God,
> the firstborn of all creation,
> For in him were created all things in heaven and on earth,

---

[61] Ignacio Ellacuría, "The Crucified People," in *Systematic Theology: Perspectives from Liberation Theology*, ed. Jon Sobrino and Ignacio Ellacuría (Maryknoll, NY: Orbis Books, 1996), 261.

the visible and the invisible,
whether thrones or dominions or principalities or powers;
all things were created through him and for him.
He is before all things,
and in him all things hold together.
(Col 1:15-17; cf. Eph 1:10).

How this will come about remains mystery, though we can understand more than we can imagine. Efforts to harmonize biblical texts with cosmological theories are bound to fail; they address different questions. The resurrection of Jesus is a clue to the ultimate transformation, not just of our embodied existence but of creation itself in God's future. Scripture suggests that the God who brought our earth with all its life into existence out of love will not simply abandon it to humankind's destructive power and capacity for violence, or to the perishability and decay of nature, to the inevitable dissipation of energy and heat-death forecast by the second law of thermodynamics, or simply cease from sustaining it.

We saw earlier Teilhard de Chardin's efforts to develop a theology of creation as moving toward self-transcendence, and many have felt his influence. Karl Rahner suggests something similar, though from a different starting point—that of the fundamental unity of spirit and matter. He sees the incarnation as a moment toward the divinization of the world as a whole: "in the world as it actually is we can understand creation and Incarnation as two movements and two phases of the one process of God's self-giving and self-expression, although it is an intrinsically differentiated process." [62] As Elizabeth Johnson says, "Since gracious divine action expressed in incarnation and the giving of grace reveals the character of God, then holy Mystery who creates, redeems, and sanctifies the world brims over with the most profound respect for creatures." [63] Peter Phan asks, will there be continuity between the "first creation" and the "new creation"? Using the resurrection of Jesus as an analogy, he favors the view of continuity-in-discontinuity, with the emphasis on the latter. [64]

---

[62] Rahner, *Foundations of Christian Faith*, 178–86, at 197.

[63] Johnson, *Ask the Beasts*, 158.

[64] Peter Phan, *Living Into Death, Dying Into Life: A Christian Theology of Death and Life Eternal* (Hobe Sound, FL: Lectio Publishing, 2014), 159.

In his encyclical on ecology, *Laudato Sì* (On Care for Our Common Home), Pope Francis laments that our sister, Mother Earth, who sustains and governs us "cries out to us because of the harm we have inflicted on her by our irresponsible use and abuse of the goods with which God has endowed her" (no. 2). He calls all people to work together to preserve this home, "knowing that all the good which exists here will be taken up into the heavenly feast" (no. 244).

Conclusion

In the biblical tradition, creation and eschatology are inescapably linked, the alpha and the omega of God's work, creating, sustaining, and bringing creation to new fullness in the mystery of salvation. Thus the incarnation cannot be conceived as a "second step," to undo the damage brought about by sin, as classical theology, especially as influenced by Anselm's *Cur Deus Homo* (Why Did God Become Man?), has so often presumed. Nor can Christian eschatology be reduced to an individualistic doctrine of personal salvation, to "getting saved."

The Genesis creation stories, echoing the ancient Mesopotamian creation myths, serve as introduction to God's salvific work, linked specifically to the covenant in the Priestly account. The notion of salvation develops further under the influence of the prophets. In the Wisdom literature, creation is linked with salvation, even with the reestablishment of justice. In the New Testament, the influence of Wisdom theology is particularly evident in Paul and in the Fourth Gospel. Thus creation and eschatology are correlative concepts.

The doctrine of *creatio ex nihilo* developed later in the Christian tradition and implies the radical contingency of being, while the notion of human beings created in the image and likeness of God grounds the reverence for human life in all its forms. In *Laudato Sì*, Pope Francis distinguishes between creation and nature: "Nature is usually seen as a system which can be studied, understood and controlled, whereas creation can only be understood as a gift from the outstretched hand of the Father of all, and as a reality illuminated by the love which calls us together into universal communion" (no. 76).

If the church's relation to science has at times seemed less open, the knowledge of our world that comes from science has led to a deeper appreciation for the immensity of creation and the drama of life in all its diversity, enabling theologians like Teilhard de Chardin, John Haught, Elizabeth Johnson, and Ilia Delio to see in evolution itself signs of God's presence in creation. Johnson says that "the doctrine of continuous creation sees the natural world in its own integrity as the dwelling place of God. The Giver of life creates what is physical—stars, plants, soil, water, air, plants, animals, ecological communities—and moves in these every bit as vigorously as in souls, minds, ideas." [65]

Nor will God abandon creation to the corruptible effects of its own contingency. If we are called to everlasting life before the very face of God, to what traditional theology called the beatific vision, the fullness of salvation involves not only the elect but also all those victims of injustice whose cry is always heard, as well as creation itself, on that future day when every tear will be wiped away and God will be all in all.

For Further Reading

Creation

Anderson, Bernard W., ed. *Creation in the Old Testament*. Philadelphia, PA: Fortress Press, 1984.

Barbour, Ian G. *Religion and Science: Historical and Contemporary Issues: A Revised and Expanded Edition of Religion in an Age of Science*. San Francisco: HarperCollins, 1997.

Clifford, Richard J., and John J. Collins, eds. *Creation in the Biblical Traditions*. Washington, DC: Catholic Biblical Association of America, 1992.

Delio, Ilia: *The Unbearable Wholeness of Being: God, Evolution, and the Power of Love*. Maryknoll, NY: Orbis Books, 2013.

Francis, Pope. *Laudato Sì*. Encyclical Letter on Care for Our Common Home. 2015. http://w2.vatican.va/content/francesco/en/encyclicals/documents/papa-francesco_20150524_enciclica-laudato-si.html.

---

[65] Johnson, *Ask the Beasts*, 150.

Haught, John F. *Making Sense of Evolution: Darwin, God, and the Drama of Life*. Louisville, KY: Westminster John Knox Press, 2010.

Hayes, Zachary. *The Gift of Being: A Theology of Creation*. Collegeville, MN: Liturgical Press, 2001.

Johnson, Elizabeth A. *Ask the Beasts: Darwin and the God of Love*. London: Bloomsbury, 2014.

Miller, Kenneth R. *Finding Darwin's God: A Scientist's Search for Common Ground between God and Evolution*. New York: HarperCollins, 1999.

Eschatology

Daley, Brian E. *The Hope of the Early Church*. Cambridge, UK: Cambridge University Press, 1991.

Lane, Dermot A. *Keeping Hope Alive: Stirrings in Christian Theology*. New York: Paulist Press, 1996.

Moltmann, Jürgen. *The Coming of God: Christian Eschatology*. Minneapolis, MN: Fortress Press, 2004.

Nichols, Terence. *Death and Afterlife: A Theological Introduction*. Grand Rapids, MI: Brazos, 2010.

Phan, Peter C. "Contemporary Context and Issues in Eschatology." *Theological Studies* 55 (1994): 507–36.

———. *Living Into Death, Dying Into Life: A Christian Theology of Death and Life Eternal*. Hobe Sound, FL: Lectio Publishing, 2014.

Ratzinger, Joseph. *Eschatology: Death and Eternal Life*, 2nd edition. Washington, DC: The Catholic University of America Press, 1988.

Rausch, Thomas P. *Eschatology, Liturgy, and Christology: Toward Recovering an Eschatological Imagination*. Collegeville, MN: Liturgical Press, 2012.

Robinette, Brian D. *Grammars of Resurrection: A Christian Theology of Presence and Absence*. New York: Crossroad, 2009.

Thiel, John E. *Icons of Hope: The "Last Things" in Catholic Imagination*. Notre Dame, IN: University of Notre Dame Press, 2013.

US Lutheran-Roman Catholic Dialogue. "The Hope of Eternal Life." 2010. http://www.usccb.org/beliefs-and-teachings/ecumenical-and-interreligious/ecumenical/lutheran/upload/The-Hope-of-Eternal-Life1.pdf.

Index of Names

Index of Subjects

ahimsa, 41
Albigensians, 257, 268
Alexandria school of, 6, 92–93
Always Our Children, 38
Anabaptists, 189, 222
analogy of being, 53, 153
Antioch, school of, 6, 92–93
Apostles' Creed, 61, 168
apostolic office, 253–55
apostolic succession, 187, 195, 204, 214, 247, 249
Apostolic Tradition, 61, 114, 173, 226, 238, 248
Arianism, 92–93
Aristotelianism, 11
assumption of Mary, 175–76
atonement. *See* soteriology
Augsburg Confession, 237
Augustinian/Franciscan tradition, 53

baptism, 221–24
    and original sin, 222
bishop of Rome, 12, 167, 186, 188, 201, 208, 211
bishops, 187–88, 190, 192–93, 247–50
    as successors to the apostles, 114, 188

Cappadocians, 63, 93
catechumenate, 231–32, 236

"Catholic," 187
Catholic identity, xvi
Catholic theology, xv–xvi, 6, 16–18, 71, 104–5, 146–61, 198, 260
    and neoscholasticism, 12, 23, 44, 71, 137
    and Scripture, 4, 23–24, 50, 112
CDF, 31, 168, 176, 205, 280
Chalcedon, Council of, 6, 61, 64, 93–94
charism, *charismata*, 58, 60, 196, 257
Christian initiation, 220–31
Christianity, 206
Christology, 6, 30, 56–57, 77–106
    "Abba," 56, 58, 100, 111, 124
    contemporary expressions of, 94–104
    death and resurrection, 84–87, 285–87
    "from above," 78, 98, 103
    high, 56, 88–89
    historical Jesus, 78–80, 180–82
    reign of God, 80–84, 103–4, 124
    types, 87–88
church, 180–211
    and the papacy 12, 115, 188–89
    and the poor, 19–20, 285–86, 192
    and Vatican II, 191–98
    as communion, 18, 168, 230
    as world church, 192, 202

Lightning Source UK Ltd.
Milton Keynes UK
UKOW05f1818220517

301772UK00005B/354/P